H. H. Nells.

15 7. 58

S0-AUG-100

MOZART
IN RETROSPECT

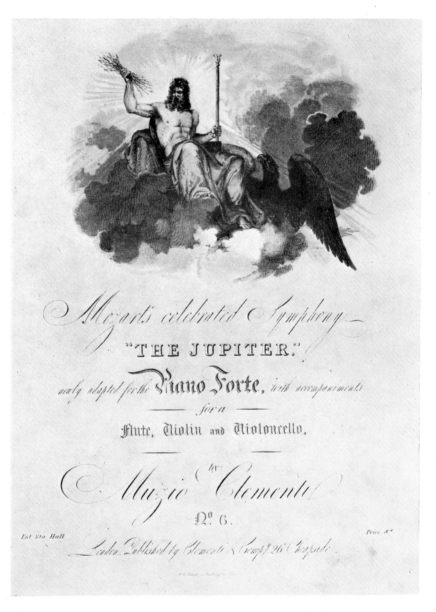

Mozart's celebrated Symphony

"THE JUPITER."

newly adapted for the Piano Forte, with accompaniments

for a

Flute, Violin and Violoncello,

by

Muzio Clementi

Nº 6.

Ent Sta Hall   Price 8ˢ

London, Published by Clementi & Compᵞ 26 Cheapside.

The 'Jupiter' Symphony. An early illustrated English edition, c. 1822

MOZART
IN RETROSPECT

*Studies in criticism and
bibliography*

BY

A. HYATT KING

GEOFFREY CUMBERLEGE

OXFORD UNIVERSITY PRESS

LONDON   NEW YORK   TORONTO

1955

Oxford University Press, Amen House, London E.C.4

GLASGOW NEW YORK TORONTO MELBOURNE WELLINGTON
BOMBAY CALCUTTA MADRAS KARACHI CAPE TOWN IBADAN

Geoffrey Cumberlege, Publisher to the University

PRINTED IN GREAT BRITAIN

ML
410
.M9K55
c.2

Library
University of Miami

6-21-89 Jngri -

To

J. ARTHUR WATSON

ἑταῖρος ἀνήρ, κεχαρισμένα εἰδώς

PREFACE

This book fills some of the gaps that still exist in English writings on Mozart, voluminous though they are. It also covers some ground not touched by French and German writers. Twelve of the chapters have appeared before as contributions to periodicals, but all have been revised and partly rewritten or substantially expanded. Chapters 1, 2, 3, and 7, amounting to over one-third of the whole, are entirely new.

The first chapter traces the fluctuating expansion of Mozart's reputation from his own lifetime to the present day, in the light of the publication of his music, its performance, various opinions of it, and the growth of critical biography. Chapters 2 and 3 enlarge on some special topics alluded to in Chapter 1 and, like it, show how bibliography, in the widest sense of the term, can contribute to musical knowledge. Six other Chapters, 4–8 and 14, are partly bibliographical in content. They contain some new information about the transmission of the texts and sources of various compositions. Chapters 9–12 give a critical account of certain aspects of Mozart's music. His lifelong interest in keyboard instruments, as teacher and performer, is examined in Chapters 15 and 16, which bring together a body of facts that are otherwise inconveniently scattered and, in part, very little known. Mozart's fruitful interest in mechanical music—a fascinating subject—is discussed in Chapter 13. This, with parts of several other chapters, lays some emphasis on his creative processes during the last years of his life. There are thus several continuous threads of interest that have shaped the presentation of an inevitably heterogeneous book and have, it is hoped, given it some unity.

My thanks for permission to reprint those chapters which originally appeared in periodicals are due to the editors of the *Monthly Musical Record* (11 and 13), *Music & Letters* (10), *Music Review* (5), *Musical Opinion* (8, 12), the *Musical Quarterly* (4, 9), the *Music Teacher* (16), the *Musical Times* (6, 13, 15). The Council of the Bibliographical Society have kindly allowed me to reprint from *The Library* the 'Subscription List to *Così fan tutte*' given in Appendix 1. I have also to thank Messrs. Macmillan & Co. and Miss Emily Anderson for generously allowing me to quote from her translation of *The Letters of Mozart and his Family* (1938); and Messrs. Novello & Co. for kindly permitting quotation from *A Mozart Pilgrimage* (1955).

A number of people have assisted me in various ways. My especial gratitude is due to Walter Emery for advice on the organs of Mozart's day: to my wife, who read and criticized the manuscript at various stages, and finally typed it: to C. B. Oldman, who read the whole in typescript and proof, and from his profound knowledge of Mozart made many helpful criticisms: to J. L. Wood, for elucidating some obscure points in the text of *Discours XVI* from the periodical *Aristide* (Chapter 8). To Professor O. E. Deutsch and the late Paul Hirsch I owe far more than the occasional mention of their names might suggest. Conversations and correspondence which I had with them from 1940 onwards greatly enriched my store of both facts and ideas.

A. H. K.

HAMPSTEAD
1955

CONTENTS

Preface   vii

Illustrations   xi

Abbreviations and Chief Sources   xii

1. *Mozart in Retrospect*
   INTRODUCTION   I
   1756–91
     Repute and Publication   3
   1792–1830
     I. *Publication and Performance*   10
     II. *Biography and Opinion*   16
   1830–1900
     I. *Performance and Opinion*   23
     II. *Publication and Research*   31
   THE TWENTIETH CENTURY
     I. *Research and Documentation*   36
     II. *Biography and Criticism*   38
     III. *Performance*   45
     IV. *Popularity*   49

2. *Köchel, Breitkopf, and the Complete Edition*   55

3. *Jahn and the Future of Mozart Biography*   66

4. *A Census of Mozart's Musical Autographs in Great Britain*   78

5. *An Unrecorded English Edition of the Clavier Duet*
   K. 19d   100

6. *Mozart and Cramer: a facsimile of the lost autograph of*
   K. 236   112

7. *Joseph Mainzer and the Mozart Family: a postscript to the Clavier Duet K. 381*   120

8. *A Swiss Account of Mozart in 1766*   131

9. *The Melodic Sources and Affinities of* Die Zauberflöte   141

10. *The Growth and Significance of Mozart's Counterpoint*   164

11. *Creative Contrast in Mozart*   180

12. *The Nature of Mozart's Genius: some analogies and reflections*   188

13. *Mozart's Compositions for Mechanical Organ*   198

14. *Mozart's Lost and Fragmentary Compositions*   216

15. *Mozart and the Organ*   228

16. *The Clavier in Mozart's Life*   242

APPENDIX 1. *A Subscription List to* Così fan tutte   260

APPENDIX 2. *The Figure*

as used by Mozart and by earlier and later Composers   262

APPENDIX 3. *The Origin of the Title* 'The "Jupiter" Symphony'   264

General Index   265

Index of Sources and Authorities cited   276

Index of Publishers   279

ILLUSTRATIONS

Pls. 3, 4, 7, and 8 are reproduced by courtesy of the Trustees of the British Museum.
Pls. 1, 2, 5, and 6 are from originals in my own collection

1. Engraved title-page of the 'Jupiter' Symphony, arranged by Muzio Clementi. Drawn by W. Collard: watermark date, 1822   *Frontispiece*

2. Bars 58–79 of the solo part of the Andante of the Clavier Concerto K. 467. (From '*Andantes, Adagio et Larghetto, tirés des six grands concertos de Mozart œuvre 82, amplifiés dans la partie du piano-forté par P. C. Hoffmann*'. André: Offenbach [1801])
                                                                                facing page 80

3. Figured bass progressions in Mozart's autograph. (*BM Add. 14396 f. 14*)   *facing page 81*

4. Johann Andreas Stumpff (1769–1846). (From '*Die Gartenlaube*', no. 32, 1857: *BM PP. 4736 il*)   *facing page 96*

5. Title-page of the Birchall edition of the Duet Sonata K. 19d
                                                                                facing page 97

6. Facsimile of the Autograph of the Andantino for Clavier K. 236. (Page 2 of the facsimiles in *Apollo's Gift or the Musical Souvenir for MDCCCXXX*)   *facing page 112*

7. Joseph Mainzer (1801–51). (*BM Add. 35027 f. 61*) *facing page 113*

8. Facsimile of the Autograph of the Duet Sonata K. 381, bars 1–45 of the primo part. (From '*Mainzer's Musical Times*', Jan. 1843: *BM PP. 1945 i*)   *facing page 128*

ABBREVIATIONS AND CHIEF SOURCES

TITLES OF BOOKS

Abert	Hermann Abert. *W. A. Mozart. Neubearbeitete und erweiterte Ausgabe von Otto Jahns Mozart*. 5. Auflage. 2 vols. Leipzig, 1923–4.
Anderson	*The Letters of Mozart and his Family*. Chronologically arranged, translated, and edited by Emily Anderson. With extracts from the letters of Constanze Mozart to J. A. André translated and edited by C. B. Oldman. 3 vols. London, 1938.
Einstein	Alfred Einstein. *Mozart. His character, his work*. New York, 1945.
Holmes	Edward Holmes. *Life of Mozart*. London, 1932. ('Everyman' edition.)
Jahn	Otto Jahn. *Wolfgang Amadeus Mozart*. 4 vols. Leipzig, 1856–9.
Keller	Otto Keller. *Wolfgang Amadeus Mozart. Bibliographie und Ikonographie*. Berlin, 1927.
Kelly	*Reminiscences of Michael Kelly*. [Dictated to Theodore Hook and edited by him.] London, 1826.
Köchel	Ludwig Ritter von Köchel. *Chronologisch-Thematisches Verzeichnis sämtlicher Tonwerke Wolfgang Amade Mozarts. Dritte Auflage bearbeitet von Alfred Einstein. Mit eine Supplement*. Ann Arbor, 1947.
Mozart Pilgrimage	A Mozart Pilgrimage. Being the Travel Diaries of Vincent and Mary Novello in the year 1829. Transcribed and compiled by Nerina Medici di Marignano. Edited by Rosemary Hughes. London, 1955.
Niemetschek	Franz Niemetschek. *Leben des K. K. Kapellmeisters Wolfgang Gottlieb Mozart. Nach Originalquellen beschrieben*. Prague, 1798 (2nd ed., 1808).
Nissen	Georg Nikolaus von Nissen. *Biographie W. A. Mozarts*. Leipzig, 1828.
Nottebohm	Gustav Nottebohm. *Mozartiana*. Leipzig, 1880.
Schiedermair	*Die Briefe Mozarts und seiner Familie*. Eine kritische Gesamtausgabe von Ludwig Schiedermair. 4 vols. Munich. 1914.

Abbreviations and Chief Sources xiii

Warde Fowler — *Stray Notes on Mozart and his Music.* [The preface signed: W. W. F., i.e. William Warde Fowler.] Privately printed by R. and R. Clark. Edinburgh, 1910.

Wyzewa and Saint-Foix — Teodor de Wyzewa and Count Georges de Saint-Foix. *Wolfgang Amédée Mozart. Sa vie musicale et son œuvre.* 5 vols. Paris, 1912–46 (Vols. iii–v by Saint-Foix alone).

OTHER REFERENCES

AMZ	*Allgemeine Musikalische Zeitung*
BM	British Museum
BM Add.	British Museum, Additional Manuscript
ML	*Music and Letters*
MQ	*Musical Quarterly*
MMR	*Monthly Musical Record*
MR	*Music Review*
MW	*Musical World*

1

Mozart in Retrospect

INTRODUCTION

WHEN Chladni was conducting his once-famous experiments in acoustics during the 1780's, he discovered that a small quantity of sand, when cast upon a glass plate set in vibration by strokes of a bow, formed itself into patterns. As the vibrations altered in intensity, the patterns changed in outline, proportion, and density, so that he was able only after long investigation to deduce laws governing their formation. Similar are the impressions we receive from examining Mozart's reputation during the last two centuries. The patterns which it has formed upon the glass of time make a fascinating but rather bewildering sequence, that has changed incessantly as the surface vibrations have altered under the impact of new states of society, new interpretations of musical history, and new aesthetic and literary concepts.

At various times Mozart's music has been illogically neglected, disparaged, and overestimated. It has been subject to contradictory reassessments and to study by musicologists as a 'problem', in ways which would probably have moved him to sardonic and disrespectful mirth. During the last part of his life his compositions engendered some controversy of the kind that is perhaps inseparable from the work of any progressive composer, though it fell far short of the bitterness of the dispute between Scheibe and J. S. Bach. While not without enemies, Mozart never suffered lampoon or caricature; only in the nineteenth century was he libelled by artists and sculptors who distorted what little is known of his appearance to suit their own fanciful vision of the 'rococo' composer.

From 1792 onwards, broadly speaking, he has always been a

classic. The reasons for the veneration accorded him may now seem to us to have been wrong—often indeed for long periods —and based on misunderstanding and restricted knowledge, but the fact remains that Mozart never experienced the wide and almost complete neglect which befell J. S. Bach. The proportion of Mozart's works printed in his life, while still a fraction of the whole, much exceeded that of Bach's. But it fell far short in quantity and circulation of what Handel, Haydn, and Beethoven saw printed of their music, even allowing for their longer span.

On the other hand, very soon after Mozart's death, his music began to be widely printed and performed. Hence it was never subject to any intensive, sudden revelation comparable to the almost apocalyptic impact of Bach caused by the dissemination of the Bach Society's edition. This may be compared to the revelation of El Greco given to art in the early 1900's when thirty-three of his canvases were gradually brought up from long obscurity in the vaults of the Prado. The progressive rediscovery of Mozart, and his rise to general popularity in the twentieth century after his more limited appeal to the nineteenth, are more appropriately matched by the gradual revaluation of Botticelli, whose paintings, long prized by only a few connoisseurs, are now widely acclaimed by critics and artists of all kinds.

The factual bases for an examination of Mozart's musical repute are sometimes scanty and often hard to interpret. Thus it must be realized that, even after 200 years and in spite of the labours of biographers and critics, any final estimate still remains an elusive task, full of paradoxes. The very universality of his art has caused him continually to be 'made all things to all men' in a greater degree, perhaps, than any other creative European artist except Shakespeare. Any attempt to explore the changes in his fame which have taken place over the past two centuries cannot avoid generalizations, because our knowledge of the musical and sociological background is still far from exact. We lack the accurate and universal statistics which are of fundamental importance for the study of the posthumous publication and performance of his music.

1756–91
Repute and Publication

All his life Mozart played and conducted his own compositions assiduously, aided in later years by pupils. But it is doubtful whether during the time of incessant travel his activity made any coherent or lasting impression even on informed minds. Only from 1781 to 1791, when his ways became more settled, did there emerge a definite musical personality of which the elements, previously so diffuse, became concentrated in the crucible of Viennese musical life. Mozart's works were intensively discussed by composers, publishers, reviewers, and dilettanti. Only a few of their observations have come down to us, sometimes through an unreliable oral tradition. Nevertheless, the resultant picture is of absorbing interest, although all the details may not be accurate.

In November 1781 Artaria of Vienna published six violin sonatas (K. 296, 376–80), of which the last five had been composed earlier in that year. A reviewer in the *Magazin der Musik* (edited by C. F. Cramer)[1] found them to be 'unique of their kind, rich in new ideas and signs of the genius of their author, brilliant'—a much more favourable judgement than later chamber works were to receive. When *Die Entführung aus dem Serail* was first performed, the Vienna correspondent of the same journal said[2] it was 'full of beauties' and went on: 'It surpassed public expectation, and the delicate taste and novelty of the work were so enchanting as to call forth loud and general applause.' But the Emperor Joseph, representing the opinion of the enlightened Viennese amateur, thought otherwise. 'Too beautiful for our ears, and a prodigious lot of notes, dear Mozart', he is reported to have said.[3]

---

[1] Hamburg, vol. i, 1783, p. 486. [2] Op. cit., 1783, p. 352.

[3] The earliest known source for this oft-quoted remark and for Mozart's equally famous reply, 'Just as many notes, your Majesty, as are necessary,' is Niemetschek, p. 34. Kelly, vol. ii, p. 72, gives a variant, said to have been told him by Mozart. It

The same criticism appears to underlie the remark of the emperor to Dittersdorf:[1] 'He has only one fault in his pieces for the stage, and his singers have very often complained of it— he deafens them with his full accompaniment.' These words probably date from about 1786, and may thus refer to *Le Nozze di Figaro*, but they hold good for all Mozart's operas from *Die Entführung* onwards, at each of which similar criticism, mingled with approval, was levelled. His raising of the orchestra almost to equality with the voices as a partner in the drama was mis-construed as a perverse increase in noise for its own sake. His powers of invention also caused perplexity, even to Dittersdorf.

I have never yet met with any composer [he wrote[2]] who had such an amazing wealth of ideas. I could almost wish he were not so lavish in using them. He leaves his hearer out of breath, for hardly has he grasped one beautiful thought than another of greater fascination dispels the first, and this goes on throughout, so that in the end it is impossible to retain any one of these beautiful melodies.

When such was the reaction of an intelligent composer, we can imagine how baffling Mozart's clavier[3] concertos, for instance, must have sounded to fashionable audiences.

Besides innovations in texture and form, his harmonic daring gave offence, particularly as exemplified in the quartets dedi-cated to Haydn. He, as is well known, after hearing K. 458, 464, and 465 privately performed in February 1785 declared to Leopold Mozart (according to the latter's letter to his daughter of 14–16 February): 'Before God and as an honest man I tell you that your son is the greatest composer known to me either in person or by name. He has taste, and, what is more, the most profound knowledge of composition.' Others were more critical. 'It is a pity', wrote the Vienna correspondent of the *Magazin der Musik*,[4] 'that in his truly artistic and beautiful com-

should be remembered that Kelly dictated his reminiscences to Theodore Hook nearly forty years after meeting Mozart.
[1] Dittersdorf, *Selbstbiographie* (Leipzig, 1801), p. 237.
[2] Op. cit., p. 237.
[3] The significance of the term 'clavier' is explained at the beginning of chapter 16.
[4] Vol. ii, 1786, pp. 1273, 1274.

positions Mozart should carry his effort after originality too far, to the detriment of the sentiment and heart of his works. His new quartets . . . are much too highly spiced to be palatable for any length of time.' The chief crux lay in the harmony of the introduction to the C major Quartet, of which passage, incidentally, the autograph is meticulously and clearly written without a single correction.[1] But the whole set gave much offence to amateur and professional alike. Prince Grassalkovics, an influential dilettante, tore up the printed parts in a rage on finding that the discords he heard were actually in print. The publisher Artaria is also said to have had the parts sent back by an Italian purchaser 'because they were full of engraver's errors'.[2]

Sarti (1729–1802), whom Mozart described to his father in a letter of 9–12 June 1784 as 'a good, honest fellow', wrote a malicious 'Esame acustico fatto sopra due frammenti di Mozart' of which only an extract appears to have been printed.[3] The salient passage of the 'Esame' (of which the tone suggests it was written in Mozart's lifetime, perhaps in 1785 when Sarti was in Vienna) runs as follows, and attacks K. 421 as well as K. 465: 'From these two passages we can decide that the composer, whom I do not know and do not want to know, is only a clavier player with a depraved ear: he is a sectary of the false system that divides the octave into twelve semitones.' Haydn, however, is reported to have remarked later of the introduction to K. 465 that, if Mozart wrote it so, he must have had his reasons for doing it.

We find a more intelligent approach to these quartets recorded in the *Anedotti piacevoli e interessanti* of G. G. Ferrari (1759–1842)[4] to whom Attwood sent the parts in Naples, and urged him to persevere:

I tried them over [wrote Ferrari] with amateur and professional

[1] Some nineteenth-century investigators of this passage are mentioned on p. 87. An organist's view of Mozart's modulations is cited on p. 235.

[2] *AMZ*, vol. i, 1798/9, col. 855, is the source for both these anecdotes.

[3] Ibid., vol. xxxiv, 1832, cols. 473 ff. The autograph was then owned by a 'Herr Asioli', possibly the composer Bonifacio Asioli (1769–1832).

[4] London, 1830, pp. 145, 146. I am indebted to Frank Walker for drawing my attention to this and other passages.

musicians, but we could only play the slow movements and even
these badly. I put into score some extracts, including the fugue in
G in the first quartet. I showed it to Latilla [*c.* 1713–89] and he, after
examining the first part, said it was a very fine thing. Scrutinising
then the modulations and ingenious combinations of the second part,
and having reached the return of the subject, he put down my copy
on the table, exclaiming, in utter astonishment: 'This is the most
beautiful, most marvellous piece of music I have ever seen in my
life!' 'Don't you think it's too ingenuous for a proper fugue?'
'What are you talking about? This is the best sort. This is a proper
fugue: it's not scholastic. It's new.'

Audacities of this kind worried publishers considerably. We
learn from Nissen[1] that Hoffmeister, after commissioning two
quartets for clavier and strings (K. 478, 493) as the beginning
of a set of four, found they did not sell, warned Mozart not to
compose any more and told him:[2] 'Write more popularly, or
else I can neither print nor pay for any more of yours.' But we
should remember that part at least of the public's difficulty may
have been due to unintelligent playing. The bad performance of
K. 478 described by the Vienna correspondent of the *Journal des
Luxus und der Moden*[3] was probably not unique. The fact remains,
however, that some publishers proved unwilling to risk a loss
on Mozart. Hummel of Berlin, an influential and experienced
publisher, who printed many of Haydn's mature compositions,
is said[4] to have boasted that he sent back some of Mozart's
works to him. We have, therefore, all the more reason to be
grateful to those who did bring out his music, no less than to
those reviewers who tempered criticism with caution.

Critics, publishers, and amateurs generally preferred the
popular composers of the day, such as Winter, Gelinek, Kozeluch, Sterkel, Wanhal, and Paisiello, most of whose works now
sound so monotonously alike to us. In 1788 the *Magazin der
Musik*[5] reported: 'Kozeluch's works hold their ground, and are
always acceptable, but Mozart's are not by any means so popu-

[1] p. 633.
[2] Rochlitz in *AMZ*, vol. xiv, 1812, col. 313.
[3] Weimar, 1788, p. 230.
[4] *AMZ*, vol. i, 1798/9, col. 547.
[5] Vol. ii, 1788, p. 53

lar.' As we find similar observations in other journals, it is worth while to try to summarize briefly the reasons which underlay the public preference for these now forgotten composers, and to examine the attitude of some of them towards Mozart.

During the 1780's music was the very breath of life to all classes of Viennese society; a large part of their existence revolved round opera, concerts, and domestic playing. The gifted, facile, and often eclectic composer who largely aimed at pleasing could hardly fail to create an incessant demand for editions of his works. Such a style of aural titillation would not easily be replaced by something which made a radically new appeal to emotion and intellect. For here lay the root of all the qualities that made Mozart's mature style so personal—kaleidoscopic changes of mood; impetuous variety of form and rhythm; strong tension of inner parts accentuated by boldness of harmony; a supreme dramatic instinct which revolutionized opera and projected itself into many instrumental forms.

By developing these characteristics Mozart moved beyond the musical ken of most of his contemporaries except Haydn and perhaps Dittersdorf. From various motives, lesser men, confronted with a bizarre, disquieting style, charged with explosive feeling, often disliked it. Sometimes the critics remained anonymous, as in two notices which, though dating from 1793, well reflect views current five years or so before. The first in the *Musikalische Monatsschrift* (p. 130) runs:

Nobody will fail to see in Mozart a man of talent and an experienced, abundant and agreeable composer. But I have as yet encountered no thorough connoisseur of art who took him for a correct, much less for a perfect artist, and least of all will tasteful criticism regard him, in the matter of poetry, as a true and sensitive composer.

The second, in the *Musikalische Zeitung* (p. 127) is even more derogatory in tone:

Mozart was a great genius, but he had little of the higher culture, to be sure, and little scientific taste, or perhaps none at all. In his theatrical pieces, original as they are, he often quite missed what is most essential to the stage—effect; and when it comes to truthful handling of the libretto, let him stand up who can say authoritatively that he always understood the proper treatment of his text and that his music always consorts in such a way with poetry that the latter may not rise and accuse him before the tribunal of criticism.

Kozeluch, who disparaged the overture to *Don Giovanni*,[1] also cast aspersions on that to *Die Zauberflöte*[2] and expressed his personal dislike of the composer openly and violently in 1791.[3] Another powerful and long-standing enemy was the influential Winter, who attacked Mozart on both moral and musical grounds.[4] Doubtless there were others, besides those whose utterances have been preserved in his own letters and in nearly contemporary accounts. Mozart's sarcastic tongue sometimes caused the shafts of antipathy to be tipped with fear and jealousy. Since adolescence he had met much hostility of this kind in varying intensity[5] but not with the concentration it acquired in Vienna. Yet his attitude never seems to have faltered; broadly, it was *oderint, dum metuant*. Because he refused to compromise either in personal relations or musical ideals, 'Tod und Verzweiflung war sein Lohn'. Herein lay the true pathos of his life.

The publication of his works during his life was, as we now know, scanty. This fits in only too well with the general trend of his ill-success. Thanks to the researches of Prof. O. E. Deutsch and C. B. Oldman[6] the basic facts have been available for nearly a quarter of a century, though their significance has been strangely neglected. The total number of Mozart's identifiable works printed during his life was 144,[7] in the following categories:

---

[1] *Bohemia*, 1856, p. 127.

[2] This has the authority of Jahn, and derives ultimately from Haydn.

[3] *AMZ*, vol. ii, 1799/1800, col. 516.

[4] Baron F. L. K. von Biedenfeld, *Die komische Oper der Franzosen und der Deutschen*, (Leipzig, 1848), p. 86, 212; *AMZ*, vol. xxviii, 1826, cols. 467, 468.

[5] Cf his letter to Artaria of 8 Feb. 1780.

[6] 'Mozart-Drucke' in *Zeitschrift für Musikwissenschaft*, Dec. 1931, April 1932. Since this article appeared, only a very few additions to its pre-1792 contents have been made.

[7] The total given by C. B. Oldman, in Anderson (vol. iii, p. 1453), is 'not more than seventy or so'. This is apparently based on the opus numbers of the original editions, which often comprised more than one work.

Sonatas and variations for clavier and violin (K. 6, 7, 8, 9, 10–
15, 26–31, 296, 301–6, 359, 360, 376–80, 454, 481, 526) .   33
Clavier duet (K. 19d, 358, 381, 426, 497, 501, 521) .   .   7
Clavier solo (K. 24, 25, 179, 180, 264, 265, 284, 309–11, 330–
3, 352–4, 398, 455, 457, 475, 485, 494, 500, 511, 533, 613,
Anh. 145a, 209)   29
Chamber music (K. 254, 285, 387, 421, 428, 452, 458, 464, 465,
478, 493, 496, 498, 499, 502, 515, 516, 542, 546, 548, 564,
581)   22
Symphonies (K. 297, 319, 385; all in parts)   .   .   .   3
Dances (K. 462, no. 3, 509, 534–6, 567, 568, 571, 585, 586,
599–602, 604, 605)   16
Clavier concertos (K. 175, 382, 414–15, 451, 453, 595; all
in parts)   8
Operas (complete: in vocal score and selections K. 384)   .   1
Operas (selection: in vocal score K. 50, 492, 527, 588, 620)   5
Songs (with orchestra K. 471, 480)   2
Songs (with clavier: K. 23, 52, 53, 472, 474, 476, 506, 517–19,
523, 524, 529, 531, 552, 596–8)   18

⎯⎯⎯
144

    Twenty-five publishers in 10 cities were concerned: 8 in
Vienna, 5 in Paris, 4 in London, 2 in Amsterdam, and 1 each in
The Hague, Mainz, Spires, Mannheim, Berlin, and Prague. The
actual total of editions fell short of 150, because a number of
pieces were issued in groups of 3 or 6. Even if we allow for the
fact that 26 of these comprised works written before Mozart
was twenty-five, the sum is small in relation to his European
fame, of which Leopold, writing to his daughter on 12 January
1787, gives us an informative glimpse: 'The report that your
brother intends going to England is confirmed from Vienna,
Prague, and Munich.'[1] Unfortunately, a good deal of this repute
came from pirated editions, which amounted to nearly thirty
of the above total. Even from works published by contract,
Mozart's earnings were negligible, and, as we have seen, publishers were not eager, in spite of his reputation, to offer him

[1] Cf. also *Magazin der Musik*, vol. ii, 1786, p. 1273.

agreements. The irony of this neglect is heightened by the fact that within little more than a decade after his death his music was to be printed in a flood unprecedented in the musical history of any age or country. This coincided with a marked advance in public taste, and a general though vague awareness of expanding musical horizons, towards which Mozart's mature works had led. Had he not succumbed to illness, the knowledge of this widely appreciative atmosphere would certainly have restored his old zest for living and might well have set him on the road to security.

1792–1830

(i) *Publication and Performance*

The two works which probably contributed most to his posthumous popularity were *Don Giovanni* and *Die Zauberflöte*, each revealing a different aspect of his genius. Their ubiquitous repetition made people more familiar with his late style and predisposed to like other works of the same period which had formerly been dismissed after a few performances as strained and obscure. The late masterpieces of Haydn and the early ones of Beethoven were known in many parts of Europe, so that a considerable public waited eagerly to play and hear the music of Mozart, now recognized as their peer and forerunner.

Soon after 1795 at least two astute publishers must have realized how receptive the potential market had become. It was J. P. Spehr of Brunswick who first announced an edition of Mozart, called *Collection complette*, at the Leipzig Easter Fair of 1797. Fear of competition spurred G. C. Härtel, the owner of the firm of Breitkopf & Härtel, to hasten his own plans.[1] Although Spehr's edition began to appear a little earlier than Härtel's, the latter's was by far the larger. By 1806 it comprised 17 volumes of works for clavier solo and duet, and violin sonatas;

---

[1] His negotiations with Mozart's widow for the use of her store of autographs fell through, but J. A. André succeeded in purchasing most of them, only to publish comparatively little. This is a fascinating story, fully told by C. B. Oldman in the preface to his annotated translation of *The Letters of Constanze Mozart to J. A. André*, included in vol. 3 of Anderson.

30 songs; 12 string quartets and 20 clavier concertos, all in parts; 3 Masses; *Don Giovanni* in full score; orchestral parts to 12 concert arias, issued in vocal score.

This remarkable achievement, though defective by modern standards of scholarship, undoubtedly formed the chief source for the editions[1] issued before 1830 by Pleyel of Paris, Steiner of Vienna, the 'Magasin de l'imprimerie chymique' of Vienna, and Simrock of Bonn. Before 1810 all the great symphonies, the most important wind concertos, serenades, and *divertimenti* were in print, and a good many clavier concertos had been reprinted in half a dozen countries. Practically all these were still in parts.[2] By 1820 nearly all the important chamber music had been printed likewise in many miscellaneous collections. Numerous clavier pieces had appeared in many countries. The variations proved particularly popular, notably in London, where nine collections were issued in barely fifteen years.

The demand for the operas was equally great. Even before 1800 there had appeared 9 vocal scores of *Die Zauberflöte*, 5 of *La Clemenza di Tito*, 3 each of *Don Giovanni*, *Idomeneo* and *Die Entführung*, 2 each of *Figaro* and *Così fan tutte*. Between 1800 and *c.* 1830 these proportions change most interestingly. *Die Zauberflöte* with 9 editions takes third place to *Don Giovanni* and *La Clemenza di Tito* with 15 and 10 respectively. *Die Entführung* and *Così fan tutte* have 6 each, *Figaro* 5, and *Idomeneo* 3. Some at least of these editions reached a very large public. One of *Così fan tutte*, an undistinguished piece of printing published by Meyer of Brunswick, included a subscription list of 274 persons scattered over the whole of northern Europe, as far as Russia and Poland.[3] Public demand is further attested by the printing of several editions of these operas in full score between

---

[1] Though styled 'complete' all these actually fell far short of Breitkopf's, for they comprised little but pianoforte and chamber music, and added only a very few new works.

[2] Only the last four symphonies had also appeared in score in 1807–09, in the London edition of Cianchettini & Sperati. These are the earliest scores of any orchestral work by Mozart.

[3] These lists are very rare in Mozart editions. Full details of this, which is of exceptional interest, are given in Appendix 1.

1801 and 1814. Between 1820 and 1830 several collections of them appeared: Frey of Paris issued seven in full score in 1822; Richault printed a similar collection in 1828; collections of vocal scores were published by Birchall of London in the early 1820's, by Schlesinger of Paris *c.* 1822, and by Heckel of Mannheim in 1827–30.

Although exact statistics for all European countries are unfortunately lacking, the following figures, some of which could certainly be augmented by local research,[1] give a striking picture of the widespread demand for Mozart's music from 1792 to *c.* 1830. In Germany 34 publishers in 19 towns were issuing it in varying quantities; in Vienna 14 firms; in Paris 37; in London 23; in Edinburgh 2; in Liverpool and Manchester 2 each; in Amsterdam 3; in Prague 4; in Copenhagen and Milan 1 each. An efficient system of international agencies ensured that a student or performer could quickly obtain almost any piece required but not on his usual dealer's list.

From this bare summary of editions, dates, and figures, we can see that by the early 1820's nearly two-thirds of all Mozart's music was easily available in print. This proportion includes all his important works in the twenty-three categories into which his output was later divided for the Breitkopf complete edition. The gaps consist principally of juvenilia in orchestral, chamber and church music, which, however desirable to the eye of history, were by no means essential for a just appreciation of his genius in the period following his death.

Widely though Mozart's instrumental music was published and, by inference, performed, it was the operas which consolidated his fame: above all, as already suggested, *Die Zauberflöte* and *Don Giovanni*. Before 1800 the former had been produced in fifty-eight towns situated in Germany, Austria, Hungary, Poland, Russia, Holland, Switzerland, Rumania, and Bohemia, and in the next thirty years spread to France, England, Ireland, Denmark, Italy, and Belgium. New York saw the

[1] Those for continental countries are derived from Whistling's *Handbuch der musikalischen Literatur* for 1817 and 1828.

opera in 1833.[1] *Don Giovanni*, though not so popular initially, easily surpassed it in lasting esteem as the nineteenth century wore on. *Figaro*, being more limited in its appeal, was heard in almost as many countries, but in fewer cities. *Die Entführung* enjoyed a flying start in German-speaking lands, for it was given in thirty towns before 1792, and within three decades had been translated into Polish, Russian, French, Danish, Czech, and English. *Così fan tutte* was mainly restricted to German-speaking and Latin countries, partly because of its troublesome libretto, but was quickly staged in St. Petersburg and Copenhagen. Even the now despised *La Clemenza di Tito* reached Lisbon, Naples, Paris, Milan, St. Petersburg, Moscow, Copenhagen, Stockholm, Amsterdam, and London before 1830. The noble music of *Idomeneo* enjoyed less popularity, but was nevertheless given in a dozen places, including concert versions at Budapest in 1803 and Riga in 1825. In fine, Mozart's operas assured him posthumously an almost universal reputation unapproached by any previous composer, and only rivalled in this period by Rossini.

But we should not forget that producers and conductors did not scruple to take drastic liberties with the music. In 1787 acts 3 and 4 of *Figaro* were completely rewritten by Angelo Tarchi for a performance at Monza. In 1827 *Die Entführung* was given its first hearing in England at Covent Garden in a fantastically garbled version[2] hardly surpassed by the maltreatment of *Figaro* and *Don Giovanni* at the hands of Sir Henry Bishop. In Paris *Die Zauberflöte* was first produced in 1801 as *Les Mystères d'Isis*, an arrangement by L. W. Lachnith[3] who included extracts from *La Clemenza di Tito*, *Figaro*, and *Don Giovanni*, 'Fin ch' han dal vino' being rearranged as a duet. This hotch-potch was given 134 times before 1828, to the total exclusion of the real opera. *Così fan tutte* suffered some of the worst outrages, because the music had to be changed radically to fit the rewriting of the

[1] These statistics are taken from Alfred Loewenberg, *Annals of Opera*, Cambridge, 1943.
[2] Described in detail by Einstein, 'The First Performance of Mozart's *Entführung* in London', *MR*, Aug. 1945.
[3] His work was dubbed *Les Mystères d'ici*, he, 'le dérangeur'.

libretto. But when even Rossini's and Weber's operas were
mutilated in their lifetime, Mozart's could hardly be considered
sacrosanct.

His Masses and other Church music seem to have been little
heard outside Germany and Austria, except the *Requiem* which
became generally popular, partly through its appeal to the romantic imagination. Six editions of it in full score and about the
same number in vocal score were printed before 1830 in France,
Germany, Austria, and England. It was performed in Rio de
Janeiro in 1820.[1] In London, Vincent Novello did his best to
popularize the Masses, by publishing eighteen in vocal score,
of which five have since been proved spurious and three doubtful. He also issued, *c.* 1822, a full score of the fine D minor
'Kyrie' (K. 341).

We know, unfortunately, far less about the performance of
instrumental music in the first part of the nineteenth century
than about opera. Exact annals of orchestral concerts are scanty;
of chamber music, almost non-existent. The records of publishing suggest that Mozart's chamber works may have been more
frequently played than his symphonies and concertos. It seems
certain that the London performance[2] of a Mozart clavier
concerto given by J. W. Hässler, on 30 May 1792, was an uncommon event. It is interesting to note that the famous *Niederrheinische Musikfeste* did not perform a single Mozart symphony
before 1835,[3] whereas Salomon had given one in London as
early as 1786.[4] Performances of Mozart symphonies were quite
regular there in the 1790's, and the Philharmonic Society had
included them in its first season of 1813. An 'E flat symphony'
reached Hereford at the Three Choirs Festival of 1827.[5]

Quite soon after Mozart's death some of his music was used
as teaching material. Many early editions of his clavier works

[1] *AMZ*, vol. xxii, 1820, col. 501. In this connexion it is interesting to note that Constanze Mozart had told J. A. André in an unpublished letter dated 19 Dec. 1801, now
in the possession of C. B. Oldman, that her husband's music was very popular in Spain.
[2] C. F. Pohl, *Haydn in London* (Vienna, 1869), p. 200.
[3] Grove, 1st ed., vol. ii, p. 457.   [4] Pohl, op. cit., p. 80.
[5] Daniel Lysons, *Origin and Progress of the Meeting of the Three Choirs* (London,
1865), appendix.

have title-pages which emphasize their suitability for the young performer. (The delusion that Mozart is easy to play still flourishes.) By contrast, the difficulty of the concertos was clearly recognized. In 1796 A. E. Müller published his *Anweisung zum genauen Vortrage der Mozartschen Clavierconcerte hauptsächlich in Absicht richtiger Applicatur.*[1] This consisted of selected passages from K. 414, 421, 415, 595, 451, with elaborate fingering based on the principles of C. P. E. Bach. The publication of such a book presupposes a fair-sized public interested in practising these concertos.

In 1803 P. C. Hoffmann, with whom Mozart had played duets at Mainz in 1790 (cf. p. 258), published through André of Offenbach an edition of the slow movements of the concertos K. 503, 595, 491, 482, 488, 467, with many passages in both hands elaborated and ornamented (pl. 2). The style of this filling-out is distinctly akin to the manner of Hummel, but probably derived in part at least from Mozart's own usage. This is the earliest attempt to solve a problem which has challenged the skill of thoughtful pianists ever since. In December 1801 there were published, also by André, Hoffmann's cadenzas to the same group of concertos:[2] they are the first published after those written by the composer himself, which were printed earlier in the same year, with two more editions *c.* 1803. This reprinting, seen in the light of the work of Hoffmann and Müller, strengthens the evidence for the early study of Mozart performance.

We find a different kind of popularity suggested by the activities of William Gardiner, the same who sent Haydn a pair of stockings embroidered with themes from his works.

---

[1] The continuation foreshadowed in Müller's preface never appeared. The opening of K. 595

as quoted by him is interesting. This suggests that in performance the minims were sometimes ornamented with gruppetti.

[2] My edition of Hoffmann's elaborations of the slow movements and of his cadenzas to the same concertos is due for publication in 1956 by Hinrichsen Edition.

Gardiner, being an inveterate arranger, included many melodies from Mozart's operas in the six volumes of his *Sacred Melodies from Haydn, Mozart and Beethoven, adapted to the best English poets*, 1812–15. Such oddities were quite regular in the early nineteenth century, and at least served to popularize fine melody. Another curious and more elaborate instance consisted of a mass compiled by C. Zulehner, *c.* 1820, for which he took all the numbers save one from *Così fan tutte*.[1]

(ii) *Biography and Opinion*

Mozart biography naturally kept in step with the popularization of his music. As all the early books were fully and sympathetically discussed by Jahn in his preface[2] only some of the more important need be mentioned here. Many persons well acquainted with the composer long outlived him. They, with his widow, became a prolific source of anecdotes, on which were based many small early writings, such as the account in Schlichtegroll's *Nekrolog* (1793), and Rochlitz's often unreliable *Über Mozart*.[3] The first book to present a picture in the round was written by Franz Niemetschek, Professor of Latin at Pilsen and of Philosophy at Prague, who knew Mozart personally. His *Leben des K. K. Kapellmeisters Wolfgang Gottlieb Mozart* appeared at Prague in 1798, with an enlarged edition in 1808.

I. F. Arnold published two books anonymously: the first, *Mozart's Geist* (1803), attempted a critical account of a good deal of the music, to a length of over 400 pages; the second, *Wolfgang Amadeus Mozart und Joseph Haydn . . . Versuch einer Parallele* (1810), though not profound, shows interestingly what differences as well as similarities the contemporary critic saw in the two men. Lichtenthal's *Cenni biografici intorno al celebre maestro Wolfgang Amadeo Mozart* (1816), while mostly derivative,

---

[1] Details are given in Jahn, 1st ed., vol. iv, p. 767, appendix 25. For the ecclesiastical flavour of some late Mozart, cf. E. J. Dent, *Mozart's Operas* (London, 1913), pp. 321, 322. The adagio of the Serenade K. 361 was arranged *c.* 1830 as an offertory, 'Quis te comprehendat'.

[2] To all the first four editions, and to the English translation.

[3] *AMZ*, 1798–9, in seven instalments; further instalments in 1801–2; published in a French translation by C. F. Cramer, Paris, 1801.

was the first substantial work in Italian. The next ten years brought many pamphlets in French and German, and articles galore in periodicals and encyclopaedias all over Europe. But nothing on a large scale appeared until 1828, when Nissen's *Biographie W. A. Mozarts* (965 pages) was published by Breit-kopf. The author, who had married Mozart's widow in 1809, died, unfortunately, in 1826. Although he was deficient in bio-graphical sense, and devoid of musical knowledge, his final revision might have put into better shape the mass of anecdotic material and important documents to which he had access. The book is still invaluable, but tiresome to use by modern standards. The subscription list proves the extraordinary interest that it roused. Nine hundred and thirty-six copies were taken by nearly 600 persons all over Europe. These included the kings of Saxony and of Denmark, each of whom bought twelve copies; the King of Prussia took six, Spontini twelve. Besides many professional musicians, the middle classes were well represented. Nissen's own erstwhile post as Counsellor to the Danish Lega-tion in Vienna doubtless induced fourteen members of various diplomatic corps to subscribe. To satisfy Viennese demand, the music publisher Mechetti took as many as 170 copies. We do not know how many were on general sale, but they can hardly have been fewer than another 500.

We may take the year 1830 as roughly marking the end of the classical period which Mozart helped to inaugurate. By then, the whole picture had come into sharper focus. His works had been extensively published and widely performed. The outline of his life was common knowledge: a detailed account had been printed for all to study who could read German; his character seemed clearly limned; in musical and literary circles his name had become a household word; he belonged to history. What, then, were the opinions of him expressed by composers and literary men in this period, some of whom remembered him personally? How unanimous were their views?

To most of the composers Mozart became an object of venera-tion soon after his death. They admired the simplicity and

seemingly effortless perfection of his music as much as its inexhaustible variety. They realized how truly he had been the
harbinger of a new era and how he had anticipated many of
the developments towards which they were striving. In particular, his successful fusion of styles, German, French, and Italian,
and his mastery of counterpoint[1] excited their admiration
Beethoven copied for himself two notably contrapuntal works,
the Fugue for two claviers, K. 426, and the 'Fantasia' for mechanical organ, K. 608. On hearing a performance of Mozart's
C minor Clavier Concerto about the year 1800, in company with
Cramer, Beethoven is said to have exclaimed, at the Finale:
'Cramer! Cramer! We shall never be able to do anything like
that!'[2]

About the same time Mozart's old rival Clementi made a
generous remark when hearing a rehearsal of the Finale of the
G minor Symphony, then recently arranged as a septet by
the London publisher G. D. Cimador: 'Mozart has reached the
boundary gate of music, and has leapt over it, leaving behind
the old masters, the moderns and posterity itself.'[3] Weber, who
much admired Mozart, particularly his Germanic tone, produced and conducted his operas assiduously: in 1818, he wrote a
noteworthy appreciation of *Die Entführung*.[4] Spohr and Danzi
found Mozart and his works 'an inexhaustible subject of conversation'.[5]

Schubert's opinion, expressed in an entry in his diary for
14 June 1816, is as follows:

A light, bright, fine day this will remain throughout my whole
life. As from afar the magic notes of Mozart's music still gently

---

[1] Discussed in Chapter 10.

[2] A. W. Thayer, *Life of Ludwig van Beethoven* (New York, 1921), vol. i, p. 219.

[3] G. G. Ferrari, op. cit., p. 148; cf. p. 5, n. 4. Ferrari himself, p. 149–52, made a
notable appraisal of the versatility of Mozart's genius, and emphasized the dramatic
qualities of the clavier concertos.

[4] M. M. von Weber, *C. M. von Weber. Ein Lebensbild* (Leipzig, 1864–6), vol. iii,
pp. 189–92.

[5] *Ludwig Spohr's Autobiography* (London, 1865), p. 109. Many similar re ferences are
given by K. Prieger, *Urtheile berühmter Dichter, Philosophen und Musiker über Mozart*
(2nd. ed., Wiesbaden, 1886).

haunt me. How unbelievably vigorously, and yet again how gently was it impressed deep, deep into the heart by Schlesinger's masterly playing. Thus does our soul retain these fair impressions, which no time, no circumstances can efface, and they lighten our existence. They show us in the darkness of this life a bright, clear lovely distance, for which we hope with confidence. O Mozart, immortal Mozart, how many, oh how endlessly many such comforting perceptions of a brighter and better life hast thou brought to our souls! —This Quintet is, so to speak, one of the greatest of his lesser works.[1]

Effusions of this vague and semi-mystical character really tell us more of the mentality of the author than of their opinion of Mozart. They become painfully frequent during the late nineteenth century.

Although the voices raised in criticism of Mozart formed but a small discord in the growing chorus of praise, they deserve mention as representing a conservative point of view.

To H. G. Nägeli (1792–1836), the Swiss music publisher, composer, educationalist, and critic, Mozart's music stood for dangerous modernism. His *Vorlesungen über Musik mit Berücksichtigung der Dilettanten* (1826) contains a number of strictures on Mozart.[2] In general, Nägeli disliked the confusion of *cantabile* with the free instrumental interplay of ideas, and the wealth of fantasy and gifts for emotional expression, which 'had a powerfully regressive effect on the art of music'. The ending of the E flat Symphony (K. 543) he found 'so noisily inconclusive, such a bang, that the unsuspecting hearer does not know what has happened to him'. He stigmatized the 'Jupiter' Symphony as being deficient in repose, and often shallow and confused, though he admired Mozart's organic use of the orchestra. Nägeli also attacked the overture to *Don Giovanni* for its exaggerated and licentious contrasts, and asserted that it contained a bar too much[3] which destroyed the rhythm. Of the double

---

[1] O. E. Deutsch, *Schubert. A documentary biography*, translated by Eric Blom, p. 60 (J. M. Dent, London, 1946; W. W. Norton, New York, 1947).

[2] The passages quoted occur on pp. 99, 157, 158, 160, 162.

[3] A curious criticism on Nägeli's part, as he was actually guilty himself of adding four bars to the first movement of Beethoven's Sonata, op. 31, no. 1, when he published the first edition in 1803.

Fugue in the *Requiem*, he wrote that the violent changes of key turned it into 'a barbarous confusion of sounds'.

The *Requiem* was also criticized by the eminent theorist Gottfried Weber (1779–1839) who was shocked by the 'wilde Gurgeleien' of the 'Christe eleison'.[1] For different reasons the convivial oboist W. T. Parke disliked this work, which he found to be 'of infinite science and dulness'.[2] The violent controversy about the authorship of the *Requiem*, was possibly due partly to the displeasure it caused, Mozart's admirers being anxious to dissociate some of it from his name. At all events, it was this work which provoked several books and numerous articles before 1830, and so gave the composer's ghost its baptism in the *palus inamabilis* of musicology.

However various the views of musicians, the literary world of this period took Mozart enthusiastically to its heart. Only a few of the more important writers can be mentioned here. Goethe, though seven years older, survived him by over forty years, and left many opinions recorded in his own writings and in J. P. Eckermann's *Gespräche mit Goethe*.[3] Goethe divined the universality of Mozart's genius, and the prophetic quality of his late works, especially *Die Zauberflöte*. In 1829 he said[4] that he represented 'something unattainable in music, even as Shakespeare does in poetry'. He found in him 'a latent, procreative force which is continuously effective from generation to generation, and is not likely soon to be exhausted'.[5] Goethe also felt that Mozart would have been well fitted to set to music his *Faust*,[6] whose inner meaning he compared to that of *Die Zauberflöte*. In January 1796, as is well known, his admiration for that opera induced him to write a sequel, and to ask Paul Wranitzky

---

[1] *Cäcilia*, Mainz, vol. iii, 1826, p. 216.

[2] *Musical Memoirs* (London, 1830), vol. i, p. 290. But in 1825 Parke observed (vol. ii, p. 207): 'the return of Mozart's music [i.e. a performance of *Figaro*] was like the return of spring weather: it vivified and delighted our senses, which had been previously satisfied with the continued repetition of Rossini's operas.'

[3] References are to the 6th edition, Leipzig, 1885. Cf. also H. Abert, *Goethe und die Musik*, Stuttgart, 1922; P. Nettl, *Goethe und Mozart*, Esslingen, 1949.

[4] Eckermann, vol. ii, p. 104.　　　　　　　　[5] Eckermann, vol. iii, p. 157.

[6] Eckermann, vol. i, p. 64.

to compose the music, but in vain.[1] Goethe believed sincerely, but surely erroneously, that Mozart at his early death had, like Raphael and Byron (he might have added Purcell), fulfilled his mission in life.[2]

Goethe's opinions are interesting as having widely influenced the thought of the new intellectual bourgeoisie. The views of romantics, like Hoffmann and Stendhal, reached a more restricted public, but all three writers made an important, not essentially musical, section of it aware of new aspects of Mozart's music. E. T. A. Hoffmann (1776–1822), who ranks for our present purpose more as a poet than as a musician, confessed[3] that Mozart led him 'into the depth of the spirit world', to which *Don Giovanni* above all held the key. Of the E flat symphony, which he called the 'swan song' he said: 'Love and melancholy breathe forth in purest spirit tones: we feel ourselves drawn with inexpressible longing towards the forms which beckon us to join them in their flight through the clouds to another sphere.' In September 1812 he wrote his own *Don Juan, eine fabelhafte Begebenheit, die sich mit einem reisenden Enthusiasten zugetragen.*[4] One of the most remarkable pieces of prose ever inspired by an opera, Hoffmann's imaginative interpretation of Mozart's music foreshadows the powerful appeal which it was to make to a 'generation brought up on Byronic Satanism';[5] it also anticipates the 'daemonic' idea of nearly a century later.

The view of Mozart taken by literary dilettanti was likely to be based mostly on the operas. Perhaps the most representative and certainly one of the most intelligent musically was Stendhal

[1] See E. J. Dent, *Mozart's Operas* (London, 1947), pp. 255, 256 (the date 1798 given here is wrong); also V. Junk, *Goethe's Fortsetzung der mozart'schen Zauberflöte*, Berlin, 1899. An English translation by Eric Blom appeared in *ML*, July 1942.

[2] Eckermann, vol. iii, p. 165. The error of this view has been discussed by Dyneley Hussey, *Wolfgang Amade Mozart* (London, 1928), pp. 308–11.

[3] *Gesammelte Schriften* (Berlin, 1887), Bd. 7. *Fantasiestücke in Callot's Manier*, Tl.i, pp. 55, 56.

[4] Op. cit., Tl. i, pp. 91–108. Translated by Abram Loft in *MQ*, Oct. 1945.

[5] E. J. Dent, *Opera* (London, 1940), p. 62. Hoffmann's view approximated to that of Schopenhauer, who in *Die Welt als Wille*, first published in 1819, referred to *Don Giovanni* as a sublime expression of the supernatural (5th ed., Leipzig, 1879, vol. ii, p. 46).

(1783–1842), on whose philosophy they exercised a strong influence. In them he found a profound knowledge of the human heart and a subtle variety of erotic sentiment remarkably akin to his own theories as expressed in *De l'amour* (1822). He had many interesting observations to make on the reception of Mozart's operas in Italy, where he realized that the gay temperament of audiences was unsympathetic to the fundamental melancholy of the music.[1] From their very different standpoints, Stendhal and Hoffmann show how eagerly the romantic movement in literature could proclaim the affinity of Mozart's genius with its own emotional outlook.

In the poetry of this period his uneuphonious name seldom appears, but his music (again probably synonymous with the operas) was in the back of many a poet's mind. For instance, in October 1818 Keats wrote to George and Georgiana Keats of an unnamed young woman: 'She kept me awake one night, as a tune of Mozart's might do.'[2] Although few, if any, artists expressed an opinion of Mozart, many critics invoked a comparison from art in their estimate of him, chiefly with Raphael. The earliest seems to have been made by Rochlitz in 1799.[3] 'Mozart and Raphael' remained a favourite comparison throughout the nineteenth century, and was sometimes worked out at great length, as by C. E. R. Albert,[4] and by A. B. Bach.[5] These books and many other articles emphasize the nearly identical age of the two men at their death, the effortless universality of their art, the simplicity and purity of their nature. The comparison lapsed in the 1890's when Raphael's stock in the art world dropped and a more realistic view of Mozart began to prevail. To the early nineteenth century, however, the parallel seemed real and sincere. It is said that Cimarosa, when flattered by a painter who told him he was greater

---

[1] Numerous references are given in an excellent article 'Stendhal and Mozart' by John P. Harthan, *ML*, July 1946.

[2] *Complete Works of John Keats*, ed. H. B. Forman (London, 1911), vol. iv, p. 181.

[3] *AMZ*, vol. ii, 1799/1800, col. 641.

[4] *Mozart und Raphael. Eine Parallele*, Stettin, 1856.

[5] *Mozart, Raphael and the Renaissance*, privately printed, Edinburgh, 1887. Cf. also Pohl in Grove, 1st ed., vol. ii, p. 398.

than Mozart, retorted: 'Sir, what would you say to a man who told you that you were greater than Raphael?'[1] We find other comparisons to minor painters very different in style and epoch. Thus Stendhal, though an admirer of Raphael, likened Mozart for 'sweet melancholy' to Domenichino (1582–1641),[2] while Carpani, Haydn's biographer, preferred a comparison with Giulio Romano (1499–1546).[3]

1830–1900

(i) *Performance and Opinion*

Very soon after Mozart's death visible monuments to his memory took shape. Before 1800 private persons had erected symbolical tablets in Graz, Roveredo, and Tiefurt. In 1837 Prague devised a practical memorial which was placed in the Imperial Library. It consisted of large glazed book-cases, containing his complete printed works, for public use. Between the cases, backed by an inscription in gold upon the wall, stood a bust by Emanuel Max. The idea of a statue seems to have been proposed first at Salzburg in 1805, and finally materialized there on 4 September 1842 when the full-length statue by Schwanthaler was unveiled. This heavy, uninspired piece of work, which still stands in the Mozartplatz, shows the composer clad in what Jahn charitably called 'the traditional toga'. Ceremonies lasted four days. The actual unveiling was followed by a performance of a cantata for two four-part choirs, specially arranged by W. A. Mozart the younger from his father's music. The arranger, who conducted,[4] provided the words, beginning

---

[1] C. A. von Gruber, *An Mozarts Geist* (Vienna, 1823), p. 17.

[2] *Lettres écrites de Vienne sur le célèbre compositeur Jh. Haydn* (Paris, 1814), p. 260.

[3] *Le Haydine* (Milan, 1812), p. 215. He mentioned no qualities, but further equates Pergolesi with Raphael, Piccini with Titian, Cimarosa with Veronese, Handel with Michelangelo, Haydn with Tintoretto!

[4] L. Meilichhofer, *Das Mozart-Denkmal zu Salzburg und dessen Enthüllungsfeier* (Salzburg, 1843), pp. 21 ff. A copy of the cantata is in BM; it is entitled *Fest-chor zur Enthüllung der Mozart-Denkmals in Salzburg aus Compositionen des Gefeierten zusammengestellt und mit passenden Texte versehen von dessen Sohne W. A. Mozart*. In MW 1842, p. 334, it is stated, alternatively but without authority, that the Archbishop of Salzburg wrote the text.

'Hier seht ihn dargestellt den Meister, hier seht ihn, er ist es! Den ihr geliebt und bewundert'—which suggests that his poetical inspiration moved on much the same level as his music. The middle section of the cantata, set to his father's Adagio for clavier in B minor (K. 540), begins: 'Ach, dass die Parze den Faden so bald zerschnitt.' Mozart's widow missed the occasion by six months only, having died on 6 March 1842 in her eightieth year, a few hours after the arrival of the model for the statue.[1] Of the important memorials elsewhere, that in Vienna came next, in 1859, when a plinth by Hans Gasser was placed in the cemetery of St. Marx.

These monuments and ceremonies, however quaint or sentimental they may appear to the eye of the twentieth century, were important contemporary events. Some of them were widely reported in the European press. They helped to establish Mozart's memory in the general consciousness of the age, though their influence has been outlived and far exceeded by various commemorative institutions and festivals bearing his name. The earliest foundation was the *Mozartstiftung* set up at Frankfurt, in 1838. Its aim was to assist needy, talented musicians to complete their education; it had no specific connexion with Mozart research or performance. But in 1841 the *Mozarteum* in Salzburg began its long and useful career, of which the principal stages are admirably summarized by Walter Hummel, *Chronik der Internationalen Stiftung Mozarteum* (Salzburg, 1951). It combines the work of an important musical training college with the administration of an incomparable Mozart archive. It has assumed responsibility for the eloquent and tasteful museum, arranged in the birthplace in the Getreidegasse, which today includes a series of vivid dioramas showing the staging of the operas as done at various times all over Europe.

The first of the Salzburg Mozart festivals was held in 1856: others followed in 1879 and 1891. But some less famous towns

[1] The extraordinary ceremony held previously at Munich in July 1841, to mark 'the arrival of the statue' (or rather, it may be presumed, the model for it), is described in *MW*, 1841, p. 9, where J. A. Stumpff quotes a letter from a Munich correspondent.

anticipated Salzburg. Koschirsch, a small place in Bohemia, had held a festival in 1836: Darmstadt and Elberfeld followed suit in 1837. The first of the great Viennese festivals took place in 1841, with others in 1856, 1888, and 1891. Although the programmes for the earliest of these events have not been preserved, and may not have consisted entirely of Mozart, they must have helped to arouse new and much-needed interest in his music.[1] For as the century wore on, its performance became so restricted in scope as to belie the wide interest in the man aroused by the efforts of biographers and publishers. His operas alone retained some of their erstwhile popularity, but after about 1860 a sharp drop in the number of vocal scores printed reflects a waning interest. In Germanic lands, *Figaro*, *Don Giovanni*, and *Die Zauberflöte* head the list, with *Die Entführung* as a bad fourth. Elsewhere, we find the first two done fairly regularly, the rest infrequently.

It is less easy to form an exact picture of instrumental performance all over Europe, because so very few records of concerts given continuously through the middle of the nineteenth century have been printed. But a tentative deduction can be made from the figures available from England and Germany for such large towns as London,[2] Manchester,[3] Leipzig,[4] and Vienna.[5] Allowing for some difficulty of identification, it seems clear that the number of symphonies generally heard did not

---

[1] Some concerts given during the 1856 centenary were organized by the Erfurt *Mozart-Verein* whose directors included Spohr, Reissiger, Meyerbeer, Marschner, Lindpaintner, Lachner, and Hiller. Cf. C. Haushalter, *Geschichte des Mozart-Vereins*, Erfurt, 1856.

[2] M. B. Foster, *The History of the Philharmonic Society of London, 1813–1912* (London, 1912). In early programmes symphonies and concertos were not precisely identified; Joseph Bennett, *The Story of Ten Hundred Concerts. Being a short account of the . . . Monday Popular Concerts at St. James's Hall, London, 1859–1887* (London, 1887). Also, the programmes of John Ella's *Musical Union*, 1845–80. It is unlikely that smaller towns in any country would have had a wider repertoire of Mozart than the large ones.

[3] *The Life and Letters of Sir Charles Hallé* (London, 1896), pp. 407–26.

[4] Alfred Dörffel, *Geschichte der Gewandhausconcerte zu Leipzig, 1781 bis 1881* (Leipzig, 1884).

[5] Richard von Perger, *Denkschrift zur Feier des fünfzigjährigen ununterbrochenen Gestandes der Philharmonischen Konzerte in Wien, 1860–1910* (Vienna, 1910). Statistics here quoted go back to 1842.

exceed ten at the most. Of these, the last five were far more popular than the earlier ones. The clavier concertos were explored more adventurously, but the D minor overshadowed all the others. The serenades, dances, and divertimenti were seldom performed: chamber music was practically restricted to the last ten string quartets, plus the G minor Quintet. There are hardly any records at all of the range of pieces heard at pianoforte recitals, but publication suggests that all the solo sonatas were played, with a fair selection of the miscellaneous pieces.

On the vocal side the picture is rather clearer. The *Requiem* remained universally popular, but the other Masses were hardly ever given. To the ears of Victorian England the sweetest of all Mozart's sacred or vocal works was undoubtedly the spurious 'Twelfth Mass', ubiquitous in church and hall. Between 1844 and 1884 eight editions appeared in vocal score, and another fifteen in instrumental arrangement; selections exceeded a hundred. Although the great concert arias were generally unknown, there were frequent performances of numerous excerpts from the operas, ranging as far back as *Idomeneo* and *Il Re Pastore*. This fully accords with the taste of the age, although the numerical preponderance of these vocal items over instrumental works did not necessarily increase the depths of public appreciation and understanding of Mozart in general.

By the 1870's the attraction of Mozart's instrumental music, restricted as it was in performance, seems to have begun to fade everywhere before the mounting popularity of Beethoven, Mendelssohn, Chopin, Schumann, and Brahms. In opera, public taste became alienated from the ideals of the eighteenth century by changes in the style of singing and in the balance between voice and orchestra brought about by the successive innovations of Rossini, Spontini, Auber, Meyerbeer, Verdi, and Wagner. Small wonder, then, that only one or two of Mozart's operas held the stage even in Germany.

In many Catholic countries another obstacle came from the powerful influence of the Cecilian Society which was founded by Proske at Regensburg in 1853 with the double object of reviving the sacred music of the sixteenth century, and of persuading modern composers to imitate it. The successful pursuit of these aims helped incidentally to depreciate Mozart's (and Haydn's) church music, which was stigmatized as theatrical and frivolous. Hence, partly, grew up the conception of Mozart as a 'rococo' composer, a term which is, in any case, almost as silly as 'baroque'. But the edifice of Mozart's fame, though weakened, did not collapse. The work of scholars such as Köchel and Jahn, of which more will be said in Chapters 2 and 3, helped ultimately to strengthen its foundations with truth and historical accuracy, enabling their successors to build still more strongly.

Simultaneously, many composers and men of letters continued to express opinions about Mozart which showed that changing taste by no means submerged the finer values of his music. Ironically enough, the great musicians who venerated it most were those whose own works contributed much to the radically new ideas and standards which made the public disinclined to listen to Mozart. The farther the romantics moved away from classical ideals, the deeper became their admiration for them, and for his music especially. Sometimes this feeling was tinged with a certain envy of qualities which they sought in vain to recapture.

Rossini, when living in old age at Paris, made two characteristically amusing but penetrating remarks about Mozart. The first, to Moscheles in 1860, was:

I take Beethoven twice a week, Haydn four times, Mozart every day. . . . Your Beethoven is a colossus who often gives one a mighty thump in the ribs, but Mozart is always adorable. He was lucky enough to go to Italy when he was very young, at a time, too, when they still knew how to sing.[1]

The second, to the historian Emil Naumann in 1867:

The Germans have always been at every time the greatest harmonists, and the Italians the greatest melodists. But from the moment that the North produced a Mozart, we of the south were beaten on our own ground, because this man rises above all nations,

[1] *Aus Moscheles Leben* (Leipzig, 1872–3), Bd. 2, pp. 308, 309.

uniting in himself the charm of Italian melody and all the profundity
of German harmony. So, if this music is to cease being recognized
as supremely beautiful and sublime, we old back-numbers can
heartily bless our approaching demise, which will enable us to go
and hear it in Paradise in the company of its author.[1]

Gounod delivered himself in 1882 of the following eulogy,
curiously reminiscent, in part, of Schubert's words quoted
above (pp. 18, 19):

Oh, divine Mozart! Hast thou reposed on the bosom of infinite
beauty, as the beloved disciple reposed on the breast of Christ and
drank in the incomparable grace which marks the great and privileged few? Did even your cradle hear those words which descended
from on high, upon the Man of God transfigured: 'This is my
Beloved Son, in whom I am well pleased: Listen to him.' Oh, yes,
entirely pleased. For prodigal heaven gave thee everything, grace
and strength, abundance and moderation, luminous spontaneity and
ardent tenderness in the perfect equilibrium which constitutes the
irresistible power to charm, and has made thee the unexcelled musician—more than the first—the only—Mozart! Who has run through
the great gamut of human passions as he has done? Who has reached
the extreme limits of the scale with the same infallible precision,
equally guarded against the false refinement of artificial elegance
and the roughness of spurious force? Who has better known how
to breathe anguish and dread into the purest and most exquisite
forms?[2]

Although Wagner's writings contained numerous allusions
to Mozart's music, mostly praising it, there is no doubt that his
knowledge was distinctly limited. He referred[3] to 'the instrumental works . . . (by no means the master's true chef-d'œvres
[*sic*]: for those belong to opera)'. How many of the clavier
concertos did Wagner ever hear? Of the symphonies he said:

---

[1] Naumann, *Italienische Tondichter* (Berlin, 1883), p. 545. The translation of this
passage and of the preceeding are from Francis Toge, *Rossini* (London, 1934), p. 233.

[2] *Le Don Juan de Mozart*, Lu dans le séance publique des cinq Académies, du 25 Oct.
1882, Paris. Reprinted in *MW*, 1882, pp. 721, 736; later translated into German, Italian,
and Spanish.

[3] *Richard Wagner's Prose Works*, translated by W. A. Ellis (London, 1892–8),
vol. iv, p. 192.

'the perpetually recurring and garrulous half-closes make the impression as if I were hearing the clatter of a prince's plates and dishes set to music.'[1] Again 'Mozart knew her [the Tragic Muse] only in the work of Metastasio's "Opera seria"; stiff and arid—*Clemenza di Tito*.'[2] Did he never see the score of *Idomeneo*? Yet he could also write: 'the most prodigious genius raised him high above all masters of all arts and every country.'[3] Among several accounts of Chopin's veneration for Mozart, one of the most interesting is given by Hallé,[4] who said that when playing in a trio recital in the Salle Pleyel, Chopin invariably began with the Trio in E major (K. 542). To Tchaikovsky Mozart represented something almost divine. His letters contain some striking passages of eulogy. In one addressed to Nadejda van Meck on 16 March 1878[5] he praised especially *Don Giovanni* and the andante of the D minor Quartet (K. 421), and went on: 'It is thanks to Mozart that I have devoted my life to music.' An unfavourable, and exceptional, opinion came from Verdi, who dismissed Mozart as a mere *quartettista*. Bizet's correspondence contains many sentences of appreciation, as does also that of Brahms. One of the latter's most interesting observations was expressed in a letter to Dvořák quoted by Warde Fowler (p. 75): 'If we cannot write with the beauty of Mozart, let us at least try to write with his purity.'

Mozart's music lost none of its fascination for artists and writers. Delacroix's journal contains many penetrating remarks about Mozart, whom indeed he mentions more than any other creative artist except Rubens. From another, very different, journal, that of H. F. Amiel,[6] the following remarkably perceptive passage must be quoted:

14th May, 1853.—The quartets were perfectly clear and easy to understand. One was by Mozart and the other by Beethoven, so that

[1] Op. cit., vol. iii, p. 334. [2] Op. cit., vol. vi, p. 178.
[3] Op. cit., vol. vii, p. 95. [4] *Life and Letters, etc.*, op. cit., p. 35.
[5] Modeste Tchaikovsky, *Life and Letters of Peter Ilich Tchaikovsky* (London, 1906), pp. 287, 288.
[6] *Amiel's Journal*, translated by Mrs. Humphry Ward (London, 1899), p. 40, 14 May 1853.

I could compare the two masters. Their individuality seemed to become plain to me: Mozart—grace, liberty, certainty, freedom, and precision of style,—the health and talent of the master, both on a level with his genius: Beethoven—more pathetic, more passionate, more torn with feeling, more intricate, more profound, less perfect, more the slave of his genius, more carried away by his fancy or his passion, more moving and more sublime than Mozart. Mozart refreshes you like the Dialogues of Plato: he respects you, reveals to you your strength, gives you freedom and balance. Beethoven seizes upon you: he is more tragic and oratorical, while Mozart is more disinterested and poetical. Mozart is more Greek, and Beethoven more Christian. One is serene, the other serious. The first is stronger than destiny, because he takes life less profoundly: the second is less strong, because he has dared to measure himself against deeper sorrows. His talent is not always equal to his genius, and pathos is his dominant feature, as perfection is that of Mozart. In Mozart the balance of the whole is perfect, and art triumphs: in Beethoven feeling governs everything, and emotion troubles his art in proportion as it deepens it.

Such objective, finely balanced analysis is rare, even among the philosophers. Kirkegaard (1813–55), who idolized Mozart's operas, viewed them mainly as the basis for developing an elaborate theory of the 'musical-erotic', published in 1843, with particular reference to *Don Giovanni*. Many other thinkers, particularly in Germany, were deeply imbued with a sense of the aesthetic values of those works. Even such a comparatively minor figure as Karl Köstlin (1819–94)[1] has some interesting observations on the universality of Mozart's genius in relation to Shakespeare and Goethe. One minor classic of European fiction was inspired by the composer's life—Eduard Mörike's *Mozart auf der Reise nach Prag*, first published in 1853[2] and since printed in many countries and languages. Although idealized in treatment, it recaptures vividly much of the spirit of the late eighteenth century.

By far the best-known drama influenced by Mozart's music

[1] *Aesthetik* (Stuttgart, 1889), p. 502.
[2] In *Morgenblatt für gebildete Leser*, Stuttgart, nos. 30–33, July–Aug.

was Pushkin's *Kamennuy Gost* ('The Stone Guest'), inspired by *Don Giovanni*. Though written as early as 1826–30, it was widely read for long afterwards. At one time Alfred de Vigny, whose conversations on artistic matters frequently touched on Mozart, thought of writing a play on his life,[1] but unfortunately the idea came to nothing. In skilled hands the subject could have been invested with dignity and pathos, but has in fact too easily lent itself to mawkish, sententious treatment by lesser authors. Yet a sentimental reminiscence of Mozart, expressed allusively by a good writer, can be attractive, as we find in two striking similes of Thackeray's, which show how naturally Mozart's music had sunk into the minds of the educated middle class. The first passage[2] runs:

After you have seen it [The Ruins of Telmessus], the remembrance of it remains with you, like a tune from Mozart which he seems to have caught out of Heaven, and which rings sweet harmony in your ears for ever after. It's a benefit for all after life!

Later Thackeray wrote:[3] 'When she comes into the room, it is like a beautiful air of Mozart breaking upon you.' These few random instances suggest, by the very diversity of the writers, that throughout the mid-nineteenth century Mozart became more and more a living part of European consciousness.[4]

(ii) *Publication and Research*

This diffusion of his musical personality, however limited, was partly due to the new generation of critics and biographers the trend of whose work can now be clearly discerned. In 1843 Semen of Moscow published in three large volumes Alexander Ulibichev's *Nouvelle Biographie de Mozart*, for which the pages of Nissen provided some material. The author, an enthusiastic

---

[1] *AMZ*, 1875, col. 762.
[2] *Notes of a Journey from Cornhill to Grand Cairo* (London, 1846), p. 158.
[3] *Sketches and Travel in London*, London, 1879. *Works*, vol. xiv, p. 311.
[4] Many other references are given by Hans Engel, 'Mozart in der philosophischen und ästhetischen Literatur', *Mozart-Jahrbuch*, 1953, pp. 64–81.

Russian amateur, being unfortunately over-anxious to assert Mozart's superiority to Beethoven, sustained violent attacks from Lenz and Serov whereby his life was shortened. Partial judgements, which distorted Ulibichev's view of musical history, led him to suggest that the music of Palestrina, Handel, and Bach only justified its existence as leading up to the *Requiem*! He also proposed judicious emendations[1] to temper the harmonic audacities of the Quartet K. 465 mentioned before (p. 5).

Nevertheless, some of his criticisms were shrewd, and his book enjoyed an unprecedented success, being translated into Swedish (1850–1) and into German (selected passages on the operas were published in 1847, the complete book in 1859–64). A series of twenty-four extracts appeared in the *Musical World* in 1854; a similar selection entitled 'The Mission of Mozart' had been printed some time earlier in the American periodical *Dwight's Journal of Music*.[2] The circulation of Ulibichev's book attests the growing demand for information about Mozart. In English the earliest distinctive and balanced biography was written by Edward Holmes, a friend of Keats, Leigh Hunt, Shelley, and Novello. Though this *Life of Mozart*, first published in 1845, drew on Nissen, it also included the results of some original research and personal investigation in Austria and Germany. Its merits are attested by the association of Ebenezer Prout and Ernest Newman with the later editions of 1878 and 1912.

In 1856, the centenary of Mozart's birth, Breitkopf issued the first volume of Jahn's *W. A. Mozart*. The background, scope, and influence of this book are too important for brief summary here, and are discussed at length in Chapter 3. Like Ulibichev's work, it was translated into Swedish, in 1865, to meet a growing Scandinavian interest. In 1857 there appeared in Paris a curious pastiche entitled *Mozart. Vie d'un artiste chrétien du XVIIIe siècle. Extracte de correspondance authentique*, by one Isidore Goschler, described on its title-page as 'Chanoine hono-

[1] Vol. ii, pp. 254, 255, footnote.   [2] *MW*, 1856, p. 137.

raire. Directeur du collège Stanislas'. The text, taken wholly from Nissen, is interesting as showing a new emphasis on Mozart's religious virtues. This thread runs right through the nineteenth century, mostly in popular and rather unimportant books, and has taken on new life in the twentieth.

Ludwig Nohl may perhaps be regarded as the first to popularize Mozart. His *Mozarts Leben* of 1863 went into a third edition as late as 1906. He wrote five other books on the same subject and numerous articles; in 1865 he published the first substantial collection of the letters, of which Lady Wallace made an inexact English translation in the same year. We owe to Franz Lorenz, a Viennese physician, the first sizeable book of any critical merit on Mozart's instrumental music, *Mozart als Klavierkomponist*, 1866. Two other admirable monographs were C. F. Pohl's *Mozart in London* (1867), a masterly piece of re-search largely based on newspaper notices and one of the first of its kind, and William Pole's *The Story of Mozart's Requiem* (1879). In 1869 Constantin von Wurzbach, editor of the *Bio-graphisches Lexikon des Kaiserthums Oesterreich*, published his *Mozart-Buch*, a concise, systematic, and still valuable summary of everything written about the composer up to that date, with lists of some printed editions and manuscript sources.

Thus the broad pattern of Mozart literature took shape. The beginnings of objective biography and criticism, based on re-search, emerged from anecdote and personal reminiscence. But between 1830 and 1875 publication of the music proceeded slowly, only a few new sources coming to light. Some valuable autographs remained in the André family, and this firm brought out first editions of such works as *Zaide* (1838), the *Mass in C minor* (1840, vocal score), *L'Oca del Cairo* (1855), and *Lo Sposo deluso* (c. 1855). In 1852 André attempted a complete edition of the clavier concertos in full score, but only managed to issue twelve. Richault of Paris succeeded a few years later where André failed, and printed all twenty-one of these neg-lected works edited by Henri Roubier, professor of the piano-forte at the Convent of the Sacred Heart. In England Cipriani

Potter made a notable attempt (1838–*c*. 1845) to edit the complete clavier works and chamber music with keyboard. In Salzburg Otto Bach, sometime artistic director of the Mozarteum, completed and published some important fragments, such as the *Sinfonia concertante à tre* (K. 320a) and a fine movement for string quintet (K. 613a). But the age of Mozartian archaeology had still to come.

When Wurzbach summarized the position of printed editions in his *Mozart-Buch* of 1869, nearly a third (partly juvenilia, it is true) remained unpublished. The most important deficiencies were: 8 out of 20 masses; 19 out of 48 various church compositions; all 17 organ sonatas; 5 out of 10 cantatas; 39 out of 66 arias, choruses, &c.; 8 out of 23 operas; 30 out of 49 symphonies; 16 out of 33 divertimenti and serenades; 16 out of 27 various orchestral pieces; 23 out of 39 dances; 17 out of 55 concertos. But by the early 1870's the position had become much more hopeful than it was even 10 years before. For in 1862 Ludwig Ritter von Köchel had published his *Chronologisch-thematisches Verzeichniss sämmtlicher Tonwerke Wolfgang Amade Mozart's*, which had assigned a sequence to Mozart's whole output and had attempted to indicate printed or manuscript sources for practically every composition. This catalogue proved of inestimable value when Breitkopf began to issue their definitive collected edition of Mozart in 1877. So greatly did Köchel influence its inception that its progress can best be examined in Chapter 2 as a logical consequence of the life's work of this remarkable man. By 1883 all except a few pieces in the 24th, and last, series of the complete edition had been printed. The gaps were filled by 1905.

The very sight of this Breitkopf edition, occupying nearly $5\frac{1}{2}$ linear feet of shelf-space, lent dignity to Mozart's stature. (In sheer quantity, his output patently did not fall far short of Bach and Handel, and exceeded that of Beethoven, the three composers whose complete works the same firm was then publishing.) Here lay a mass of music to be studied and revived. There is no doubt that this revival gained impetus from the reaction against the more strident excesses of the romantic style, and from the consequent search for restraint in musical values. Conductors, composers, scholars, and writers all hastened to book their tickets, as it were, for excursions along the quiet branch lines of classicism away from the terminus of late romanticism. 'The name of the engine that drew us', they might have said with Samuel Butler, 'was Mozart'.

Thus, about the turn of the century, there was formed a complex of strong impulses which gradually broadened the basis of Mozart's popularity, and which are still far from being exhausted. Definitive publication coincided with a climacteric in musical taste and history, and with the growth of new forces that widened interest in the classics and raised the general level of taste in music. One very important influence was the recognition of musicology as a many-sided discipline in its own right. Hence came fresh insight into musical history, higher standards in criticism, biography, and bibliography. Simultaneously, science slowly aided the dissemination of musical learning; as the twentieth century wore on, the gramophone and radio, the scientific toys of its very early years, developed into intricate branches of technology, rich in possibilities for the spread of musical knowledge. These factors combined to foster a new, often profound interest in Mozart's life, character, and music. Not only did men perform his music with new hands, and listen to it with new ears; they thought about it with new minds. They began to understand what an immense reserve of power was concealed by its polished surface, how rich was its formal invention, how subtle its apparent simplicity, how timeless and illimitable its aesthetic and philosophical significance, how aloof yet attractive the personality of its creator. Gradually both audiences and executants realized that Mozart's musical thought could be profound when expressed in other keys than D minor and G minor.

THE TWENTIETH CENTURY

(i) *Research and Documentation*

This widening of general interest was a process that initially owed much to the cumulative effect of the work done by researchers in many fields, sometimes in conjunction with societies founded for special study and propaganda. The various branches of the international *Mozart-Gemeinde*, established at Salzburg in 1888[1] helped first to stimulate local activity. Its organization quickly reached a membership of over 2,100 in sixty-four branches. Two of them published valuable transactions—one at Berlin from 1895 to 1925, the other at Salzburg from 1918 to 1921. These contained hundreds of articles on the most astonishing range of topics, bearing closely or remotely on Mozart. Some were important, some trivial. The latter betrayed the same lack of a sense of proportion as was seen in the numerous articles devoted to Mozart's skull in the German press between 1890 and 1906. His iconography also became the subject of intensive, and sometimes extravagant study, for, with few exceptions, extant portraits are bad, both as art and as representation, and most of their late, much-investigated copies are quite ludicrously inept. A more profitable type of scholarship took the form of the Mozart Yearbooks edited by Abert in 1923, 1924, and 1929, and by Erich Valentin in 1941–3, followed by the volumes of 1950 onwards issued by the Mozarteum. Thus, having attained the status of a complete edition, Mozart shared with Gluck, Handel, Wagner, and Beethoven the high distinction of these intensive special studies.

Research of this kind gradually stimulated, and later itself received fresh stimulus from, a new factual and historical outlook, which urged scholars, editors, and authors to strive continually towards higher standards. They re-examined many of the known sources bearing on the biography and criticism of Mozart, and tirelessly pursued new ones. Mozart bibliography,

[1] *Neunter Jahresbericht der . . . Internationalen Stiftung Mozarteum in Salzburg*, 1889, p. 30.

in the broadest sense of the term, came into its own. Waldersee's revision (1905) of Köchel's catalogue represented a substantial advance on the original, though not as great as did Einstein's later revision of 1937 on Waldersee's.[1] The study of printed sources in relation to autographs and manuscript copies led to a tardy recognition of their importance. For it was discovered that the first edition sometimes embodied definitive corrections made in proof by the composer, and often had to be regarded as the primary source if the autograph were lost or fragmentary. Hence arose the need for the exact dating of first and early editions as a basis for their evaluation. To collect them became a matter of increasing importance.

After the death of Aloys Fuchs in 1853, no collector specifically or primarily concerned with Mozart appeared until 1897, when Paul Hirsch, then a youth of sixteen, began to include many Mozartiana among the foundations of his great library in Frankfurt. In 1906 he published a small but valuable *Katalog einer Mozart-Bibliothek*, the first of its kind. Among the general collectors of the late nineteenth and early twentieth century who included Mozart among their subjects were Charles Malherbe in Paris, Wilhelm Heyer in Cologne, Edward Speyer in Frankfurt, Antony van Hoboken in Vienna, and Daniel Scheurleer in The Hague. From the early 1920's onwards C. B. Oldman in London built up a notable collection of Mozart editions and literature. After Wurzbach, the next scholar to attempt a list of books and articles on the composer was Henri de Curzon, whose *Essai de bibliographie mozartine* (1905) remains a most useful work despite many inimitable misprints. More comprehensive was Otto Keller's *Mozart-Bibliographie* of 1926, which included much information drawn from a remarkable collection of newspaper cuttings.

Bibliographical study stimulated the collection of fresh documents relating to Mozart's life, and served as a basis for the critical estimation of them. As early as 1880 Nottebohm published his *Mozartiana*, the first important new source material

[1] Discussed in Chapter 2.

since Nissen (1828). Nottebohm's new letters were included by Schiedermair in the four volumes of his *Die Briefe Mozarts und seiner Familie* (1914), to which he added a fifth volume of portraits and facsimiles. Although far more accurate than previous editions of the letters, this collection suffered from sparse annotation. This defect was not remedied for over twenty years until Emily Anderson's rather larger and most liberally annotated edition of 1938. This masterly English version included many of Leopold Mozart's letters. Then at last Mozart's character was revealed through his own words, in English. Josef Kreitmaier, S.J., had used the original German documents in 1919 for his admirably balanced study, *W. A. Mozart, eine Charakterzeichnung des großen Meisters*. In 1919 Schiedermair edited *W. A. Mozarts Handschrift in zeitlich geordneten Nachbildungen*, which illustrated the development of his musical calligraphy, and through it shed light on its relation to his character, a topic that has still not received the close attention which it deserves. The great possibilities of visual documentation have been shown in Robert Bory's *La Vie et l'œuvre de W. A. Mozart par l'image* (1948), a skilful and scholarly book.

(ii) *Biography and Criticism*

Largely on the basis of this great wealth of research and documentation, new ideas and standards in biography and criticism grew up in the first two decades of the twentieth century. (Some of this growth was, of course, a general feature of musicological development in this period.) When, therefore, the third and fourth editions of Jahn appeared respectively in 1889 and in 1905–7, it was unfortunate that fresh ideas and data were only used within the existing framework of the book.[1] But about 1900 Teodor Wyzewa, a Russian-born scholar living in Paris, began to study Mozart's style from an entirely new angle. In collaboration with Count Georges de Saint-Foix, he considered the growth of it in relation to every scrap of music which he might have heard or played. The result was *W.-A.*

[1] Cf. Chapter 2, pp. 68, ff.

Mozart. Sa vie musicale et son œuvre, of which the first two
volumes appeared in 1912, and carried the work up to 1777,
examining twenty-four of the thirty-four periods into which it
had been divided. The three later volumes, written by Saint-
Foix alone and issued in 1936, 1939, and 1946 proved rather inferior to the first two.

Although the whole book, running to well over 2,000 pages,
was a landmark in musical criticism, its weakness lay fundamentally in its method of minute, bar by bar, verbal analysis
unaided by a single musical quotation (apart from an *incipit*) or
bar reference number. While the general discussion preceding
each period was brilliant and stimulating, many of the longer
analyses were difficult to follow, even with a score. The interest,
too, flags towards the end, once the formative periods have
been passed.[1] Nevertheless, the book made people aware of the
importance of Mozart's early music, and paved the way for its
ultimate revival. It also established, largely on grounds of style,
a more exact chronology for compositions written prior to
1784. Its basic methods went unchallenged until 1930, when
Fausto Torrefranca published *Le Origine del romanticismo musicale*, a considerable part of which he devoted to the sources of
Mozart's style. He showed that Wyzewa and Saint-Foix had
ignored a large mass of Italian music which had just as much
claim to be considered a formative influence as the French and
German composers whom they had adduced.

Wyzewa and Saint-Foix idolized both the composer and his
works, even as had Jahn before them, from a different stand-
point. In 1913 came a partial corrective—Arthur Schurig's
Wolfgang Amadeus Mozart, which represented a strong reaction
against the idealized, half-heroic image built up by the nineteenth century. Although Schurig certainly had a case, he over-
stated it; he modified his asperities in the second edition of his
book (1923), to which his *Konstanze Mozart. Briefe, Aufzeichnungen und Dokumente* (1922) formed a valuable complement.

---

[1] Further points were discussed in my article, 'Wyzewa and Saint-Foix: conclusion and restrospect', *MMR*, Jan. 1947.

Abert's revision of Jahn went some way towards restoring the balance. The great bulk of this edition lent it a misleading air of finality, for despite Abert's consummate scholarship, the book contained many unsolved problems. (These are discussed in Chapter 3.) Since the reissue of Abert in 1923–4, no full-scale general book on Mozart has been written.

Among the spate of monographs that began early in the century, E. J. Dent's masterly *Mozart's Operas* (1913, 2nd ed., 1947) was outstanding. It has become a standard work, was translated into German in 1922, and has strongly influenced performance. In 1921 Ernst Lert published the third edition of *Mozart auf dem Theater*, a penetrating examination of the problems of modern staging and performance in relation to the social and aesthetic background of the eighteenth century. One by-product of revived interest in the operas deserves mention, Lowes Dickinson's fantasy *The Magic Flute* (1920), a most moving flight of imagination, which took the form of an elaborate allegory on the problems of modern life. This unique book forms a link with E. J. Dent's work on Mozart's operas. For he, like Dickinson, derived his early love of the composer from Oscar Browning, an inspiring amateur of an earlier generation, and all three were Fellows of King's College at Cambridge.

Of other monographs Robert Lach's *Mozart als Theoretiker* (1918) was an enduring piece of constructive criticism, giving a brilliant analysis of one aspect of his work as a teacher. His creative processes received their first systematic study in 1948 when Jean Chantavoine published *Mozart dans Mozart*, an investigation of the repeated use of certain types of melodic material.[1] By far the most valuable study of any group of the instrumental music was C. M. Girdlestone's magisterial *Mozart et ses concertos pour piano* (1939, English translation 1948). Einstein's very important *Mozart, his Character, his Work* (first published in an English translation, 1945; in the original German, 1948) wisely omitted biography, and summed up a lifetime's thoughtful study of the music. While rich in new ideas

[1] Cf. p. 142.

and stimulating criticism, it lacked the documentation demanded by its importance, and was partly marred, for English readers, by a somewhat cloudy style. Numerous general books appeared in the 1920's and 1930's in English, French, and German, mostly on a high level of accuracy and scholarship. Biographers turned their attention to a minute examination of every aspect of Mozart's social, personal, and masonic life.[1]

Apart from books wholly devoted to Mozart, some interesting critical opinion is to be found in musical textbooks, as well as in general literature. In England, the musical articles contributed by Bernard Shaw to the London press from 1889 to 1894 sparkled with an appreciation of many finer points in Mozart's music which showed how far Shaw's mind ranged beyond the knowledge of some of his more erudite contemporaries. For instance, Parry's article 'Variation' in the first edition of Grove[2] contained the following sentence: 'He [Mozart] was not naturally a man of deep feeling or intellectuality, and the result is that his variation building is neither impressive nor genuinely interesting.' One cannot help wondering if Parry had ever looked at the scores of the Clavier Concertos K. 453, 456, or 491, or the Andante of the A major String Quartet. The same patronizing tone is found in his historical writings, which show that he viewed all eighteenth-century composers as the forerunners of Beethoven. A similarly negative attitude to Mozart marked Hadow's approach in his volume on the Viennese period in the *Oxford History of Music* (1904) where the Masses, concertos, quintets, and serenades are practically ignored. On the other hand, Tovey's famous analysis of the great Clavier Concerto in C (K. 503), which formed the basis of his essay of 1902, 'The Classical Concerto: its nature and purpose', shone as a beacon in the fog which then shrouded English Mozart scholarship.

On rare occasions, enthusiasm went too far and was reproved.

---

[1] Cf. Carola Belmonte, *Mozart und die Frauen* (1905, 2nd ed. 1924); E. K. Blümml, *Aus Mozarts Freundes- und Familienkreis* (1923); Paul Nettl, *Mozart und die königliche Kunst* (1932); O. E. Deutsch, *Mozart und die Wiener Logen* (1932).

[2] Vol. iv, 1890, p. 224.

Rockstro had defended the apparent bareness of the constructional details in Mozart's sonatas on the ground that 'he left them boldly exposed to view, as a great architect delighted to expose the piers upon which the tower of his cathedral depends for its support'.[1] Later, Macdowell retorted somewhat irritably[2] that, so far from resembling cathedrals, these sonatas were 'compositions entirely unworthy of the author of the "Magic Flute" or of any composer with pretensions to anything but mediocrity'. He went on: 'They are written in a style of flashy harpsichord virtuosity such as Liszt never descended to.' But this was exceptional. Quite early in the twentieth century, Mozart was firmly established as 'the musicians' composer'.

Most of the articles printed in periodicals at this time were not of great importance, but one dating from the anniversary of 1906 deserves mention. Written by Alfred Heuss, it was entitled 'Das dämonische Element in Mozarts Werken',[3] and drew attention to the dark undercurrents of passionate feeling that can be discerned in both familiar and unfamiliar compositions. This view, which looks back to the ideas of E. T. A. Hoffmann, has been accepted and enlarged upon by many critics in the last fifty years. Heuss's bold article came out at the same time that Busoni (a fervent disciple of Hoffmann, and much influenced by his ideas on Mozart) was writing down his own opinions.[4] These 'aphorisms', which form a landmark in Mozart criticism, but do not seem to have been quoted *in extenso* in any book, run as follows:

'This is how I think of Mozart: he is up to the present the most perfect manifestation of musical talent.

---

[1] *General History of Music* (London, 1886), p. 269.

[2] *Critical and Historical Essays* (Boston, 1912), p. 194.

[3] *Zeitschrift der Internationalen Musikgesellschaft*, vol. vii, pp. 175–86.

[4] Though written mostly in 1906, it seems that they did not appear in print until 1921. They were then published in a special Busoni number of *Musikblätter des Anbruchs* (pp. 19–27) forming a large part of his 'Aufzeichnungen und Tagebuchblätter'. The present translation is reprinted by permission of Messrs. Curwen & Sons, from *The Sackbut*, vol. ii, 1921, pp. 33–36. On p. 169 of E. J. Dent's *Ferruccio Busoni*, London, 1933, they are referred to as 'Mozart-Aphorismen', but never seem to have been published under this title.

The pure musician looks up to him disarmed and content.

His short life and fecundity enhance his perfection to the point of the phenomenal.

The untroubled beauty of his work irritates.

His sense of form is almost superhuman. Like a masterpiece of sculpture, his art, viewed from any side, is a perfect picture.

He has the instinct of the animal to adapt his task to the utmost limit, but not beyond that of his powers.

He does not attempt anything rash.

He finds without seeking and seeks not what is undiscoverable, that is to say perhaps rather undiscoverable for him.

He possesses an unusual wealth of material but never exhausts it.

He can express a great diversity of things, but never attempts to utter too many at once.

He is passionate, but preserves chivalrous form.

He bears all characters in himself, but only as their exponent.

With the riddle he provides the solution.

His standards are astonishingly true, but they can be measured and defined.

He disposes of light and shadow, but his light does not pain, and his darkness shows a clear outline.

He has a witticism ready to meet any situation, even the most tragic; in the merriest he can present a solemn mien.

He is universal through his adroitness.

He can draw upon any glass because he never drinks one to the dregs.

He stands so high that he sees further than all, and therefore sees everything on rather a small scale.

His palace is immeasurably great, but he never steps outside the walls.

Through the windows of it he sees Nature. The window frame is also the frame of nature.

Gladness is his predominant feature. He covers even the most unpleasant things with a smile.

His is not the smile of a diplomat or an actor, but of a pure mind, yet that of a man of the world.

His mind is not pure through lack of knowledge.

He has not remained simple and has not become *raffiné*.

He has a temperament but not a nervous one, he is an idealist but not unmaterial: a realist without unpleasantness.

He is a burgher as well as an aristocrat, but never a peasant or a rebel.

He is a friend of order: miracles and devilries preserve with him their 16 and 32 bars.

He is religious as far as religion is identical with harmony.

In him the antique and the rococo are combined to perfection, though without resulting in a new architecture.

Architecture is the art most akin to his.

He is the prime and round number, the sum total, a conclusion and not a beginning.

He is as youthful as an adolescent and wise as an old man— never out of date and never modern: carried to the grave and yet ever alive. His very human smile transfigured still beams upon us.'

Towards the end of the same 'Aufzeichnungen' (p. 21), Busoni asked:

'Does my *Brautwahl* with its 700 pages of score achieve more than *Figaro* with its six wind instruments playing accompaniments?'

These words betray a whole world of wistful admiration, shared by many late romantic composers.

Not all, perhaps, even of Mozart's most devoted admirers would accept the implications of each and every one of Busoni's dicta, but the fact remains that in the twentieth century Mozart, like Bach and Beethoven, has passed beyond controversy into the realms of exegesis. Any dispute now turns not upon merit, but upon the basis and latitude of aesthetic values. It is strange, nevertheless, that no reasoned, comprehensive case has apparently yet been made,[1] setting out the weaknesses that are inherent in Mozart's music.

(iii) *Performance*

The branches of the International Mozart Society at Berlin and Salzburg, mentioned above, interested themselves as much in performance as in the publication of their proceedings. Another very active branch was that at Dresden, founded in 1898, whose members by 1900 amounted to over 1600. A similar society was active in Düsseldorf in the next decade. A Mozart Society in London gave a number of special concerts in 1898, duly chronicled by the *Musical Times*. In Paris, an independent *Société d'études mozartiennes* began to publish a bulletin in 1930, and during its short existence gave six concerts of neglected masterpieces, including *Idomeneo*. All over Europe the centenary of 1891 and the 150th anniversary of Mozart's birth, observed in 1906, gave new impetus to special concerts and festivals which have flourished spasmodically until the present time. These activities have all played their part in making audiences progressively more ready to be led from the familiar to the unfamiliar.

The spread of musicological ideas helped to bring about a new outlook on the revival of 'old' music. Mozart gained most, perhaps, in operatic performance. Not only did the stock favourites—*Figaro*, *Don Giovanni*, and (outside England and France) *Die Zauberflöte*, benefit from a fresh approach to problems of staging, dress, and ensemble, but neglected ones began to win favour. Before the First World War, Beecham in London, Mahler in Vienna, and Richard Strauss in Munich all contributed to the re-education of the public in operatic appreciation. At Cambridge in 1911 Clive Carey's production of *Die Zauberflöte*[2] in E. J. Dent's translation marked the begin-

---

[1] Paul Zschorlich's *Mozart-Heuchelei* (Leipzig, 1906) makes out only a limited case.

[2] This opera had not been heard in London since 1869. Loewenberg records a production staged in Egypt, at the Pyramids, in 1912. Cf. also A. Cœuroy, *Appels d'Orphée* (Paris, 1929), pp. 46, 47, for an imaginative account by Gérard de Nerval of such a performance.

ning of a new epoch in England. Their efforts to reinstate
Mozart as popular entertainment bore fruit in the gradual
adoption of the five great operas as part of the regular repertory
first at the Old Vic, later at Sadler's Wells.

Equally notable was the work of John Christie at Glyndebourne, where the early festivals from 1934 to 1937 were devoted entirely to Mozart, though later the repertory included
other composers. This superlative service culminated in 1951
with triumphant proof of the power of *Idomeneo* to move
modern English audiences. The revival of this noble opera
given at Munich in 1931 under Strauss had caused its restoration
to the stage of other German cities, and in Switzerland, Austria,
and Belgium. Three English revivals during the same period,
being by amateurs, failed to surmount completely the extreme
technical difficulties of the work, but at least served to open the
eyes of all but the most obtuse critics to its inherent beauty. No
less interesting is the fact that between 1925 and 1938 *Così fan
tutte* was produced in Latvia, Poland, Hungary, Czechoslovakia,
Argentina, and Belgium.

Compared with the operas, the instrumental works gained
ground slowly everywhere, but ultimately their fine, varied
qualities, particularly as found in the chamber music and concertos, have become widely appreciated by audiences and performers. As early as 1891 Carl Reinecke wrote *Zur Wieder-
belebung der Mozart'schen Clavier-Concerte*, with particular
reference to the difficulties offered by K. 537. Though the
pamphlet was several times reprinted, his plea fell on deaf ears.
In 1910 Saint-Saëns, then seventy-five years old, came to London, and in three concerts, conducted by his pupil Benno
Hollander, played twelve Mozart clavier concertos, each with
three cadenzas of his own.[1] But the time was not yet ripe in
England, although in Edinburgh Tovey played most of the
great concertos regularly at his Reid Concerts from 1914 until

---

[1] K. 413, 449, 456, 453, 466, 467, 482, 488, 491, 503, 537, 595. The complete
programmes, forming part of a collection made by Hollander himself, are now in
the BM.

his death in 1940. As late as 1928 Cecil Gray could write that these works were 'wayward and nonchalant in form, full of charming ideas which he hardly takes the trouble to work out' —a curious echo of what Dittersdorf had said *c.* 1785.[1] It was left to a sounder English critic, C. M. Girdlestone, writing in French, twenty-nine years after Saint-Saëns's visit, to state a reasoned case for these magnificent works.

Abroad, only two or three of them were regularly heard, principally the D minor. Exceptionally, from 1873 onwards Busoni's astonishing repertory included nine of the concertos (which he once thought of editing complete, in conjunction with Egon Petri) as well as the Rondo in A minor (K. 511) and the Gigue in G (K. 574). His playing raised Mozart to a majestic level.[2] Nor were the concertos alone slow to make their way. Only after 1920 did the symphonies which Mozart wrote before 1780 appear with some frequency in concert programmes; equally slow recognition came to the serenades and divertimenti, of which Gray[3] wrote that they were little more than what the Germans call *Galanteriekunst*. The clavier rondos, fantasias, and duet-sonatas remained almost unknown, although a few of the solo sonatas kept their place. The nineteenth century regarded this type of work as 'thin'. (It was presumably this notion which prompted Grieg to try to popularize them by publishing, from 1879 onwards, the Sonatas K. 283, 545, 533 with 494, K. 457, and the Fantasia K. 475 with a part for second keyboard.) This rather condescending attitude to Mozart's clavier pieces has lasted well into the twentieth century. As in earlier periods, modern performance has stimulated publication. A considerable number of definitive editions of known works appeared after 1905, when the supplement to the Breitkopf edition was completed. But discoveries of unknown Mozart

---

[1] Cf. p. 4. Gray, *The History of Music* (London, 1928), p. 180, was referring to the pre-1782 concertos but did not correct the implication that his words applied equally to the later ones.

[2] Busoni also wrote cadenzas to these nine clavier concertos, and to two flute concertos. The influence which intensive study of Mozart exercised on his own music is discussed by E. J. Dent, *Ferruccio Busoni* (London, 1933), p. 111.

[3] Op. cit.

compositions were comparatively few.[1] The printing of large numbers of miniature scores (some containing a critical revision of the text) has afforded some measure of his popularity.[2]

The scope of modern Mozart performance is a matter that requires a more detailed consideration than can be attempted here. Briefly, however, it may be asked—of the total of roughly 650 works (including the extensive, playable fragments), what proportion deserves regular performance in the concert repertory? The answer, in round figures, may be given as half his large output; for the total of masterpieces, in many different categories, is upwards of 300. Among these, even the old favourites have not yet yielded up all their secrets, and, indeed, wider knowledge of many fine, neglected works will shed fresh light on the familiar, and the unfamiliar will in turn gain popularity, for the one cannot fail to set the other in perspective. Among the less important and early pieces, it is hard to say, by applying a rigid yard-stick, which deserve regular performance and which do not. Many compositions are unequal in themselves, having perhaps two out of several movements that are outstandingly fine. To include them entire in concerts can hardly be justified, for, with few exceptions, the works of Mozart's childhood and adolescence are interesting mainly for the light they shed on his development.

Nevertheless, in recent years, many of those lesser compositions have been given in England, and some have been hailed, rather uncritically, as masterpieces. While such performance is undeniably interesting it may involve two real dangers. It may do Mozart some disservice by blunting the appreciation of his greatest music, and is very likely to militate against the revival of the best works written by such interesting contemporaries as Pleyel, Beck, Schobert, Gossec, Rosetti, and the Stamitz family. For, although it cannot, of course, hold a

---

[1] Cf. Chapter 2, p. 64.

[2] Mozart has shared the general vulgarization of the classics. Two of many extraordinary arrangements may be noted—the Andante of the clavier Trio K. 564 as a song 'O come sweet spring', and the *Rondo alla turca*, from the sonata K. 331, as a vocalise.

candle to the masterpieces of Mozart, this delightful music does deserve an occasional hearing in its own right, as being distinctly superior to his second-rate works. It would also remind us how subtle were the varieties of style in the later eighteenth century, and would show how talent even of a high order differs from genius.

In style of performance, there is still generally much to be attained because in the past too much has been taken for granted. Until the last few decades, the apparent simplicity of Mozart's music has often led to ill-considered and ill-rehearsed renderings. Even now, when conductors, players, and soloists attain a high technical standard, many of them still betray the most incongruous and contradictory ideas of 'interpretation'. There is some excuse in the fact that modern research into the theory and practice of the eighteenth century hardly goes beyond the year 1760, although the problems of the era that followed the end of the so-called 'thorough-bass period' are quite as difficult as the earlier ones. The patient study given to the authentic rendering of Bach and Handel is still a desideratum for Mozart and his contemporaries. Such matters as tempi, phrasing, ornamentation, the repetition of formulae, nuances, and emphasis in scale-playing all need much study in contemporary sources before we can claim to have recaptured some of Mozart's own standards and ideals in performance.[1] Meanwhile, the present variety of styles could surely be reduced.[2]

(iv) *Popularity*

Looking back on the first half of the twentieth century, we can now see that during this time Mozart became generally accepted as a great and popular musician. The width of this acceptance has largely been due to the fact that he wrote more fine music in a greater variety of forms than any other composer. But it might be argued, somewhat paradoxically, that this very variety has militated against his universal popularity.

---

[1] Some aspects of clavier performance are discussed in Chapter 16.
[2] Cf. William Glock, 'Some Notes on Performance', *Score*, Dec. 1952.

For there is no doubt that in forms apart from opera and chamber music many others have written works more compelling than comparable ones by Mozart, and capable of attracting consistently larger audiences. (Whether these works are necessarily greater than his, is another matter.) A further limiting factor has undoubtedly lain, and still lies, in national temperament. While his music has a great appeal for Germanic lands, Britain, and America, it remains far less popular in Latin countries. Italian audiences of today find Mozart's formalism and *morbidezza* as uncongenial as they did in Stendhal's time,[1] so that the proportion of his works regularly heard remains small. In France they appeal mainly to the intellectual classes:[2] the better-known instrumental pieces are popular, but only one or two operas are usually given. It seems improbable that these or other national antipathies towards Mozart are likely to change very much.

Some special causes underlying the growth of his popularity call for comment. From the very range of his music, he stood to gain more than many other composers from the development of radio and gramophone. For he wrote so much, still little known in the late 1920's, which was of high quality and ideally suited in length and medium for exploration by the enterprising record company or planner of radio programmes. Universal statistics for broadcasting are not, unfortunately, available, but even a casual survey of programmes for England and Germany shows how much greater is the range of Mozart now played than twenty-five or thirty years ago. A similar expansion can certainly be detected in recorded music from the late 1920's onwards, when an ever-increasing quantity appeared in the lists of continental companies, particularly Polydor, and in the memorable 'connoisseur' catalogues of 'His Master's Voice'. Some interesting proportionate figures can be extracted from the definitive *World's Encyclopaedia of Recorded Music*[3] which

[1] Cf. p. 22, n. 1.
[2] *The Journals of André Gide* (translated by Justin O'Brien, London, 1949) contain many interesting observations on Mozart; cf. especially vol. i, pp. 32, 282.
[3] Ed. F. C. Clough and G. Cuming, London, 1952, including the first supplement.

comprised all classical disks issued in Europe and America from 1925 to 1950. Mozart, with twenty-five pages of entries, ranks second only to J. S. Bach, with twenty-seven pages. Verdi and Schubert come next with twenty-one pages each, Wagner fourth with eighteen, and Brahms and Beethoven fifth with fourteen pages. In the second supplement (1953) Mozart occupies fifteen pages, Bach twelve. Allowing for differences in variety and productivity between one composer and another, these figures give a fair indication, from a very wide field, of the relative demand for classical music in general, and for Mozart in particular.

In Britain, partly under the influence of gramophone and radio, a notable change has taken place in public taste for several branches of his music. For the first time in our operatic history, the five great operas have won a seemingly permanent place in the repertoire. This is principally due to the cumulative, long-term effect of the work done by Sir Thomas Beecham at Covent Garden, mentioned above (p. 45), by the Carl Rosa company playing in many cities, by E. J. Dent and Clive Carey at Sadler's Wells, and by John Christie at Glyndebourne. (In this connexion, we should notice a surprising difference between England and Germany. Professor Friedrich Blume has mentioned[1] that, although Mozart's operas received 3,610 performances in German theatres from 1935 to 1940, and were more popular than any others, they have declined since the war to fifth place, after those of Wagner, Verdi, Lortzing, and Puccini.)

At the same time, Mozart's orchestral music has come into high favour with British audiences. From about 1927 onwards 'Mozart nights' were established at the London Promenade Concerts. In Edinburgh during the 20's and 30's Tovey

[1] *Wolfgang Amadeus Mozart, Denkrede* (Wolfenbüttel, 1948), p. 28; cf. also Erich Valentin, 'Geschichtliches und Statistisches über Mozartpflege', in *Neues Mozart Jahrbuch*, 1943, pp. 247–63, dealing mainly with the operas. For post-war performances in Vienna at the 'Theater an der Wien' Otto Fritz, *Almanach der Staatsoper, 1945–1954*, (Vienna 1954), provides the following figures: Verdi (9 operas), 494; Mozart (6) 314; Wagner (4), 273; R. Strauss (8), 217; Puccini (4), 187.

successfully revived many neglected works at the Reid Concerts. Particular interest was aroused by the London Theatre
Concerts from 1937 to 1939, which, in association with
Beecham, were devoted very largely to Mozart's forgotten
masterpieces. Harry Blech's London Mozart Players founded
in 1949 have carried on this tradition. Of any group, the
clavier concertos, of which at least a dozen have become firm
favourites, are clearly the most popular. The best of the
divertimenti and serenades, again mainly owing to the spirited
advocacy of Beecham, were much appreciated, but he and
other conductors were less successful in reviving the numerous
early symphonies. Charming though many of them are,
barely half a dozen have kept their place. It is, however, the
chamber music that has undoubtedly made the deepest and
widest appeal. The amount currently played is probably
greater, even considering what a large part of his instrumental output it forms, than that of all the other groups
together. Its expansion began in the 1920's[1] and culminated in
the remarkable range and frequency of performances heard at
the National Gallery Concerts.[2] This level of popularity has
hardly waned since, and may be taken as a fair index of the
attraction that the chamber music has for players and audiences
throughout Britain.

Apart from actual performance, Mozart also gained from an
affinity between his music and certain contemporary movements in other arts, which created a new enthusiasm for formal
values. In England this was seen in the revival of interest in
Milton, Pope, and Donne, and in the intensive study of
Georgian architecture: in Germany, in the work of Gropius and
the influential ideals of the Bauhaus. A new, and widespread,
though perhaps imprecise, appreciation of formalism found
itself in sympathy with the achievement of the classical composers. For during the inter-war period, musicians of many

[1] Cf. W. S. Meadmore, *The Story of a Thousand Concerts, 1887–1927* (the South
Place Concerts), London, 1928.
[2] *Music performed at the National Gallery Concerts, 10th October 1939 to 10th April 1946*,
privately printed, London, 1948.

schools were pursuing ideals that did not commend themselves to the average music-lover. In that distracted epoch, with the future so uncertain, faith in tradition seemed at a low ebb, and many extremes of artistic experiment lacked purpose and coherence. The music with the widest appeal proved to be that which had certainty of style and direction, which was organic in growth and affirmative in spirit. So to Mozart came his full share of a great wave of enthusiasm for all the Viennese 'classics'.

This steady, manifold increase in his popularity has been to his undoubted benefit. But may not the pendulum have swung too far? 'We are all Mozartians nowadays', wrote Professor Peter Latham,[1] implying that we can have too much of a good thing. There is indeed some danger, particularly in English- and German-speaking countries, that Mozart's music may be taken over-seriously for its ultimate good. It would be sad if sheer enjoyment of its technical skill, its wit and humanity should be submerged in a welter of interpretation and annotation. It would be ironical if its vitality, having survived the partial neglect of the nineteenth century were to be endangered by the mummifying assiduity of the twentieth.

Yet such foreboding may be unjustified. For as the kaleidoscope of taste has revolved, Mozart's place in musical history has seemed at some times clear and steady, while at others the pattern on the glass has been blurred and, in some respects, still is. Our position, at the bi-centenary of his birth, is not unlike that of a listener to the first movement of one of his clavier concertos. Most of the themes have been stated: their relative importance seems to have been partly defined: but as the development approaches, who can tell what new ideas, with unpredictable modulations, contrasts and regroupings, may appear? Nearly seventy years ago it was said[2] that Mozart was a young man with a great future before him. Whether spoken in jest or earnest, those words have come profoundly true. In

---

[1] *ML*, Jan. 1953, p. 77, review of the Penguin book *The Concerto*.
[2] The remark has been variously attributed to von Bülow and Richter.

the present and foreseeable circumstances of musical life, when fertile European traditions are continually spreading to distant parts of the world,[1] all the classics seem assured of long life and renewal, at many different levels of musical experience.

What place Mozart may hold in the musical hierarchy of the future, in 1991, 2056, and beyond, is really immaterial and to attempt to divine it now by asserting his superiority to one composer or another, is mere sciamachy. But if greatness may be measured by the very deep affection in which a man's memory is held, by the real happiness which his works have given to countless millions, then Mozart is surely to be reckoned among the greatest of the earth.

[1] Active branches of the International Foundation Mozarteum have been established in Tokyo, in Sydney, and in the Argentine.

2

Köchel, Breitkopf, and the Complete Edition

FEW men of the nineteenth or any other century have become universally known through a single letter of their name. Outside the field of science—where, for instance, the 'M' numbers of certain nebulae have perpetuated the name of Charles Messier, the French astronomer—it is doubtful if this honour has come to anyone save Ludwig Ritter von Köchel, the 'K' of whose surname is seen in print wherever Mozart's music is played. Such literal distinction is of course now facilitated by the passion of the twentieth century for compressing organizations and persons into strings of unpunctuated letters, GATT, GBS, SHAPE, and so on *ad nauseam*. After some sixty years of general acceptance as 'K. V.', Köchel's great Mozart catalogue has now become known simply as 'K'.

Ludwig Alois Friedrich Köchel, the son of an official in the Austrian Imperial Treasury, was born on 14 January 1800 at Stein, a small town on the Danube, some forty miles north-west of Vienna. From early youth he showed intellectual and personal qualities, which, as they later developed, were to mark him as one of the great men of his age. Having taken his doctorate in law, Köchel became a private tutor. His third appointment came in 1828 when, together with his lifelong friend Dr. Franz von Scharschmied, he was chosen by the Archduke Carl to supervise the education of his four sons. With one of them, the young Archduke Friedrich, Köchel later visited many parts of Europe, including Scotland and England, where he and his charge were entertained at Windsor Castle. When his tutelage came to an end in 1842, he received the Knight's Cross of the Order of Leopold in recognition of his services. Thereafter he built up a European reputation as a mineralogist and botanist. (The names of several species of plant, such as the *Bupleurum Koechelii*, commemorate his work.) He also found time for serious musical study. Thus in versatility of mind he had much in common with his close friend Otto Jahn.

In 1851 Franz Lorenz,[1] another friend of Köchel's, had drawn attention in an anonymous pamphlet *In Sachen Mozarts* to the urgent need for the systematic investigation and preservation of his works. To this stimulus Köchel, trained in scientific classification and imbued with a deep love of Mozart, responded at once. From 1850 to 1863, Salzburg served as his chief place of residence, whence he travelled all over Europe in order to further botanical research and to collect materials for his catalogue. He had some foundations on which to build.[2] The most comprehensive was a thematic, classified catalogue of all Mozart's works, completed by Aloys Fuchs in 1837, invaluable, though necessarily imperfect. Mozart's own *Verzeichnüß aller meiner Werke vom Monath Febrario 1784 bis Monath—* (of which Johann Anton André had printed two editions, the first in 1805, the second in 1828) formed a basis for its own period. But for the years 1762 to 1783 the pursuit of autographs and manuscript copies was very difficult, despite some further help derived from André himself. In 1841, when sixty-six years old, he was anxious to sell as a whole his collection, which he had purchased from Mozart's widow early in 1800, and issued a *Thematisches Verzeichniß derjenigen Originalhandschriften von W. A. Mozart . . . welche Hofrath André in Offenbach besitzt*. After André's death in 1842, his collection remained intact for eleven years, but in 1854 his heirs began to disperse it. Thus in 1856, the centenary year, there was no sign of any library's making a systematic effort to collect and preserve Mozart's autographs,[3] still less to relate them to early printed editions.

---

[1] Cf. p. 33.

[2] Jahn tells in the preface to his second edition how he himself began to collect materials for a thematic catalogue, but gave them all to Köchel when he learnt of the latter's plan.

[3] So Ferdinand Hiller complained in an article written in the *Kölnische Zeitung*, quoted by *MW*, 1856, p. 101. The situation was partly remedied in 1873 when the

All the more credit, therefore, must go to Köchel for his pertinacity. Apart from this, his great achievement lay in the chronological order which he established, on a basis of musical style and palaeography, for the works composed before February 1784, for many of which the autographs, even if they could be traced, bore no date. He enumerated all Mozart's works in chronological order of composition, with thematic identification of, and the numbers of bars in, each movement: he gave the manuscript sources, where known, for each composition: he listed early and other important printed editions: and he commented shortly, with references to Jahn, upon the style and value of each piece. In order to round off the whole, Köchel classified Mozart's entire output into the twenty-three categories which were later adopted unchanged for the publication of the complete edition, and added appendixes, giving invaluable lists of lost, fragmentary and doubtful works. Prolonged research and planning gave him material for an important article 'Ueber den Umfang der musikalischen Produktivität W. A. Mozart's'[1] which he printed in 1861. It served as a *prolegomenon* to the monumental catalogue which Breitkopf published in 1862 under the title *Chronologisch-thematisches Verzeichniß sämmtlicher Tonwerke Wolfgang Amade Mozart's* with an appropriate dedication to Jahn. A lesser man might have rested content with these laurels, but Köchel's final service was still to come.

He realized that the publication of his catalogue marked only the first stage in making Mozart's genius fully and widely known. The second stage necessarily entailed the establishment of a definitive text of each composition, to be published in a standard edition. It must have been tantalizing to Köchel to watch the progress of the Breitkopf editions of Bach, Handel,

Prussian State Library purchased all the Mozart autographs still in the possession of André's heirs. By 1900 an extension of this policy had augmented their holding to 422: cf. Oskar Fleischer, *Mozart* (Berlin, 1900), p. 185. A list of all owners of Mozart autographs known in 1889 is given in Breitkopf's *Nachtrag* to Köchel.

[1] In *Mitteilungen der Gesellschaft für Salzburgsche Landeskunde*; it was reprinted separately in 1862.

and Beethoven, which had been begun, respectively, in 1851, 1858, and 1862. (The first two, moreover, had no thematic catalogue, and that compiled anonymously for Beethoven in 1851 gave but scant bibliographical detail.) But, as shown in Chapter 1, current interest in Mozart was still limited. Clearly a definitive edition could not be undertaken as an ordinary publishing venture. Enthusiasm and financial support were essential. Köchel supplied some of the latter himself, and devoted all his energies to arousing the former.[1]

His eminence in the world of learning and his privileged position in court circles enabled him to evoke some interest among musicians and the aristocracy. (The thirteen patrons ultimately included eight German crowned heads.) He himself gave Breitkopf 15,000 gulden (approximately £1,500) to finance the project, but had his name withheld until later. Thus emboldened, Breitkopf issued the following appeal in 1875:[2]

MOZART'S WORKS.

PUBLICATION BY SUBSCRIPTION

of the

FIRST COMPLETE AND CRITICALLY-REVISED

EDITION OF

W. A. MOZART'S COMPOSITIONS

The undersigned firm have the satisfaction of announcing, that

[1] Köchel's part in the enterprise is made clear in Waldersee's preface to the second edition of the Mozart catalogue, and in the article on him in the *Allgemeine Deutsche Biographie*, written by C. F. Pohl. It is to be presumed that Köchel collaborated with such bodies as the *Gesellschaft der Musikfreunde*, which is said to have been designated by Liszt as the supporter of the plan for a Mozart edition, originated by him during the Vienna festival of 1856. Cf. H. J. Moser, *Das musikalische Denkmälerwesen in Deutschland* (Kassel, 1952), p. 14. According to Walter Hummel, *Chronik der Internationalen Stiftung Mozarteum* (Salzburg, 1951), p. 8, the first impulse towards the complete edition came from a conversation in London between Joachim and Sigmund Menken. Cf. also *Briefe von und an Joseph Joachim*, ed J. Joachim and A. Moser (Berlin, 1913), vol. iii, p. 160.
[2] The English version quoted is from an issue now in the BM and bound up with a copy of Köchel's 1862 catalogue. The italics, capitals, &c., are those of the original.

they have undertaken the first *complete*, and at the same time *critically-revised* edition of Mozart's works.

'No monument more worthy of Mozart's genius could be suggested'—thus wrote VON KÖCHEL, the indefatigable collector of his works—'than a correct edition of the *whole* of his compositions'. Yet, up to the present time—86 years after his death—such a memorial has been denied to him. For, although his name, as well as a great portion of his compositions, has become a household word everywhere, yet the full extent of his productiveness as a composer, embracing, as it did, all branches of vocal and instrumental music, is even now, scarcely known. Thus: of the 626 compositions by MOZART, enumerated in the list here appended, *one third*, i.e. more than 200, have never been published[1] while among those published, some are spurious, and others incorrect.

Within recent years we have had the satisfaction of publishing a complete and critically-revised edition of BEETHOVENS [*sic*] works—which has met with general approval. To this, the present *Mozart-edition* is to form a companion, not only as regards intrinsic correctness and external appearance, but also as to price and the manner of publication. It will comprise all genuine and finished compositions by MOZART: the text of which will be established by competent musicians from the Original Manuscripts (where procurable), and thus the distinctive features of the present edition will be *authenticity, completeness,* and *cheapness.*

Authenticity will be ensured by a scrupulous determination of the text from the Autographs and original publications: and we tender to all owners of Autographs our earnest request for their temporary loan. We shall thus be able to stem the tide of incorrect and distorted reading, which has befallen so many of the immortal master's compositions: and as an earnest of our endeavours in this respect, we may point not only to our edition of BEETHOVEN'S works, but also to the *Eight Operas* by MOZART, edited by J. Rietz, recently published, which will be incorporated in the present complete edition.

We have obtained already the promise of assistance for the editorial portion of the undertaking, from the following eminent musicians and *savants*, viz: Dr. JULIUS RIETZ (of Dresden), F. ESPAGNE (of the Royal Library, Berlin), G. NOTTEBOHM (of Vienna), and Professor C. REINECKE (all of whom have been en-

---

[1] This figure has been reduced by later research: cf. p 9.

gaged on the *Beethoven-edition*), as also of J. BRAHMS (of Vienna), Professor J. JOACHIM (of Berlin), OTTO GOLDSCHMIDT (of London), VON KÖCHEL (of Vienna), Professor RUDORFF, Professor P. SPITTA (of Berlin), and others.

Completeness will be attained by including in this edition all MOZART'S authentic compositions, whether previously printed or not, while fragments, sketches, and unauthenticated pieces will be excluded, as also his transcriptions and instrumentations of other composers.

VON KÖCHEL'S well-known *Chronological and Thematic Catalogue of Mozart's Works*, will form the basis of our edition, which will be divided into *Twenty-three Series* (in a similar way to the *Beethoven-edition*), while each composition will bear the number corresponding to that with which it appears in KÖCHEL'S exhaustive work.

A supplementary *series* will subsequently contain the Editor's report, as also such fragments of compositions as it may appear desirable to publish, and any other genuine compositions that have not yet been traced. KÖCHEL'S labours, like those of JAHN, the famous biographer of MOZART, have undoubtedly facilitated the object we have in view, and so has [sic] the praiseworthy efforts of the Royal Library of Berlin, which has [sic] been directed towards collecting autographs and authenticated copies of autographs—still we would call upon all, who are in a position to do so, to aid us in the promotion of this great undertaking, by giving information as to the existence of any autographs, authenticated copies, or original editions, which are not mentioned in KÖCHEL'S *Catalogue*.

Cheapness also will be a feature of the present edition, which, since it will comprise all MOZART'S works, and consequently those that sell less, as well as the more popular ones, should of course not be compared with the ordinary cheap editions of the latter only.

In shape and type it will satisfy the requirements of a Standard edition—while the price will be at the rate of about fourpence only for a large music sheet of four pages.

The sum of £50—subscribed beforehand—will cover the total expense of a copy of the complete edition—whatever its extent may be, and these subscribers' copies will be printed direct from the plates, before the customary transfer upon stone has been effected.

The list of patrons, as well as of subscribers, will head the new edition. £100 will entitle to a complete copy, elaborately bound, bearing the donor's name as a patron and co-founder of this Mozart-Memorial.

In order to meet the requirements of the musical public, the work will be issued in instalments: containing, alternately, compositions from the different series or groups into which the whole is divided. The preliminary work of critical revision having already commenced, the public will be in possession of the first instalments within the next few weeks. We hereby pledge ourselves to bring all possible energy to bear upon a speedy-publication, so that the completion of the whole may be looked for in the course of a few years.

Thanks to the magnanimous support of a wealthy patron, we have been able to approach an undertaking, the very dimensions of which must, of necessity, separate it from all speculative publications; still we have to enlist the generous support of all admirers of MOZART, i.e. the music-loving public in general.

Surely we are not too sanguine in anticipating that the countless admirers of the master, who are indebted to his genius for so much lofty enjoyment, will unite in manifesting their gratitude by cheerfully contributing to this monument to the great composer, while acquiring for themselves at the same time a rich and permanent treasure.

LEIPZIG.   BREITKOPF & HÄRTEL.

This exceptionally interesting document shows how ludicrously cheap, by mid-twentieth century standards, was the cost of high-class music engraving in the 1870's, even when partly subsidized. But notwithstanding the low price, few subscribers came forward, and the somewhat anxious tone of the prospectus proved to be justified, for the first list, published in 1877, contained only eighty-five names. Clearly, the edition could hardly have been undertaken but for Köchel's generosity. Even by 1883 the total had only risen to ninety-three (barely one-third of the subscribers to the German Handel Society's edition), made up of forty-four in Germany and Austria, fourteen in France, eighteen in England,[1] seven in America, and ten elsewhere. The progress of the undertaking was sadly marked by

---

[1] Namely: Oscar Browning, R. Pendlebury, Herbert Oakley, the Maharajah Duleep Singh, Messrs. Augener, Arthur G. (presumably J.) Balfour, Edward Baring,

the deaths of several of the editors, the first being that of Köchel himself on 3 June 1877. As a final tribute to his services to Mozart, the *Requiem*, which he had lived to see published a month before in the edition prepared by Brahms, was sung at his funeral. He died revered by all who knew him for his deep and varied learning, for his dignity and nobility of character, and for the generosity of his mind and fortune. Of the other editors, Rietz died later in 1877, Espagne in 1878, and Nottebohm in 1882.

But publication went on steadily. By 1883 twenty-three series had been issued completely. (This was by far the speediest of all Breitkopf's great undertakings, not excepting their Schubert edition which was begun and completed within the twelve years 1883–95.) Whatever faults changed standards and wider knowledge have found in the work of editors of nearly eighty years ago, who can doubt that this policy of rapid publication was then right? The protracted incompleteness of the collected editions of Haydn and Liszt surely points the moral. The year 1905 saw the completion of series 24 of the Mozart edition, containing works described as 'rediscovered, un-certified or unfinished', to a total of seventy-one numbers, of which all but five had appeared before the end of 1889. At the same time Count Paul Waldersee completed his revision of Köchel's catalogue, which he augmented with rather fuller bibliographical information, but in which, apart from a few redatings and a score of insertions based on series 24, he left the main plan untouched. About the same time or a little later, Breitkopf reprinted most of the twenty-three series (into some of which corrections and revisions were introduced) in order to meet the growing demand.

Waldersee's edition of Köchel ran to 676 pages, an increase of only 125 on the original. But when Einstein published the third edition in 1937 his text amounted to 984 pages. Besides

W. A. Barrett, Sir W. G. Cusins (for Queen Victoria), Messrs. Chappell, Messrs. Dulau (for the BM), Charles Hallé, Miss Nisbet Hamilton, F. Justen, Messrs. Novello, Ebenezer Prout, G. S. Löhr, and E. W. Whinfield. The 1877 list included also George Henschel.

meticulous presentation of juvenilia, two general factors had caused this remarkable expansion—the advance of musical bibliography in general with its intensive application to Mozart, and the far-reaching growth of Mozart scholarship referred to in Chapter 1. Einstein's edition of Köchel was the result of more than seven years' work, during which he brought to light many lost autographs, and some early copies of lost works. He incorporated much new information about first and early printed editions, although his principles of selection were rather inconsistent. Close study of Mozart's musical handwriting, coupled with the evidence of style and a modified use of the *nouvelle classement* of Wyzewa and Saint-Foix, enabled Einstein to establish a chronological order of impressive exactitude, into which, for the sake of completeness, he introduced nearly a hundred fragments, previously relegated to an appendix.[1] Elaborate notes on the circumstances of performance and composition of each piece, references to a select range of Mozart literature, and a finely documented appendix of doubtful and supposititious works rounded off a book of thematic and bibliographical reference to which, at that time, there was no rival in scholarship or scope.

The first person to dispel any illusion of finality which 'Köchel–Einstein' might seem to have was Einstein himself. In five successive issues of *Music Review* (November 1940–November 1941) he published copious additions and corrections, with further notes in the issues for February 1943 and November 1945. All these were reprinted in 1947 as an appendix to the reissue of the whole 1937 edition undertaken by Messrs. Edwards Bros. of Ann Arbor, U.S.A. In 1951 Breitkopf published *Der kleine Köchel*, a useful abridgement of the 1937 text, giving only titles, dates, and incipits for works of a similar type in the same key. There, for the present, the history of Köchel's catalogue has come to a stop.[2]

---

[1] This notable feat is discussed in a closer context on p. 217.

[2] The edition of 1951 published by Kaltschmied of Vienna, and entitled *W. A. Mozart. Gesamtkatalog seiner Werke. 'Köchel-Verzeichnis'. Neubearbeitet und heraus-*

The expansion and revision of the corpus of Mozart's music kept pace, for the most part, with bibliographical research. Several new works came to light. As early as 1909 Georg Schünemann published the fascinating 'London sketchbook' of 1764–5, under the title *Mozart als achtjähriger Componist*. In 1921 Saint-Foix published an account of an early Duet-Sonata (K. 19d).[1] Einstein discovered an early Symphony of 1768 (K. 45b). In 1936 he edited the Rondo in A major for clavier and orchestra (K. 386), which he reconstructed from a nineteenth-century reduction for pianoforte solo and a few leaves of the autograph score traced by C. B. Oldman (cf. pp. 94, 95). Einstein also published a new Flute Quartet (K. 285a) and found two lost Organ Sonatas (K. 241, 263).[2] The need to study every phase of Mozart's activity has resulted in the printing of some pieces which, although known for some time past, have previously been felt to be of only secondary interest. (The spirit of paragraph 6 of Breitkopf's 1875 prospectus died hard.) Such were the ballet *Le Gelosie del Seraglio* (1772) first published in 1942[3] and the four fine preludes composed in 1782 to Bach fugues (three by J. S., one by W. F.), which were edited by J. N. David in 1938. Some interesting compositions of doubtful authenticity which have been printed at various times include a bassoon concerto (K. App. 230a), edited by Max Seiffert in 1934, six 'Milanese' string quartets (K. App. 210–13), edited by H. Wollheim in 1932, and an overture (K. 311a), edited by Adolf Sandberger in 1937.

The need for new editions of standard works began to make itself felt in the mid-1920's. The Breitkopf text of some of the operas was the first to be called in question. Kurt Soldan published a new edition of *Don Giovanni* in or about 1925, and Einstein brought out another in 1931. Abert re-edited *Le Nozze*

---

gegeben von K. F. Müller is retrogressive and of little value. The antecedents of Köchel and some implications for its future were discussed in my article 'The Past, Present and Future of the Thematic Catalogue', *MMR*, Jan., Feb. 1954.

[1] Cf. Chapter 5. [2] Printed in *ML*, Jan. 1948.

[3] As a supplement to vol. i of E. H. Müller von Asow's edition of the Mozart letters.

di Figaro and Soldan *Die Zauberflöte.* From 1937 onwards Professor Friedrich Blume re-edited twelve of the great clavier concertos, commencing with K. 271. In 1945 Novello's published a definitive edition of the ten last string quartets prepared by Einstein; he then began to revise the early Masses, of which volumes 1–4 were published by Messrs. Edwards Bros. in 1951, in a corrected photo-lithographic reprint of the Breitkopf volumes. The cumulative effect of all this revisional work has been to show that the Breitkopf edition can no longer satisfy modern needs. It has served its great purpose, but the haste with which it was produced has conspired with an ineluctable rise in standards to impugn its authority.

It is now over a hundred years since Köchel began work on his thematic catalogue. We can see that the destinies of this book have become closely linked with the complete edition, which has tended to lag behind bibliographical progress. Every lover of Mozart must hope that they will soon proceed *passibus aequis*, and that the *Neue Mozart Ausgabe*, which began publication in the spring of 1955 under the general editorship of Dr. Ernst Fritz Schmid, will reach its goal as speedily as its predecessor. For in the year of the bi-centenary, and for some time afterwards, we are likely to be very much *In Sachen Mozarts*, both in the literal sense and in that for which Lorenz coined the phrase in 1851, when he spurred Ludwig Ritter von Köchel to his missionary task.

3

Jahn and the Future of Mozart Biography

In order to set Jahn's life of Mozart in proper perspective we should try to see it in relation not only to similar contemporary works, but also to the general literary background of the mid-nineteenth century. It is sometimes forgotten that the biography of musicians, written on a scale large enough to be considered as a branch of literature, is barely a century old. The beginnings were small. After Mainwaring's chatty life of Handel (1760), there was a gap of forty-two years before Forkel's *Bach* appeared in 1802. Two notable works of much larger size followed, Baini's *Palestrina* (1828), and Winterfeld's *Giovanni Gabrieli* (1834), the latter in three large volumes. Schindler's life of Beethoven (1840) and Holmes's of Mozart (1845) both reverted to a single volume.

Thenceforward the field was dominated by German biographies of German composers, all written on a heroic scale, all based on intensive research, and all published within a remarkably short time. Within twenty-six years there appeared Jahn's *Mozart* (1856–9), Chrysander's *Handel* (1858, 60, 67), Marx's *Gluck* (1863), Thayer's *Beethoven* (in German, 1866, 72, 79), Weber's life of his father (1864–6), Spitta's *Bach* (1873, 80), and Pohl's *Haydn* (1878, 82). Some of these were left unfinished by their authors, others waited long for completion. Chrysander's *Handel* still remains a great torso. Jahn also collected material for lives of Beethoven and Haydn, as well as Mozart, but after his death his Beethoven papers passed to Thayer (whose biography had to wait until 1921 for publication in its definitive and original English form), and his Haydn papers to Pohl, whose work was not rounded off until Botstiber published the third volume in 1927. Facts like these do not detract from the greatness of the original achievement.

In range of mind these and other German writers on music stood very high. At that time it was quite as practicable for scholars to specialize in several vast tracts of history, art, or literature, as to attain some degree of universal knowledge. While Humboldt was working on his *Kosmos* and Burckhardt on his *Cicerone* and other monumental books about the Italian Renaissance, Ambros was collecting materials for a history of music on the largest scale ever planned by a single author. The fourth massive volume, when ultimately issued in 1878, only carried the design up to about 1640. Thus, for one man to attempt the definitive biography of a single composer was by no means presumptuous.

Today the picture is very different. Gone are several advantages which facilitated and inspired the work of the pioneers— leisure for academic scholar and private researcher alike to amass material, to think and plan on a generous scale; a general and personal sense of security and faith in a stable future; a burning faith in their mission as biographers writing on an heroic scale. All the more notable appear the few great biographies published in the last fifty years or so, such as Radiciotti's life of Rossini, Kalbeck's life of Brahms, and the lives of Wagner written by Glasenapp and Newman. As new works on the nineteenth-century scale became less frequent, there has been an increasing tendency to revise the old. Is there not, however, a definite limit to the extent to which this is practicable or indeed beneficial to the study of the subject? Of none of the nineteenth century German 'classics' is this truer than of Jahn's *Mozart*, the most revised of them all.

Born at Kiel in 1813, Otto Jahn typified both the strength and the weakness of his generation. His education, based on Greek and Latin, secured him a succession of academic posts in archaeology and philology at Greifswald, Leipzig, and Bonn, interrupted only by the disturbances of 1848 and 1849.[1] He published over sixty books on his professorial subjects and edited

<hr />

[1] There is an excellent article on Jahn, written by his nephew A. Michaelis, in the *Allgemeine Deutsche Biographie*, vol. xiii, 1881, pp. 668–86.

sixteen classical texts; his works on music number less than half a dozen. He tells in the preface to his life of Mozart how he had resolved to write the book as a result of a conversation which he had with his friend Gustav Hartenstein at Mendelssohn's funeral on 7 November 1847. Jahn's orderly mind made for a lucid and logical presentation of the immense quantity of material which he collected during the next six years or so. (It is not clear how long the actual task of writing took him, but Breitkopf timed the first volume to coincide with the centenary of Mozart's birth in 1856; three more followed in successive years.) But Jahn's limited and rather desultory musical training lent his great book a bias in favour of the historical and biographical aspects. As musical criticism it fell short even of the highest standards of its own era, best exemplified perhaps in what Chrysander had to say about Handel's music.

Jahn himself produced a second edition in 1867, in two volumes, into which he incorporated a good deal of new material, and made numerical and factual use of Köchel's *Chronologisch-thematisches Verzeichniß sämmtlicher Tonwerke Wolfgang Amade Mozart's* which had appeared in 1862. (An English translation by Pauline Townsend, published in 1882, was made from this second German edition.) Then in 1869 Jahn died, at the regrettably early age of fifty-six. In due course the responsibility for re-editing his biography of Mozart passed to Hermann Deiters (1833–1907), who combined an active life as a musical critic with his profession as a jurist. After completing a revision of Thayer's *Beethoven* on a grand scale, Deiters produced the third edition of Jahn in 1889–91. The fourth appeared in 1905. In both these, Deiters, whose musical knowledge seems considerably to have exceeded Jahn's, made progressively greater changes and additions, but the framework and proportions of the book remained substantially as Jahn had planned them in the 1850's.

Before long Breitkopf & Härtel realized that new methods and new standards of revision were needed, and commissioned Hermann Abert to undertake a fifth edition, which they issued

in two volumes in 1920 and 1921. Abert, born in 1871 at Stuttgart, had taken a classical doctorate at Tübingen in 1897 and
thereafter studied musicology at Berlin. He became lecturer at
Halle in 1909, then Professor, and finally succeeded Riemann in
the Chair at Leipzig in 1920. His special interest in the seventeenth and eighteenth centuries, coupled with a deep understanding of Mozart, his predecessors, and contemporaries, made
him very well fitted for the task. Yet the result cannot be
described as a satisfactory book. This is due partly to causes
beyond Abert's control, but partly also to his handling of the
material.

His inevitably drastic treatment of Jahn as revised by Deiters
led to a patchwork of styles, which does not make for natural
reading. Even without comparison of editions, it would not be
hard to distinguish the three strata, for although Deiters writes
differently from Jahn, they have some similarity of outlook. In
mind and manner, Abert was quite unlike either. Being of a
later generation, he was trained to a less idealistic, more rational
biographical attitude, and was far more scientific in musical
temper. He appears, on the whole, to have been much more
interested in Mozart's music than in his life, so that the expansion of Jahn–Deiters makes rather laborious reading. Yet
Abert retained some of Jahn's musical judgements, to which he
added his own extensive criticisms. He also wrote several excellent new chapters, discussing various aspects of Mozart's style.
He wrote at length on the great clavier concertos, yet treated
other works, such as the late chamber and keyboard pieces,
rather perfunctorily.[1]

The original Jahn had a notoriously defective index. Though
improved considerably in later editions and in the English
translation, it could not compare with the index to Abert,
which is masterly, although, rather curiously, it omits some
names included in that to the second edition of Jahn. Jahn and
Deiters both provided full footnote references, and Abert fol-

---

[1] Some of Abert's best writing on the chamber music is to be found in his Mozart
article in Cobbett's *Cyclopedic Survey of Chamber Music* (London, 1929), vol. ii.

lowed suit as far as his greatly increased volume of fact and opinion allowed. Unfortunately, while adding much, he dropped not only many footnotes, but also sometimes the related sentences in the text. The appendixes present a peculiar problem, which can most suitably be considered later.

Over thirty years have now passed since Abert published his revision, which was reprinted with a few addenda in 1924 as '6. Auflage'. The considerable amount of fresh material which has accumulated since the end of the First World War shows clearly that a new definitive biography of Mozart is badly needed. Two questions may be posed. Would this need be met by a further revision of Jahn–Deiters–Abert, or should an entirely original book be undertaken? If so, on what principles should it be based, and should it include a critical discussion of the music or not?

The evolution of Jahn through the successive editions outlined above surely makes it clear that yet another expansion could only make worse an unsatisfactory and unwieldy book. Indisputably the scheme forced on Abert by preceding editions made it very hard to follow either the biographical or the critical thread. Indeed no really clear picture emerges either of Mozart's life in relation to music and character, or of the evolution of his enigmatic, Protean musical personality. Further, to graft the outlook of the mid-twentieth century on to a book which in many ways still reflects the mind of the mid-nineteenth would be bound to produce incongruities comparable to those which Horace ridicules at the beginning of his *Ars Poetica*. A new work is the only solution. So gigantic a task would now require even more thought and preparation than that which Jahn compressed into the years from 1848 onwards. Mozart's music is now available in print almost in its entirety; in 1848 neither Köchel nor the complete edition existed. Large as was the quantity of literature which Jahn had to read, sources available and necessary today are far larger. Present discussion of a possible method of working, and of the problems involved can only be in the nature of *prolegomena*, from which perhaps no absolutely valid conclusions can be drawn, still less principles which could be applied rigidly to the needs of any other composers.

Modern musical literature shows clearly how general is the acceptance of the idea that in a large-scale book biography is best treated separately from compositions. In the case of Mozart, whose life, though relatively short, was woven into complex and shifting patterns of recurrent travel, distasteful court life, intense personal relationships, and a strenuous public career, such treatment would bring inestimable gain in continuity and clarity of presentation. This would more than offset the awkward necessity of briefly repeating, in the musical section, certain dates and facts previously stated at length for biographical purposes. The question of authorship must be faced. The practice of the past, when all the German classics of musical biography were severally written by one man, was based on the assumption that this produced the best of all possible worlds. But it has since been realized that, while a biographer, however brilliant in style, sympathy, and acumen, may also have the qualities of a fine analytical critic, this is not necessarily so. Could biography and criticism be entrusted to two separate authors, each the best of his kind, the interrelation of the two might well be fruitful and mutually helpful. If, however, more than two authors were to combine, in the manner of what is now curiously called a 'symposium' (although it is hard to imagine anything less hilarious or argumentative than these sober twentieth-century monologues), the results would surely be incompatible with the needs of a definitive critical biography. The analogy with a large general history written by many hands is not really valid when applied to a book dealing with a single artist, in the treatment of whom unity of approach is essential.

Less controversial perhaps than any division of authorship is some mention of the range of sources to be consulted. One of the most serious gaps in modern Mozart scholarship is the lack of any up to date or cumulative bibliography printed since 1927 when Otto Keller's invaluable but rather uncritical volume appeared. No substitute for this desideratum can be offered here; indeed no more can be attempted than a mere outline of some outstanding new sources, and of the principles on which old ones might be used.

All primary documents used by Jahn and his editors must be consulted anew, not because the facts extracted were inaccurate, but because they were often too few. Other details besides those quoted were overlooked as lacking the relevance which modern research attaches to them. This applies to Nissen, for example, and to Pohl's *Mozart in London*. If a definitive biography of Mozart is to include some discussion of the growth of critical and aesthetic opinion, then such interesting studies as Ulibichev's *Nouvelle biographie de Mozart* (1843) will repay perusal. It must also be remembered that not a few valuable pieces of information given in footnotes by Jahn were dropped by Abert. For his revision the best edition of Mozart's letters available was that prepared by Schiedermair in 1914. Emily Anderson's translation of 1938 not only contains seven new letters, but also prints eighty others in a fuller text than any previous edition. It also gives far more copious annotation, which would be invaluable to a biographer. The Deutsch–Paumgartner edition of Leopold Mozart's letters to his daughter (1936) includes a mass of new secondary material.

Any thorough marshalling of collective sources would have to analyse the Mozart year-books, those edited by Abert in 1923, 24, 29, the new series edited by Erich Valentin in 1941, 1942, and 1943, and the issues published at Salzburg from 1950 onwards. To compile a card index of both the *Mozarteums-Mitteilungen* and the *Mitteilungen für die Mozart Gemeinde in Berlin* would be most profitable for many sections of the book, for Abert made partial but not exhaustive use of both. In order to supplement Keller's bibliography, an index should be compiled to all Mozart articles in periodicals published since 1927, not forgetting those issued in Europe between 1940 and 1945. It is true that Einstein included many references in the notes to his edition of Köchel, but these are not comprehensive.

Books on Mozart, though not so elusive as articles and merci-fully less multitudinous, have been published since 1920 in great numbers and include many indispensable works, both general and special. Foremost comes Köchel–Einstein with an in-comparable wealth of new dates for both life and works, including not a few reassessments in the supplement. All this would add to the biographer's burden. Abert made full use of the first two volumes of Wyzewa and Saint-Foix. Although these, by general consent, exceed in value the three volumes subsequently written by Saint-Foix alone, the latter remain a primary source not to be ignored, but to be used with caution. Books published since 1920 have struck a fairly even balance between those devoted wholly to criticism or wholly to bio-graphy and those compounded of both. There is much to be read and learned in the books by Schurig, *Wolfgang Amadeus Mozart* (1913, rev. ed. 1923); R. M. Haas, *Wolfgang Amadeus Mozart* (1933, rev. ed. 1950); E. K. Blümml, *Aus Mozarts Freundes- und Familienkreis* (1923); Paumgartner, *Mozart* (3rd ed. 1945); Einstein, *Mozart, his Character, his Work* (1945), to name some of the most important. The fascinating topic of Mozart's ancestry has been exhaustively treated in E. F. Schmid's *Ein Schwäbisches Mozartbuch* (1948). The *Augsburger Mozartbuch* of 1942–3 (vols. lv–lvi of the *Zeitschrift des Histo-rischen Vereins für Schwaben*), edited by H. F. Deininger, contains as much curious information as did Smith and Farmer's *New Mozartiana* of 1935. There is no lack of specialized studies such as G. Hauswald's *Mozarts Serenaden* (1951), E. Komorzynski's *Schikaneder* (1951), H. Dennerlein's *Der unbekannte Mozart. Die Welt seiner Klavierwerke* (1951), and other earlier books men-tioned on pp. 33, 39, and 40.

These represent a fair sample of the ground to be covered in the main body of the work. Its appendixes, however, could have an even wider range. Whether they would in fact do so depends on the view taken of the function of the appendix, a topic on which there seems to be little agreement among bio-graphers. At its most useful, perhaps, the appendix serves, or should serve, as a repository for matter often not easily found elsewhere, which is germane to the text, but which, there introduced, would tend to disturb its balance and break its continuity. The contents of the appendixes in successive editions of Jahn and in the English translation present a curious study in the handling of biographical and critical material, and offer something of a challenge to posterity. As they have always, with one exception, amounted to a small book in themselves, their past and possible future merit a summary discussion.

Jahn himself originally devised twenty-seven appendixes, to a total of 295 pages, which in his second edition he reduced to nineteen (including four new ones), amounting to 156 pages.[1] Deiters in both his revisions restricted the number to sixteen, four of which were new, with a length of 172 pages. In Abert the contents remained the same, but a rather smaller type reduced the length to 150 pages. Of Jahn's original twenty-seven appendixes, ten consisted wholly of letters, which soon proved to be dispensable. Some, though dropped by Deiters and Abert, are worth retaining, namely: (17) Opinions of contemporaries on *Die Entführung*. (21) Mozart's letter (now generally considered spurious, but still sometimes quoted in part as genuine) to 'Baron von P.', on his method of writing and composing. (23) Italian operas produced in the Vienna Court Theatre, 1783–91. (24) Fragment of a German translation, purporting to be by Mozart himself, of a portion of *Don Giovanni*. (25) A Mass in C derived from *Così fan tutte*. (26) Reviews of *La Clemenza di Tito* and of the concerts given by Mozart's widow in Berlin (1796).

Abert's final sixteen were as follows: (1) Family Documents. (2) Marianne Mozart. (3) Testimonies: (*a*) laudatory poems on Mozart as an infant prodigy, (*b*) two letters by Baron Grimm, (*c*) an article published in Verona on 8 January 1770, (*d*) honorific diplomas, (*e*) testimony of Padre Martini, (*f*) opera con-

---

[1] In the English translation these were reduced to three! It is not clear whether this was done by Grove, the writer of the preface where the appendixes are mentioned, or by the translator, Pauline Townsend.

tracts. (4) Dedications [i.e. to some editions of Mozart's works printed in his lifetime]. (5) Texts of Church Music. (6) Arrangements of Mozart's Church Music. (7) Wolfgang's 'Bäsle'. (8) Mozart as a comic poet. (9) Mozart and Vogler. (10) Two letters from the time of Mozart's first love affair. (11) The choruses from *König Thamos*. (12) On the growth of *Idomeneo*. (13) The Controversy about the *Requiem*. (14) Mozart's residences in Vienna. (15) Mozart's Portraits. (16) A list of Mozart's juvenile works. Of these, nos. 7 and 10, which consist of letters, can now be jettisoned. So, too, can no. 16, now printed in Köchel and in Müller von Asow's edition of Mozart's *Verzeichnüß*. The remainder could justifiably be retained (revised as necessary) under the definition given above of the purpose of an appendix. But logically this would open the door to a good many cognate topics untouched by Jahn or his successors, and it would be rather difficult to know where to stop.

The allocation of an appendix to Mozart's sister, Marianne, surely makes it desirable to devote similar appendixes to his wife and children. Marianne was important for nearly forty years after Mozart's death: Constanze, in a different way, for even longer. The latter, it is true, has been the subject of a study by Schurig (1922), but some new information has come to light since then, and the salient facts of her life and activity could be profitably summarized in an appendix. The publication of her letters to André[1] has shown how notable a part she played in the dissemination and printing of Mozart's works. This topic could indeed be treated in its own appendix, divided into two sections, the first devoted to pieces printed in Mozart's lifetime, in both original and arrangements, the second to those published after 1820. Not the least valuable result would be a conspectus of the growth of Mozart's popularity within thirty years of his death.

A purely musical topic, which could be suitably presented in a summary appendix, is Mozart's re-use of his own melodic

[1] Edited by C. B. Oldman, in vol. iii of Anderson.

material. Admittedly Chantavoine's *Mozart dans Mozart* (1948)
presents many instances of this. But these, being largely drawn
from vocal works and naturally having verbal associations, are
perhaps less informative than instrumental examples would have
been. Tabulated results of a thorough investigation would
throw light on Mozart's creative process at different times of
his life.

The performance of his music presents a number of problems
well worthy of statement in an appendix, even if briefly.
Nowhere, for instance, does there appear to exist a comprehensive study of the tone-qualities of the various instruments[1]
used in Mozart's day, of the differences between them and their
modern counterparts; of tempi, dynamics, orchestral balance,
and other matters that need to be studied if historically accurate
performances of his music are to be given.

Perhaps some of these matters might seem to call for lengthier
treatment than appendixes could give, but if nearly 300 pages
were deemed necessary in 1856, some expansion could surely
be justified over a century later. If the material for some of the
subjects suggested here did prove too bulky, calling rather for a
separate book, other ideas would doubtless emerge as the Jahn
of the twentieth century pursued his immense task. So vast,
even in outline, are the elements from which a new critical biography of Mozart would need to be constructed. The checking
of sources, the selection of facts and documents to be quoted,
the planning of chapters in relation to the scale of the whole,
would all surely occupy many more years than the seven devoted by Jahn to this and to the actual task of writing.

Even in the most favourable conditions that the mid-
twentieth century can offer, at least two decades would be
needed for the whole work. Planning and construction may be
made easier with the scaffolding, as it were, erected in a 'documentary biography' of Mozart which O. E. Deutsch is understood to have in preparation, on the lines of his volume devoted

---

[1] An exception is H. Brunner's book *Das Klavierklangideal Mozarts und die Klaviere
seiner Zeit*, Augsburg, 1933.

to Schubert (1946). But even with this, it would be a formidable undertaking, a challenge to the highest qualities of literary power and musical scholarship. Germany has given us the grand succession of Jahn, Deiters, and Abert: France has paid tribute in the two volumes written by Wyzewa and Saint-Foix, crowned by the final three from the latter's solitary pen. May it not be suggested that the honour might pass to England, a country for which Mozart felt such deep affection[1] and where his music is played with ever-increasing frequency?

[1] H. J. Ullrich, 'Mozart and England', *MR*, Feb. 1943.

4

A Census of Mozart's Musical Autographs in Great Britain

By the middle of the twentieth century the total of the autographs of Mozart's compositions that had found a home in Great Britain was upwards of fifty. This modest assemblage does not, of course, bear comparison in quantity with the far more numerous and diverse treasures of the Mozarteum in Salzburg, or with the riches of the great musical libraries in Vienna, in Paris, or in Berlin as it was before 1939. But in total quality and interest the English heritage of Mozart stands high. In addition to a bare enumeration of manuscripts in public and private ownership, some account of the gathering of its largest single holding—that of the British Museum—makes a most interesting excursion into the bypaths of musical history. Moreover, apart from any sentimental value that these autographs may have, many of them will serve to provide a primary source for the new complete edition of Mozart's works now in progress. They also shed some light upon his creative processes.

PUBLIC COLLECTIONS

I. BRITISH MUSEUM

(i) *Department of Manuscripts*

This holding is given, as far as possible, in chronological order of acquisition, in order to preserve unity of ownership which would be broken if the manuscripts were described in order of Köchel numbers. Despite the growth of Mozart's posthumous reputation in England, he was but poorly represented in the Museum's collections until the nineteenth century was well advanced. In 1843, Vincent Novello, a generous benefactor, presented a volume of musical manuscripts, Add. 14396, containing, *inter alia*, four Mozart autographs. These are:

K. 176 (f. 13). The minuet No. 3 and the trio of No. 6 of a set of sixteen dances for small orchestra, arranged for clavier, 1773. This is a narrow strip, on two staves only, obviously cut from a larger sheet.

K. ? (f. 14). A single sheet containing comparative figured-bass progressions, in D minor (pl. 3). It is twelve bars long. The style of the hand-writing suggests that this is a youthful work. The leaf is signed by Constanze Nissen: 'Scritura di mio marito Mozart, per il carissimo amico Novello. Salzburgo, il 3 Augusto. 1828.' It appears to be that mentioned in Köchel on p. 833, Anh. 109d.

K. 577 (ff. 12–21). A copy, in vocal score, in the hand of a copyist named Lausch, of the rondo 'Al desio, di chi t'adora' 1789, followed by the recitative from *Figaro*, 'Giunse al fin il momento', with clavier accompaniment. The cadenza at the end is in Mozart's autograph. Novello has added the following note: 'This is the identical copy from which Mozart used to accompany his wife when she sang this beautiful composition.' Constanze Nissen has added an inscription similar to that at the end of f. 14.

K. 358 (ff. 22–28b). Sonata in B flat for clavier duet, 1774. F. 22 bears the inscription: 'From Mozart's sister to Winslow Young, Esq., from Winslow Young to his brother Charles Young, from Charles Young to Miss May Tomkison (now Mrs. Fouché), and from Mrs. Fouché to Lydia B. Hunt, from Lydia Hunt to her highly respected friend Vincent Novello 1832.' F. 28b bears the inscription: 'Dass diese Composition von meinem Bruder componiert und geschrieben ist, bezeuget seine Schwester Maria Anna Freifrau von Berchtold zu Sonnenburg.'

The second and third of these autographs, and possibly the first also, were given to Novello by Mozart's widow when he visited Salzburg in the summer of 1828 for the purpose of presenting to Mozart's sister, then seventy-eight years old, a sum of money that he had collected in London to relieve her poverty. Novello travelled with his wife, Mary Sabilla, and they both kept a diary and notes of their doings and impressions which were published in 1955 by the firm of Novello.[1] It would be interesting to know more of those who were the successive owners of the autograph of K. 358 before it passed to Vincent Novello, but nothing can be discovered about them. Particularly one would like to know when Winslow Young visited Salzburg and saw Mozart's sister.

In 1881 the Trustees purchased from Julian Marshall Add. 31748, 31749, 31750, which contain two genuine Mozart autographs, one recently called in question, and others now attributed to Beethoven.

Add. 31748 contains:

K. 93 (f. 1–2b). The motet *De Profundis*, for S.A.T.B., first and second violins (these staves are left blank), and organ figured bass, 1771. In an article[2] in *Die Warte*, 29 August 1953, 'Mozart hat kopiert', K. Pfannhauser attributed this work to Georg Reutter (1708–72). In the same article K. 93a, 'Memento Domine David', is ascribed also to Reutter, and K. 93b–d to Eberlin.

K. 406 (f. 25–27). The String Quintet in C minor, arranged by Mozart himself from the Wind Octet, K. 388, 1787. This autograph is further discussed on pp. 85, 86.

K. App. 284g (f. 10–12). Gavotte in F, allegro in B flat, and *marcia lugubre* in C minor, for clavier duet, variously attributed to Beethoven or Kozeluch.[3]

K. App. 284h (f. 3–9b). Two movements of a trio for clavier and strings in D, now attributed to Beethoven.

K. App. 284i (f. 13–14b). Rondo, for clavier, in B flat, now attributed to Beethoven.

[1] *A Mozart Pilgrimage*. Short extracts were previously printed in Mary Cowden Clarke's *Life and Labours of Vincent Novello* (Novello, 1864); some of Mary Novello's letters were published in *MW* for Aug. 1838.

[2] Reprinted in an expanded form in *Acta Mozartiana* (Augsburg), Jahrg. 1, 1954, Hft. 2, 3.

[3] See O. E. Deutsch, *Kozeluch ritrovato*, in *ML*, Jan. 1945: but cf. also correspondence in the issues for Apr. 1945, Jan., Apr., July, and Oct. 1952.

Mozart's Clavier Concerto in C major, K. 467. Part of the Andante with P. C. Hoffmann's elaboration, 1801

Figured bass progressions in Mozart's autograph

Add. 31749 comprises: K. 172. The String Quartet in B flat, 1773. An exquisite piece of calligraphy, worthy of Mendelssohn.

Add. 31750 comprises: K. App. 293a. A minuet and trio in C, for full orchestra, now attributed to Beethoven.

Before we consider the next group of autographs, which consists principally of Mozart's ten 'celebrated' string quartets, some account must be given of how they came to be in England, and how they passed to the British Museum. Though not perhaps strictly germane to the present census, this curious and protracted affair is so interesting as to deserve a slight digression, for two particular reasons. First, the principal person concerned, Johann Andreas Stumpff (Pl. 4), is a shadowy though very interesting figure, known chiefly through his friendship with Beethoven, and secondly, the curious sequence of events has to be reconstructed from very scattered sources, for it is not mentioned in English books on Mozart, and only sporadically by German writers.[1] Stumpff was born at Ruhla, in Thuringia, in 1769, on 27 January, the same day as Mozart, a fact that gave him pride. Early in life he became one of the thirty musicians who formed the band of the Elector of Cologne. After coming to London in 1790, he set up as a manufacturer of harps and (if the evidence of the sale-catalogue of his effects is to be believed) of keyboard instruments. Before his death in 1846 he had enjoyed a wide musical acquaintance, including Weber, Sir George Smart, Dragonetti, Vincent Novello, and others who were founder-members of the Philharmonic Society. It is clear from a reference in the English translation of Schoelcher's *Life of Handel*[2] that Stumpff kept a manuscript journal, which is now most unfortunately lost.

[1] My own article, 'The Mozart Autographs in the British Museum', in *ML*, Oct. 1937, included the first discussion of the subject in English. This article contained, however, several errors which have here been corrected. I am indebted to O. E. Deutsch for helpful information. Other sources used for this Stumpff episode are: Thayer, *Life of Beethoven* (New York, 1921), vol. iii, pp. 182, 277, &c.; Einstein, 'Mozartiana und Köcheliana', in *MR*, vol. iv, no. 1; A. Hughes-Hughes, *Catalogue of Manuscript Music in the British Museum* (London, 1909), vol. iii, p. 347; Frimml, *Beethoven Handbuch* (Leipzig, 1926), Bd. 2; *Grove*, 4th ed., vol. i, p. 261a.

[2] London, 1857, p. 395, note 1.

Abroad, his friends included, besides Beethoven, Constanze Mozart, Hummel, Schindler, and J. B. Streicher. Later, one Ludwig Storch contributed to a periodical *Die Gartenlaube* (1857, nos. 32–34) an article on Stumpff entitled 'Ein hochherziger Mann aus dem Volke'. It includes a letter from Stumpff to Storch in which he states that in 1811 he purchased a number of Mozart autographs for £150. The sale catalogue of his musical property[1] states that he bought them for £350 in 1811 from Mozart's widow, the exaggeration in price being presumably intended to raise their importance. While Einstein is probably right in saying that the purchase was made from J. A. André of Offenbach, on the grounds that Constanze had sold most, though not all, of her husband's autographs to him, he hardly appears justified in doubting Stumpff's own statement as to the date of purchase and suggesting that he really meant 1814.[2] Musicians of all nations could and did travel on the Continent during the Napoleonic Wars. This, however, is a small matter. Much more important is a broadsheet, unfortunately without date, but probably printed *c.* 1815, of which a copy is in the British Museum. It runs thus:

P R O P O S A L
FOR
DISPOSING
OF THE
INVALUABLE AND ORIGINAL MANUSCRIPTS
OF THE
IMMORTAL MOZART

J. A. STUMPFF takes the liberty of acquainting the Amateurs and Lovers of Music that he has lately received from Germany a quantity of undoubted Manuscripts of this great Master (accompanied by proper testimonials of their being in his own

---

[1] Two copies in BM, both priced: S.C.P. 2 (7) and C. 61. h (3). A second sale, held 18 June 1847, was devoted entirely to Stumpff's extensive general library. Catalogue BM S.C.P. 3 (8).

[2] Storch, loc. cit., p. 439, mentions another journey to Germany in 1814.

hand-writing) which he is about to dispose of, on a plan by which any Gentleman or Lady paying a given sum, may have a chance of possessing a part of these invaluable Works; the full particulars of which may be known on application to him at No. 44, *Great Portland Street, Portland Place*; or at CHAPPELL and Co.'s Music Shop, No. 124, *New Bond Street*, where a List of the Pieces may be seen, and the Manuscripts viewed.

N.B. Independant [*sic*] of the testimony above alluded to, Mr. STUMPFF has had the pleasure of submitting the whole to Mr. ATTWOOD'S inspection (who studied under MOZART for several years, and has some of his writing still in his possession) and who, after comparing them with his own, has permitted him to add that he (Mr. A.) has no doubt whatever of the whole being in MOZART'S own hand-writing.

C. Richards, Printer, 48, Warwick-street, Golden square.

This raises some interesting points. We may conjecture that the plan of disposal was probably a raffle, which aroused little or no response. In support of this is the fact that Stumpff tried again some thirty years later, when he made a second announcement:[1]

MANUSCRIPTS
IN THE HAND-WRITING OF
W. A. MOZART.

No. 1. Six Quartetts, dedicated to Haydn.
  ,,   2. Three Quartetts, dedicated to the King of Prussia.

---

[1] A copy of this broadsheet is in Add. MS. 37766, f. 2. (F. 1 of this MS. appears to be a draft for the second proposal, and ends with the sentence 'the property since the year 1811 of J. A. Stumpff . . . purchased for £350 sterling'.) The announcement also appeared, as O. E. Deutsch discovered in 1942, in John Ella's *Record of the Musical Union*, vol. i, no. 2, p. 12, 1845; cf. also *MW*, 27 Mar. 1845, p. 156. *MW*, 14 Feb. 1843 describes a private quartet party given by Stumpff, at which the Mozart autographs were used for performance, and the composer's health drunk at 4 a.m.

No. 3. Quartett in D major.
 „   4. Quintett in E flat major.
 „   5. Quintett in C minor.
 „   6. Quintett in D major.
 „   7. Fantasia and Sonata in C minor.
 „   8. Favourite Sonata in B flat major.
 „   9. Fugue in C minor.
 „ 10. Variations on the Air 'Le [*sic*] Berger [*sic*] Célimène'.
 „ 11. A Fugue.
 „ 12. An Adagio for the Piano-Forte.
 „ 13. Theme for the Piano-Forte and Violin.
 „ 14. An Adagio for two Violins, Tenor, and Violoncello.

The above extraordinary Collection of Manuscripts was purchased, from the Widow of MOZART, in the year 1811, by Mr. J. A. STUMPFF, since which time it has remained in his possession.

Independent of the interest which must ever be attached to any productions from the hand of this great Master, these Manuscripts contain copious alterations (also in his handwriting) showing his first conceptions, and subsequent improvements, furnishing a valuable source of study to the Composer or the Amateur; and will likewise supply an authentic standard, whereby the errors of the various printed editions may be corrected.

Mr. J. A. STUMPFF, having determined on parting with these choice relics, has been advised to dispose of them by Raffle, on the following conditions, viz:—

The number of Subscriptions will be *Four Hundred*, at ONE POUND each.

The Manuscripts, as enumerated above, will form Fourteen Prizes.

Due Notice will be given to every Subscriber of the time of Drawing.

Subscribers' Names, and Subscriptions of One Pound for

each Chance, are to be forwarded to Messrs. CALKIN and BUDD, 118, Pall Mall, London.

The Manuscripts (which are in the finest state of preservation) may be seen at Mr. J. A. STUMPFF'S, 44, *Great Portland Street, Oxford Street*; and the Drawing will take place as soon as the number of Four Hundred Subscribers is completed.

Printed by T. Brettell, 40, Rupert Street, Haymarket.

But the public, once again, was not interested; Stumpff died on 2 November 1846, and the autographs, which he had bought as a speculative investment, came under the hammer at Puttick & Simpson's on 30 March 1847, with the rest of his effects. From the sale catalogue and the second broadsheet, the identification of the fourteen manuscripts is almost beyond doubt. The list, with prices, names of purchasers ('money' = cash payment) and identifications, is shown on p. 86.

The total realized for these manuscripts was £34. 10s. 0d., so that it would seem either that Constanze had developed a strong business sense since the death of her first husband or that the value of famous composers' manuscripts had sunk to a purely sentimental level at this time. Perhaps the latter was the case, for at this same sale Lot 64 was 'the initials of Mozart and his wife worked in their own hair', which went for £1. 2s. 0d.

An amusing error has arisen from the use of the term 'money' in this list. Somehow, perhaps from Pohl, Jahn got hold of the details of this sale (cf. Bd. iv, p. 68 of the first German edition), and reproduced 'money' as *Baar*, which is the older German spelling for the equivalent of 'cash down'. This is the source of the error in the catalogue issued by the Department of Manuscripts in the Museum, which states that the autograph of the Quintet K. 406 was in the hands of ——Baar. It is interesting that the first edition of Köchel has the German equivalent *bar angekauft*. The 1937 edition repeats the error of the second and of Jahn, but it was corrected in the 1947 reprint.

1. 6 Quartets dedicated to Haydn.	£5. 15. 0. (Plowden)	K. 387, 421, 428, 458, 464, 465.
2. 3 Quartets dedicated to the King of Prussia.	£4. 6. 0. (Hamilton)	K. 575, 589, 590.
3. Quartet in D major.	£3. 3. 0. (Plowden)	K. 499.
4. Quintet in E-flat major.	£3. 10. 0. (Schmidt)	K. 614.
5. Quintet in C minor.	£2. 0. 0. (money)	K. 406.
6. Quintet in D major.	£2. 11. 0. (money)	K. 593.
7. Fantasia and Sonata in C minor.	£2. 0. 0. (money)	K. 475, 457.
8. Favourite Sonata in B-flat.	£3. 3. 0. (Caulfield)	K. 454.
9. Fugue in C minor.	£3. 15. 0. (Vickery)	K. 546.

5 different pieces in one parcel, i.e.:

10. Variations on the air *La Bergère Célimène:*		K. 359.
11. A Fugue.		K. App. 109, XI.
12. Adagio for the pianoforte.	£3. 17. 0. (Caulfield)	K. 540.
13. Theme for the pianoforte and violin.		K. 360.
14. An Adagio for two violins, tenor, and violoncello.		K. 546.

The subsequent history of these manuscripts, as far as the British Museum is concerned, can be briefly summarized. The three Prussian quartets were sold on the day after the sale by Mr. C. J. Hamilton to the same Mr. C. H. Chichele Plowden, F.R.G.S., F.S.A., who had purchased the other seven quartets. On the latter's death in 1866, all ten autographs passed to his daughter Miss Harriet Plowden, by whom, largely through the good offices of Barclay Squire, they were bequeathed to the British Museum at her death in 1907. An action at law was undertaken by Miss Plowden's heirs in order to upset the bequest, but it was unsuccessful.[1]

The disposition of the autographs is as follows:

Add. 37763.	K. 387, 421, 428, 458, 464, 465.	The six quartets dedicated to Haydn.
Add. 37764.	K. 499.	The 'Hoffmeister' quartet in D.
Add. 37765.	K. 575, 589, 590.	The three quartets dedicated to the King of Prussia.

In Add. 37766 there are, besides the broadsheet quoted above, two letters written to Mr. Plowden by John Ella. Part of the one dated 2 December (without year, but almost certainly 1858)[2] is worth quoting: 'A German professor is anxious to see the MSS of the Mozart quartets, etc. His object is [to] communicate to a writer at Frankfurt his occular [*sic*] evidence of Mozart's scoring of the Adagio of the C quartet [K. 465] the printed copies of which are said to be defective.'[3]

As a final tribute to Stumpff, there must be quoted the verses which he inscribed on a leaf inserted in Add. 37763:

A ray had flashed from yonder lucid sphere
On Mozart's youthfull [*sic*] brow. What heartfelt strains
Awoke now from his lyre, gay, grave and clear:
The soul is waft to realms where fancy reigns:
That sky-born quest nor love nor tears could stay,
Who yearning for that home beyond the sky
He started pouring forth his last, a sacred lay,
That fills the soul with awe, with soothing tears the eye.

To judge from the number of items in the 1847 sale catalogue that were accompanied 'with verses by Mr. Stumpff', he had a weakness for these effusions. (Lot 29, 'A chased silver snuff-box

[1] Edward Speyer, *My Life and Friends* (London, 1937), p. 208. Some of the details given here are not wholly accurate.

[2] I owe this date to Mr. John Ravell, who has deduced it from a minute study of Ella's life, and discovered some facts about Mr. Plowden. The second letter refers obscurely to the 'Professor' as the pianist 'Schlosser', who is possibly C. W. A. Schlösser, 1830–1913.

[3] Edward Holmes had himself visited Stumpff to investigate the same point: cf. Holmes, p. 205; and also Warde Fowler, pp. 20, 21. Joachim consulted the autographs of the quartets for editorial purposes when in London in 1869. See *Briefe von und an Joseph Joachim*, ed. Joachim and Moser (Berlin, 1913), vol. iii, letter dated 13 Mar.

with a lock of Beethoven's hair set in a locket outside and original verses by J. A. Stumpff engraved within' sold for seven guineas!)

The autographs of these quartets provide a fascinating study in Mozart's methods of composition. Their relation to the early printed editions has been discussed in detail by Einstein in the long preface to his critical edition, which was published by Novello in 1945 as vol. 12, ser. 1 of the *Publications of the Paul Hirsch Music Library*. Einstein mentions every one of Mozart's corrections and first drafts, which amount to nearly 200 in all, and provide ample refutation of the widespread but erroneous idea that all his autographs are flawlessly written as, for instance, is that of the 'Jupiter' Symphony. It is true that in many compositions Mozart knew exactly what he wanted before he began to write, and only needed to correct slips of the pen. But in others, his preliminary thought was hurried and the autograph served both as draft and final version. It may be remarked that his use of odd leaves for sketches seems to have been far larger than was formerly believed.

In the course of time, No. 9 of the Stumpff sale found its way into the British Museum, as Add. 28966, K. 546. It comprises an arrangement for strings, made in 1788 by Mozart himself, of his Fugue in C minor for two claviers, K. 426. Besides a complete and most unusual lack of any expression marks whatever, the manuscript has several features of exceptional interest. The top four staves are occupied by a copy of the Fugue in its original form, which apparently Mozart originally intended to have written by an amanuensis, for on the first leaf the clefs are added and on all the other leaves the staves are braced by a hand that is indisputably not Mozart's. Then he seems to have changed his mind, for the writing in the clavier version is very probably his. (One can only say 'very probably', because there are certain features in it that are not characteristic of his autograph at this period.)[1] Beyond question the arrange-

---

[1] Dr. E. F. Schmid considers the whole MS. to be in the hand of a copyist identical with the one who wrote the MS. of the Fantasia for mechanical organ K. 594, now in the New York Public Library.

ment for string quartet below is written by Mozart himself. Some time later, he added with a different pen a part of six bars marked 'contrabassi', ten bars before the end, possibly to pile up the climax. But on the first leaf there are five staves braced together for the string version. Perhaps this and the addition of 'contrabassi' suggest that Mozart had intended in the first place to make the arrangement for a string orchestra.

In 1928 the British Museum acquired from the Perabo Collection, presented by E. P. Warren, Add. 41633, which contains copies of nineteen pieces of sacred music composed by Michael Haydn and Ernst Eberlin. These were made by Mozart at Salzburg early in 1773, in a clear, elegant hand. The full list of contents is given in K. App. 109, VI.

In 1953 the Museum received two Mozart autographs from the E. W. H. Meyerstein bequest:

Add. 47861. K. 570. Clavier Sonata in B flat, 1789. A single leaf, two sides, containing bars 64–209 of the first movement. A facsimile of one side was published in Martin Breslauer's catalogue, 7 April 1950. Previously the manuscript was owned by Dr. Eric Millar. Only one other leaf of the autograph of this sonata is known at present (1955).

Add. 47873. K. 626a. C (Köchel, p. 822). Cadenza to the first movement of a clavier concerto, K. 40, consisting of arrangements made by Mozart in 1767 from movements by various composers. The mature, closely formed style of the handwriting suggests, however, a date somewhat later than 1767 for this cadenza. The back of the strip, which consists of two staves only, contains sixteen measures of sketches for an unidentified instrumental piece. It has been mounted in a frame together with a letter from Constanze Mozart, dated 30 April 1835, sending the autograph as a present to a judge named Sattler.

Royal College of Music Collection: No. 402

K. 491. Clavier Concerto in C minor. In 1946 there was deposited in the British Museum on permanent loan the whole collection of the manuscripts of the Royal College of Music, of which this autograph is one. It had been acquired from André's stepson, J. B. Streicher, in 1856 by Otto Goldschmidt, the husband of Jenny Lind.From him it passed to Sir George Donaldson, who bequeathed it to the R.C.M. This concerto certainly cost Mozart many pains, for the autograph is full of corrections, some of the *bravura* passages having been altered two or three times. Comparison of the autograph, in conjunction with the first edition printed by André in 1800, with the current editions shows how faulty they are in points of detail.

(ii) *Department of Printed Books*

Two autographs are preserved here, both comprising single sheets.

K. 20. Motet, *God is our Refuge*, 1765. Bound up with the Paris edition of Mozart's violin sonatas (K. 6, 7: 8, 9; pressmark: Music Room K. 10. a. 17 (1)). This motet was composed specially for the British Museum, and was presented, together with the sonatas, by Leopold Mozart, in the summer of 1765. The official receipt given to him is worth quoting (it is reproduced in Tenschert's *Mozart: ein Künstlerleben in Bildern*, from the original in the Mozarteum):

Sir,

I am ordered by the Standing Committee of the Trustees of the British Museum to signify to You that they have received the present of the Musical performances of Your very ingenious Son, which You were pleased lately to make to Them, and to return You their Thanks for the same.

M. MATY, Secretary, July 19th 1765.

K. 508a. Eight vocal canons without text, in two and three parts, composed in 1786. These, incorrectly described in a hand probably that of Nissen as 'Uebungen in Contrapunkt', are on one side of a single leaf that is bound into the second of three large volumes (pressmark: Music Room K. 6. e.) containing programmes, letters, photographs, and other documents relating to the Wandering Minstrels, an amateur musical society which gave concerts in aid of charity, and flourished from 1860

to 1895. How this Mozart sheet came into the society's possession is not known for certain, but it probably belonged at one
time to Karl Mozart, who obtained it from his mother as a keep-
sake. The verso of the sheet contains a sketch, in rough score,
for the string parts of the opening subject of the last movement of the Clavier Quartet K. 493. Its melodic line is given
in connexion with another sketch for the same, on p. 93.

II. CAMBRIDGE.[1] FITZWILLIAM MUSEUM

The library contains seven Mozart autographs.

K. 166h. Psalm, *In te, Domine, speravi*. Four-part unaccom-
panied, 1773. Acquired at Sotheby's, 12 August 1942, by the
Friends of the Fitzwilliam. Two sheets, the verso having been
used ten years later in 1782 for the beginning (27 bars) of a
fugue for clavier, K. 375g.

K. 267. Four German Dances for orchestra, 1776. Previously
owned by André's heirs, and acquired in 1936 from Hinterberger of Vienna. An exquisite piece of calligraphy, comparable
to Add. 31749, the String Quartet K. 172.

K. 293. Unfinished Concerto for oboe and orchestra, in
F, 1783. Sixty-one bars of the first movement, allegro.
Acquired at Sotheby's auction, 21 April 1943, by the Friends of
the Fitzwilliam.

K. 497. Sonata for Clavier Duet in F Major, 1786. Presented
in 1925 by Ralph Griffin (1854–1941), a barrister, formerly of
St. John's College. Of previous ownership, nothing is known
save that the manuscript had been auctioned by French, *c.* 1840,
and later was owned by Joseph E. Street. It is written with the
greatest care, and bears copious evidence of revision.

K. 521. Sonata for Clavier Duet in C major, 1787. Presented
in 1926 by Ralph Griffin, and previously owned by Joseph E.
Street. The manuscript was obviously written in haste.

K. 562e. An unfinished movement of a string trio, in G major,
1788. One hundred bars, allegro. Acquired at a Puttick &

---

[1] No Mozart autographs can be traced at Oxford.

Simpson sale in 1939. This manuscript had been in England
since 1850, was owned by T. A. Walmsley, a pupil of Mozart's
pupil Attwood, and then passed to Dr. Reginald Steggall, who
exhibited it in 1904 at the Loan Exhibition in Fishmongers'
Hall.

K. App. 109x. A four-part canon by Kirnberger, with two
resolutions by Mozart, one in G and one in F. Date unknown.
A single sheet, presented by Ralph Griffin in 1917. The other
side of the sheet contains five-finger exercises for clavier and a
draft for a four-part vocal canon, without text.

PRIVATE COLLECTIONS[1]

CAMBRIDGE

Mrs. Olga Hirsch

K. 593. String Quintet in D major, 1790. This is an extremely
important manuscript, for two reasons. It shows how inaccurate
the current editions are in points of detail, and contains some
most interesting examples of Mozart's revisions. Some of the
inaccuracies are described in my article 'Mozart Manuscripts at
Cambridge' (*MR*, vol. ii, no. 1). It formed no. 6 in the Stumpff
sale of 1847 (cf. p. 86). Both this and the following autograph
were acquired by the late Paul Hirsch at the Heyer sale in 1927.

Robert P. Hirsch, Esq.

K. 507, 508. Two three-part canons, without text, 1786. A
single leaf, also containing a sketch for the Finale of the Clavier
Quartet K. 493. Another version of this theme is in the British
Museum (cf. p. 91). Since this is, apparently, the only instance
of an instrumental piece for which Mozart made two distinct
versions before arriving at a satisfactory solution, it is worth
quoting both here (Ex. 1, 2, 3).

---

[1] My thanks are due to the owners of these manuscripts for having allowed me to
see them, and for having furnished me with various particulars.

Ex. 1.
Cambridge Draft

etc.

Ex. 2.
British Museum Sketch

etc.

Key signature and time signature have been supplied

Ex. 3.
Final version

etc.

HOVE, SUSSEX

J. E. Kite, Esq.

K. 246b. A single leaf, comprising twenty-one bars of an un-published divertimento in D major for two violins, viola, and cello, 1776. This is the last of four leaves recorded in Köchel, of which the other three appear to have vanished. It was acquired by J. E. Kite in 1937 from Otto Haas, having formerly belonged to André's heirs.

LLANDUDNO, N. WALES

William Barrow, Esq.

K. 386. Rondo in A major for clavier and orchestra, 1782. One leaf containing bars 155–71 of the full score. Formerly owned by Kellow J. Pye (a pupil of Cipriani Potter), passed later to the collection of Arthur F. Hill. (Sotheby's sale, 17 June 1947, lot 296.)

LONDON

Clifford Curzon, Esq.

K. 516. String Quintet in G minor (1787). A single leaf, numbered 21 in the top right-hand corner, containing bars 282–97 of the finale, with Julius André's seal and note of authenticity. The leaf was previously owned by Mr. A. Curtis Brown.

Mrs. Inge Henderson

K. 353. Variations, for clavier, on 'La belle françoise', 1779. The 8th and 11th variations only, one on each side of a narrow strip, cut from a larger sheet.

W. E. Westley Manning, Esq.[1]

K. 492. *Le Nozze di Figaro*, No. 27, 1786. Twenty-nine bars of a sketch, vocal line and unfigured bass only, of the aria 'Deh, vieni non tardar', which differs from the later version in both text and music.

A single leaf, without date, containing a transcript of seven canons by Caldara. It is referred to by Köchel (p. 704) as 'ein angeblich autographes Blatt', but it is unquestionably in Mozart's hand. It is headed 'canoni di Caldara', and bears a note of authentication by Haslinger, the well-known music publisher in Vienna. Mozart made his own setting of the text of three of these canons 'Lacrimoso son' io' (K. 555), 'Caro, bell' idol mio' (K. 562), and 'Nascoso e mio sol' (K. 557).

[1] After Mr. Manning's death, this collection was sold by auction at Sotheby's in Dec. 1954 and Jan. 1955.

Messrs. Novello & Co.

K. 562a. Four-part canon, without text. A single leaf, possibly owned by J. A. Schlosser, who reproduced it in facsimile as early as 1828, in his *Wolfgang Amad. Mozart* (Prague). The leaf later passed to the Abbé Stadler, who gave it to Vincent Novello. Novello inserted it in his personal album of autographs, letters, &c., which came up for auction at Sotheby's on 13 December, 1950, and was purchased *in toto* by the firm of Novello. This autograph was unknown to Köchel.

T. Odling, Esq.

K. 386. Rondo in A major for pianoforte and orchestra, 1782. Two leaves containing bars 23–62 of the full score. A relative of T. Odling possesses another leaf (actually the first of this autograph) from which a strip, containing several bars, has been cut off. Köchel is in error in tentatively identifying the leaf formerly in the Hill collection (cf. Llandudno, above) with one of those now in T. Odling's possession.

C. B. Oldman, Esq., C.B.

K. 485a. Minuet, without trio, for string quartet, written by Thomas Attwood when Mozart's pupil in 1786. Mozart corrected the exercise and amplified it with additions in canon. The leaf, forming part of a large exercise book which Attwood gave to Sir John Goss, and Goss to Sir Frederick Bridge, has been described by C. B. Oldman in 'Thomas Attwood's Studies with Mozart'.[1] Two more minuets by Attwood, from the same collection, with corrected versions by Mozart, were printed by C. B. Oldman in *MR*, August 1946, 'Two Minuets by Attwood with Corrections by Mozart'.

K. 626a. 2e (Köchel, p. 813). A cadenza to the Andante of K. 246, one of two that Mozart wrote for this movement.

William Reeves, Bookseller, Ltd., S.W.16

K. 364. *Sinfonia concertante* for violin and viola, 1779. Cadenza to the first movement, in score, twenty-seven bars.

---

[1] *Gedenkboek aan Dr. D. F. Scheurleer*'s Gravenhage, 1925, pp. 227–40.

Formerly owned by André, Fuchs, J. Kafka, and Speyer. The reverse of the sheet, which has been cut from a larger leaf, bears what are probably, according to Köchel, the horn parts to two *Contredanses*. The handwriting of the parts is totally different from that of the cadenza. William Reeves also possesses an autograph letter from Fuchs sending the cadenza to an unknown correspondent.

The Heirs of Stefan Zweig

Besides three Mozart letters, this collection, formed largely from dispersals of the collections of C. A. André of Frankfurt and Wilhelm Heyer of Cologne, includes also two other documents which, though not musical compositions, must be briefly mentioned. The first is the famous thematic catalogue of his works which Mozart kept from February 1784 until the time of his death. Mozart wrote on the cover: 'Verzeichnüß aller meiner Werke vom Monath Febrario 1784 bis Monath .' A fine collotype facsimile of the whole catalogue, with a separate commentary by Prof. O. E. Deutsch, was published by Reichner of Vienna in 1938. The second document is Mozart's marriage contract, which was reproduced on p. 114 of Robert Bory's *La Vie et l'œuvre de W. A. Mozart par l'image* (Geneva, 1948), where the owner is incorrectly given as Edward Speyer of Ridgehurst, who died in 1934.

K. 104. No. 3 of six minuets for orchestra, scored for strings, horns, and trumpets, 1769. (Unpublished.) Sold at Sotheby's 5 April 1949.

K. 173. String Quartet in D minor, 1773, Three leaves comprising an unpublished version of the Finale, which differs in many respects from the printed text.

K. 408. Three marches for orchestra, 1782. No. 1 only.

K. 447. Concerto for horn and orchestra, 1783. The ownership of this autograph, formerly the property of C. A. André in Frankfurt, was unknown to Köchel.

K. 492. *Le Nozze di Figaro*, 1786. 'Non so più cosa son cosa faccio.' Two leaves, comprising (1) a draft of this aria, giving

Johann Andreas Stumpff, 1769–1846

Mozart's Duet Sonata in C major, K. 19d. The title-page of the first English edition

vocal line and string parts; (2) on the verso of the last leaf, sketches, in score, of two unidentified orchestral pieces not connected with the opera.

K. 559, 560b. *Difficile lectu mihi Mars*, and *O du eselhafter Martin*, 1788. Two canons, on a single sheet, the first in three, the second in four parts.

K. 609. Five *Kontretänze* for violins, bass, flute, and drums, 1791.

K. 614. String Quintet in E flat, 1791. This autograph appeared as No. 4 in the Stumpff sale of 1847 (cf. p. 86): his signature is on the cover. An unusual feature is that the last leaf bears Mozart's description of the work and his signature.

K. 617. Quintet (adagio and rondo) for armonica, flute, oboe, viola, and cello in C minor-major, 1791. The autograph is followed by a copy of the armonica part in a later hand, which a note, signed by H. Henkel (who was J. A. André's amanuensis), testifies to be not that of Mozart.

K. 621. *La Clemenza di Tito*, 1791. 'Deh prendi in dolce amplesso.' This duet was extracted from the complete autograph by Mozart's widow and presented to Christian Exner of Zittau. After passing through various hands, it came up for auction at Liepmannssohn's in 1929, but its present whereabouts was unknown to Köchel.

WINDSOR CASTLE, ROYAL LIBRARY

K. 35. *Die Schuldigkeit des ersten Gebotes*, 1767. Purchased in 1841 by Prince Albert from J. A. André, and in 1863 added by Queen Victoria to the Library at Windsor, where in 1864 it was discovered by C. F. Pohl.

It is all too seldom that the private collection passes complete, or largely so, into the hands of a national institution. A search through the pages of Köchel and a comparison with the list of owners given in the supplement of 1889 reveal the fact that before 1914 there were some dozen more Mozart autographs in England than were known in 1940. Most of these have found more permanent homes elsewhere, but some have disappeared. Apart from the Clavier Fantasia in C minor and the Adagio for String Quartet (No. 7, item 1, and No. 14 in the Stumpff sale), the String Trio in E flat (K. 563), the Duet Sonata in D major (K. 381), and the Divertimento in E flat (K. 289), were all at one time in England. Where are they now?

Though several of these were fine works, they were not of the order of *Don Giovanni*, of which the autograph might have come to England and stayed there. This curious and lamentable episode is so little known that it is worth relating here. It was first told in print by John Ella in his *Musical Sketches* (1869, p. 179). The passage is as follows:

> The original manuscript of Don Giovanni I have examined at the residence of Madame Viardot at Baden-Baden. I may mention that I had in 1866[1] a secret mission to purchase the autograph of Don Giovanni: but Madame Viardot refused to part with it. The Austrian Government have been anxious to purchase it for the National Library in Vienna. It was first offered to the British Museum for a much smaller sum than I was authorized to give Madame Viardot for it. To the surprise and regret of all English musicians Signor Panizzi allowed the MS. of Mozart's finest lyrical work to go out of England into private hands.

It is to be feared that Sir Anthony Panizzi, for all his fine record of service as Director and Principal Librarian of the British Museum, had limited views on the importance of musical autographs. This manuscript, which had been purchased for £180 by Madame Viardot-Garcia from André's heirs, was bequeathed by her in 1910 to the Conservatoire, Paris.

Hardly any aspect of Mozart's life and work can be entirely free from speculation as to what might have happened had he not died young. One cannot refrain from wondering how greatly the English store of his manuscripts might have been enriched had he been able in 1790 to accept the invitations extended to him first by Salomon and secondly by R. B. O'Reilly,

---

[1] According to *MW*, 1856, p. 486, the autograph of *Don Giovanni* was previously offered to Queen Victoria.

the director of the Pantheon. O'Reilly's letter,[1] to which no reply of Mozart's has survived, invited him to compose 'au moins deux opéras, ou sérieux ou comiques'. What other works as well might he not have written had this second visit to London taken place? By analogy with the result of Haydn's visits, some of the autographs would surely have found a permanent home in this country.

[1] Nottebohm, p. 67.

5

An Unrecorded English Edition of the Clavier Duet K. 19d

THE history of Mozart's Clavier Duet in C major, K. 19d, is perhaps more curious than that of any other of his juvenile compositions, and is particularly interesting to English readers since there is little doubt that the work was written in London. But the very first mention of it raises a problem of a kind which characterizes its whole rather chequered career. During the summer of 1765, when the Mozart family was still in London, but preparing to return to the Continent via The Hague, several advertisements had appeared in the daily press, announcing concerts by Wolfgang and his sister. The last announcement of all, inserted in *The Public Advertiser* on 11 July 1765, ended with the sentence: 'The two children will play also together upon the same harpsichord, and put upon it a handkerchief, without seeing the keys.'

As a corollary to this, there must be quoted two sentences which, according to Nissen,[1] occur at the end of a letter written on 9 July in London by Leopold Mozart to Lorenz Hagenauer, his friend and landlord in Salzburg. They run as follows: 'In London, little Wolfgang has composed his first piece for four hands. Up till now, no four-hand sonata had been composed anywhere.' Apart from the questionable truth of the latter statement[2] it appears most improbable that these sentences belong to the letter of 9 July. The salient words in German are: 'In London hat Wolfgangerl . . . gemacht.' Leopold, if actually writing in London, would have had little reason to place such

---

[1] p. 102.

[2] It was strictly true only for works in sonata-form. Some account of early duets is given in my article 'Mozart's Piano Music', *MR*, May 1944.

emphasis on the place, or on the past tense. Schiedermair suggested[1] that the sentences might be an addition of Nissen's. But it would seem more likely that Nissen either muddled his sources, or, for some obscure reason, manipulated them as was his wont, and transferred these sentences to the London letter of 9 July from a subsequent letter, perhaps written at The Hague, and now lost. Forgery cannot be ruled out, but it is hard to divine what he stood to gain. The corroborative facts (of which he could not possibly have been aware) stand against this possibility and, besides, what did the unmusical Nissen know of the historical antecedents of the duet-sonata? But it must be mentioned that the letter as given in the early copies in the former Preussische Staatsbibliothek, and used by Emily Anderson in her translation,[2] does not contain the crucial sentences.

At all events, there is no reference to this sonata in the documents covering Mozart's lifetime. But on 23 March 1800 his sister, then Baroness Sonnenburg, wrote to Breitkopf and Härtel:[3] 'I have now nothing more to send you than the three [two-hand] sonatas, as requested, and two pieces which were his first work for four hands.' The words '2 Stücke, welche seine erste Composition für 4 Hände waren' hardly seem to apply to a sonata in *three* movements, but may have been written loosely. Further correspondence, as partially quoted by Köchel on K. 19d, mentions other pieces for four hands. It is not known whether K. 19d was among them, and whether Baroness Sonnenburg did actually send any or all of them to Leipzig. The autographs have all disappeared, and for over a century after Mozart's death none of this juvenile duet-music was known in any form. The earliest surviving sonata for four hands was assumed to be that in D (K. 381), probably composed in 1772. Baroness Sonnenburg once possessed this autograph too, but most of it has likewise vanished (cf. Chap. 7).

On 1 May 1921, however, Saint-Foix published in *La Revue*

---

[1] Vol. iv, p. 395.
[2] Vol. i, p. 83. I am indebted to Miss Anderson for discussion and verification of this point.
[3] Nottebohm, p. 139.

Musicale an article entitled 'Une sonate inconnue de Mozart', giving an account of the Sonata now known as K. 19d, of which he had discovered a unique copy in the Bibliothèque Nationale in Paris. The title-page of this edition reads as follows:

> Sonate / à quatre mains / pour le piano forte / ou le clavecin composée / par A. Mozart / œuvre - / gravé par Melle Rickert / prix 3l 12s / A Paris / chez M. de Roullede, rue St. Honoré, près l'Oratoire / au duc de Valois, no. 614 /.

From external evidence Saint-Foix assigned this edition to a date between 1789 and 1791, which can be slightly adjusted through the discovery of an advertisement of it in Kunzen and Reichardt's *Musikalisches Wochenblatt* for June 1792 as one of the 'brand new musical works engraved in Paris'.[1] Saint-Foix's discussion of the relevant passages in the letters of Leopold Mozart and of Baroness Sonnenburg, runs as follows:

> So the worthy Leopold Mozart states that such a marvel was produced at London, for the first time, towards the beginning of July in the said year 1765, and that his son is the composer of the first sonata written to be played by four hands at the same keyboard. Towards the end of her life, Baroness Sonnenburg, *née* Marianne Mozart (doubtless remembering the countless exhibitions and sessions at which she had appeared at the side of that little fellow, so serious in his curled wig, who was the future composer of *Don Giovanni*), loved to tell that she treasured in her possession 'two pieces for clavier, four hands,' the first of this type which her illustrious brother had written'.

From this characteristically romantic flight of imagination, it is clear that Saint-Foix without hesitation not only identified the de Roullede edition with the work mentioned in Leopold Mozart's letter but also ignored the doubt previously cast upon the last two sentences of that letter. Saint-Foix's second thoughts[2] were slightly more cautious, but his basic opinion seems to have remained the same.[3] In these two points he has been uncritically

---

[1] Einstein, p. 271. [2] Wyzewa and Saint-Foix, vol. i, 2nd ed., 1936, p. 526.
[3] Cf. the note to p. 150 of R. C. Ganzer and L. Küsche, *Vierhändig* (a study of duets), Munich, 1937.

followed by those subsequent writers on Mozart who have
mentioned the work, mostly with little comment.[1] Saint-Foix
printed in full the minuet and trio of K. 19d in a later issue of
La Revue Musicale (1 Oct. 1921, pp. 286, 287).[2] In 1937 the de
Roullede edition was reproduced in a reduced facsimile by
R. C. Ganzer and L. Küsche in *Vierhändig*.[3] This was not, however, an exact facsimile, but included corrections of some of the
more obviously wrong notes. An undated edition, consisting
of a new printing of de Roullede in oblong folio and based substantially upon the facsimile in *Vierhändig*, was issued in 1941
by Dunnebeil of Berlin, and there the history of K. 19d came
to a stop. (The Schott edition listed in Alec Rowley's *4 Hands,
1 Piano*, 1940, did not in fact appear until 1951, edited by Rowley
himself.)

But in 1949 I was fortunate enough to acquire a copy of an
unrecorded English edition, published by Birchall as 'Op. 16',
which not only intensifies the problems raised by the de Roullede edition, but poses new ones, to some of which it is hard to
give a complete or satisfactory answer. Birchall's edition is noteworthy in that, though still faulty, it provides a much more
accurate musical text. Before discussing this, however, some
points of bibliography and provenance call for consideration.

The title-page is, as a glance at the illustration (Pl. 5) will
show, of the passe-partout kind, adaptable for a whole series of
Mozart duets. The number in the series and the opus number
are left blank, to be filled in by hand. Besides K. 19d, only the
following copies of this Birchall series are known at present:

Op.	No.	Köchel	W.M. date	Location, &c.
3	1	381	1797	Hirsch Library (BM) M. 1434.
3	1	381	1805	BM g. 272. 1 (10).
3	1	381	1824	C. B. Oldman's Collection.
3	2	358	1819	„ „ „

[1] Abert, vol. i, p. 62 (1919 ed.), left the reference to Leopold's letter just as it stood
in the earlier editions of Jahn, but added the words 'allerdings unrichtigen' to qualify
paternal claims for absolute priority. In the reissue of 1924 he failed to take cognizance
of Saint-Foix's discovery.

[2] Robert Haas, *Wolfgang Amadeus Mozart* (Potsdam, 1950), p. 48, incorrectly credits
Saint-Foix with publication of the whole in 1921.   [3] Cf. note 3, p. 102.

The single initial 'A' preceding Mozart's name is otherwise unknown on English editions, though Saint-Foix suggests in a note to his article in the *Revue Musicale* that it is by no means uncommon on French title-pages. Examination of the imprint reveals the fact that in all recorded copies the name 'R. Birchall' has been impressed with a stamp over an erasure, while the remainder, including the address—'133 New Bond Street'—has been left unaltered. The erased name under 'R. Birchall' does not, unfortunately, become legible under either infra-red or ultra-violet rays. But according to Köchel, Mozart's op. 3 had been issued by Birchall & Andrews, whose address was no. 129 New Bond Street.[1] Therefore we should expect either or both of these to be the erased name, and examination of all known copies of the series under a strong glass reveals enough of the original letters in fragmentary outline to make it most probable that the original imprint was 'Printed for H. Andrews'. At once, however, a difficulty presents itself. The 'No. 133' has plainly been left untouched (cf. Pl. 5) and we know beyond dispute that Hugh Andrews was never in business at this number in New Bond Street. When the partnership was dissolved in May 1789,[2] Andrews stayed at the old address no. 129 and Birchall moved to no. 133 where he remained, ever prospering, until 1819. Moreover, between 1783 and 1819 no other music publishers had premises at either no. 133 or no. 129. Perhaps we may assume that originally Andrews intended to move to no. 133, and had the title-page for the Mozart duet series engraved with this address. But in the event Birchall went to no. 133, and, taking over the series presumably by arrangement, reissued op. 3 early in 1790 with an erased imprint, and added op. 16 shortly afterwards.

The date of the first publication of op. 16 can be fixed approximately from its mention, with op. 3, in a long Birchall catalogue that forms part of his edition of Madame Delaval's

[1] K. 358 (op. 3, no. 1) was also published by Birchall & Andrews, but without opus number, as part of Stephen Storace's *Collection of Harpsichord Music, c.* 1788.

[2] The exact date has been discovered by Charles Humphries through his researches in the Burney newspapers at the British Museum.

Three Sonatas for the Harp. Op. 1ma,[1] which, it may be inferred from works mentioned on its title-page, appeared in or soon after 1790. Thus, while the present copy of Mozart's op. 16 (which is without watermark date) is probably a reissue, printed between 1795 and 1805, there is no doubt, on bibliographical grounds, that Birchall's original publication of this duet was at least as early as the edition put out in Paris by de Roullede.

Two puzzling points remain—first, the source of the number '16'. Nearly twenty years ago, it was connected with a Birchall edition (of which no copy was then known) of a Mozart duet by Prof. O. E. Deutsch and C. B. Oldman in part 2 of their 'Mozart-Drucke'.[2] Under the number '16' they otherwise identified only the Artaria edition of the Clavier Trio K. 564, an André edition of K. App. 149, and a Henning edition of K. 496. As '16' is also unknown in connexion with any English edition of Mozart issued before 1800, Birchall may well have devised it himself to fill a gap in the English series of Mozart opus numbers.[3] Later, 'Op. 16' appears to have been pirated by Lavenu & Mitchell, for *c.* 1805 they published a Mozart duet with this number as no. 47 of their *Collection of Periodical Duets for two Performers on one Pianoforte*.[4] No copy of the Lavenu edition is known, but it is probable that it was of K.19d, as opus numbers and works tended to remain in constant relationship.

Secondly—what source did both Birchall and de Roullede use for their respective editions of this sonata? Though contemporaneous, it is most unlikely, for both textual and bibliographical reasons, that either copied the other, or that there was any trade relationship between the two firms. Obviously there is a wide field for conjecture. But admittedly it is a strange coincidence that such an obscure work should have appeared in two almost simultaneous editions, twenty-five years after it was composed. Perhaps the most likely original for each is a manuscript copy, since it is almost inconceivable that in or about

---

[1] BM h. 3200 (8).
[2] *Zeitschrift für Musikwissenschaft*, Apr. 1932, p. 341.
[3] Cf. p. 106, n. 1.
[4] Advertisement on G. Wölfl's Duet, op. 37. BM H. 2815 (10). W.M. 1804.

1790 either publisher could have had access to the autograph of
K. 19d, which was then presumably still in the possession of
Mozart's sister at St. Gilgen in the Salzkammergut. For the
English source one might suggest, as a pleasant theory, that
Mozart, before leaving London in 1765, had given a copy of
the duet to J. C. Bach, himself a composer of such works, as a
souvenir of their having played together. After Bach's death
in 1782, the copy would have been discovered and, in time,
have come to the notice of the firm who showed the earliest
interest in the sonatas and duets of Mozart's maturity.[1]

Space does not permit a detailed account of the many differences between the Birchall and de Roullede editions,[2] but a few
characteristic points may be noted. The first twelve bars of the
treble of the de Roullede (= B) edition deserve quoting for
their marked divergence from those of Birchall (= A).

Ex. 4.

Primo

Secondo

---

[1] Early in 1785 Birchall & Andrews advertised some sonatas by 'Mozart' as op. 5,
of which no copy is known, but this is probably the first appearance of Mozart's name
on an English title-page since 1766. Later, besides op. 3, they also issued K. 497 as
op. 12. Birchall published K. 521 as op. 14 and K. 614, arranged as a duet, as op. 41.

[2] A full *apparatus criticus* was included in the definitive edition of this sonata, which
was published in 1952 by the Oxford University Press, edited by Howard Ferguson
and myself. Saint-Foix's discovery unfortunately came too late for K. 19d to be
included in the supplements to the Breitkopf *Gesamtausgabe*.

In bar 1 A gives the correct chords, while B, dropping the low-est note an extra third, commits a type of error which occurs several times later. But in bars 3–4, 9–10 the variously placed trills are misplaced identically: they should more probably be on the *appoggiatura* than on its resolution. In bars 5 and 10, 11 (r.h. *primo* and *secondo*), however, A gives a correct sequence of notes throughout, while B, as marked with an asterisk, rises too high. At the same time it should be mentioned that the bass in both these passages is identically corrupt with crude harmony and blatant consecutives. Two typical smaller points of differ-ence occur in the Minuet, bar 45, where B gives

Ex. 5.

but A, correctly

Ex. 6.

and in the Rondo, bar 64, where B has a misplaced grouping combined with a wrong note,

Ex. 7.

given accurately in A

Ex. 8.

Out of a total of thirty-seven misengraved accidentals, in all three movements, twenty-eight are common to both A and B: nine are found only in B, which is a further, though less weighty instance of the superiority of A. Again, at bar 160 in the Rondo, A gives 'all°' = *allegro*, for the resumption after the remarkable 3/4 episode in slow tempo (foreshadowing the Clavier Concertos K. 271, 482); B gives 'Alto'! On the other hand, one weakness common to both consists of obvious errors in the notes causing a clash of hands between the two players, which would, of course, have been easily avoidable in performance on a two-manual harpsichord. In general, however, it may be said that the discovery of the Birchall edition has much eased the restoration of a sound musical text of one of the most delightful and original of all Mozart's juvenile works. Should the autograph, or (what seems less likely) an earlier printed edition come to light, no doubt many of the puzzling points outlined in this chapter will be solved.

★   ★   ★   ★   ★   ★   ★   ★

Such was the rather inconclusive impasse to which a study of sources had led between 1949 and November 1950. But while the original article was in proof, a singular stroke of good fortune befell me in January 1951. I happened to be examining the British Museum's file of the *Analytical Review*, a literary periodical that includes some reviews of music. In the issue for September 1789 (p. 111) I came upon a notice of K. 19d. The text of this notice, and my comments on it, as published in *Music Review* for May 1951[1] were as follows:

Art. LXXV. *A Duet for two Performers on one Piano-Forte or Harpsichord.* By *A. Moyart* [*sic*]. Pr. 2s. *Andrews*.

This is a pleasing, familiar composition, and the parts are so adjusted as to move together with very good effect. It comprises three movements: the first in common time of four crochets in a bar, the second a *minuetto* 3/4 with a trio, and the third a rondo 2/4 *allegretto*. In the first movement we discover a pleasing train of ideas, well connected, and somewhat novel. The minuetto is also conceived with taste and ingenuity, while the rondo, or concluding movement, possesses a spirited subject, successfully relieved by its several digressions. This piece, we apprehend, by the ease of its style, not to be designed for proficients on the pianoforte or harpsichord, but for

---

[1] With the kind co-operation of the editor, Mr. Geoffrey Sharp, and reprinted here, as is also the original essay, with his permission.

the use of practitioners, for whose improvement it certainly is well calculated, and will be found by them as pleasing as it is profitable. We may note that the amusing misprint 'Moyart' is preceded by the solitary and unusual initial 'A'. Despite the lack of any opus number, or mention of key, there is no doubt that this is a review of op. 16, K. 19d. No other duet by Mozart has three movements corresponding exactly with the details of *tempi* given in this review, which, though not to be classed as profound criticism, is quite a perceptive piece of writing for its period. The inclusion of the name of Andrews as the publisher at the head of the review is singularly fortunate, because it justifies the conjecture that his was the name under the superimposed imprint 'R. Birchall' (cf. Pl. 5). But it still does not explain satisfactorily why a Mozart duet, or perhaps a series of them, was taken over from Andrews by Birchall. The date at which the review appeared, September 1789, is most informative. Since Andrews and Birchall broke their partnership in May of that year, Andrews must have issued this duet in the course of the summer. His edition bears the price '2s.', Birchall's reissue, '3s.'. This rise suggests that the earliest date for the latter is about 1795, since the increase of 50 per cent. in music prices did not occur till the Napoleonic Wars were well advanced.

★   ★   ★   ★   ★   ★   ★   ★

A further contribution to the somewhat episodic history of this edition was made by William S. Newman, writing in *Notes* for March 1954[1] after the revision of the present chapter had been completed. He pointed out that Eduard Reeser in *De klaviersonate met vioolbegeleiding*[2] had quoted an advertisement from the *Calendrier musical universel*[3] mentioning 'Sonate à quatre mains pour le piano par M. A. Mozart: œuv. 14ᵉ, Prix 3 liv. 12s. chez de Roullede', which he identified with K. 19d.

---

[1] p. 204, n. 3.   [2] Rotterdam, 1939, p. 32.
[3] Paris, 1789, p. 239.

From internal evidence this issue of the *Calendrier* can be dated to within the period from 20 November 1787 to 15 December 1788. (This being so, it must be assumed that the term 'brand-new' as quoted by Einstein means 'recently available in Germany' and not 'recently published'.) From these dates, Newman deduced that the de Roullede edition *must* precede that of Andrews.

But the matter cannot be taken as proven *ipso facto*. Both Reeser and Newman overlooked the vital point that, while the *Calendrier* advertisement specifies 'Op. 14', on the title-page of the only known copy of the de Roullede, there is no number following the word 'Op'. This might, of course, mean that early copies of this edition had no opus number, whether in manuscript or print, and on later ones '14' was added, but this, from what we know of publishing usage, is improbable. It is at least possible that the advertisement in the *Calendrier* refers not to K. 19d at all, but to another duet sonata, the C major, K. 521, which was in fact published by other firms with this very opus number 14.

The first edition of K. 521, composed in May 1787, came out either late in that year or early in 1788, without opus number. Schott of Mainz published the next known edition as 'Op. 14', probably in 1789. Later English editions from Birchall and Goulding also bore this same number. Within the time limits imposed by the *Calendrier*, de Roullede could still have issued K. 521 himself as op. 14, and soon followed its success with the earlier duet taken from the Andrews edition. True, de Roullede can hardly have taken the number from Schott, but there may well have been some common archetype so numbered, now lost. This is admittedly supposition. But it is surely required to explain what would otherwise be a very remarkable coincidence—that he chose an opus number in current use for another Mozart duet, but applied it to the early, then unknown, work.

Should this theory be impugned by the initiative it presupposes on de Roullede's part, there are two further arguments in favour of Andrews's priority—the facts that his text is better than de Roullede's and that it too bears no opus number on a passe-partout title-page. If Andrews had pirated K. 19d from de Roullede as op. 14, he would undoubtedly have copied the number, and he must also have had a skilful editor to correct the blunders in the French edition. But this latter, to judge again by what we know of contemporary practice, is most unlikely. What would, of course, settle the matter would be the discovery of an actual copy of a de Roullede edition of K. 521, with opus number 14, but none can be traced in the music libraries of Paris, where K. 19d is his only surviving Mozart issue.[1] Thus, though the priority cannot be decisively proven, the bibliographical evidence combined with the textual seems to tilt the scales in Andrews's favour. In either case, the primary source of K. 19d remains an unsolved mystery.

[1] I am indebted to François Lesure for this information.

6

Mozart and Cramer

A FACSIMILE OF THE LOST AUTOGRAPH OF K. 236.

AMONG Mozart's shorter pieces for clavier there is an Andantino in E flat, which is first known from its mention in the correspondence between Constanze Mozart and J. A. André,[1] to whom, about 1800, she was disposing of the bulk of her husband's works, both autographs and copies. On 26 January 1801 she sent to André, among other items, an undoubted transcript of this Andantino, which presumably passed, on his death in 1842, to his eldest son Carl August. This transcript, bearing the inscription 'Abschrift der Mozartschen Handschrift für J. B. Cramer', became the sole source available in 1862 to Köchel, who numbered it 236, with the conjectural date 1775. In 1878 the piece was published in Series 22 of the Breitkopf edition, presumably from the André copy. In his revised Köchel of 1905 Waldersee left the number and date unchanged, but added a note that the work had been printed in Cocks's *Musical Miscellany* for 1 May 1852, with the following superscription: 'An unpublished theme of Mozart, contributed by Charles Czerny of Vienna—Thema von Mozart (noch ungedruckt), und von ihm, 1791, in ein Album geschrieben.' In 1937 Einstein renumbered this Andantino 588b, and dated it early in 1790, on the apparently reasonable assumption that the album mentioned by Czerny belonged to Cramer. Einstein ends his note thus: 'Wie Czerny noch zu Lebzeiten Cramers in den Besitz des Themas kam, bleibt rätselhaft.' This puzzle, at least, is solved

---

[1] Translated by C. B. Oldman in Anderson, vol. iii. It should be mentioned here that J. A. André did not think it worth while to enter this Andantino either in the catalogue of his Mozart autographs printed in 1841, or in his manuscript catalogue of Mozart's works composed before 1784 (BM Add. 32412).

Mozart's Andantino for Clavier in E flat major, K. 236. A facsimile of the autograph

Joseph Mainzer, 1801–51

by a most interesting note in the *Musical Miscellany* for 1 May 1852, which was overlooked by Waldersee's informant. It runs:

In this posthumous relic of the great composer—for which we have to thank Carl Czerny of Vienna—will be recognized a veritable melodic gem. Its authenticity is unquestionable. 'I send you,' says Carl Czerny, 'by way of contribution, what I know will please you —an hitherto unknown *melodie* by Mozart, written by him in a Stammbuch (Album), presented to me by his son long since dead.'

This makes it clear that Czerny's source had nothing to do with Cramer, who had actually come into possession of the autograph, though in circumstances that are indeed puzzling. In addition, there were two copies, one belonging to C. A. André, the other to Mozart's younger son, Wolfgang Amadeus, who died in 1844. Nor was Czerny aware of the fact—which has likewise remained unknown to Köchel and his two successive editors—that the original manuscript of Mozart's Andantino remained in Cramer's possession until at least 1830, when a facsimile of it was published in England, twenty-two years before Cocks (who was Czerny's friend and English publisher) printed it in his *Miscellany*.

There is in the British Museum a volume with some fine lithographed illustrations, of which the title-page reads:

Apollo's Gift, or the Musical Souvenir for MDCCCXXX. Edited by Muzio Clementi and J. B. Cramer. Price sixteen shillings, or large size, with proofs on India Paper, one guinea. London, published by S. Chappell . . . Cramer and Co. . . . and Hurst, Chance and Co.[1]

At the end we find a section of autograph facsimiles, listed thus in the index: 'Weber, First Sketches of Oberon. Air by Mozart. Canon by Clementi. Musical Puzzle, to be read either way, by Haydn, Andante by Beethoven.' The 'Air by Mozart'

---

[1] Pressmark F. 150, where there is also bound up a similarly entitled volume for 1831. This, too, contains facsimile autographs of Hummel, Moscheles, Cramer, Mayseder, Spohr, Catel, Boïeldieu, B. Romberg, and Weigl. Another copy of this fairly scarce book is in my own collection.

is the Andantino in E flat, and its inclusion in a volume issued by Cramer himself jointly with his friend, teacher, and trade rival Clementi, is noteworthy. It would go some way to substantiate the accepted conflation of the statements of André and Czerny, were this not invalidated by evidence written on the autograph itself.

For it is, beyond all doubt, a facsimile of Mozart's original autograph (Pl. 6). The bold natural sign, the hooked tail to single quavers, the double strokes at the lowest brace of each pair of staves, the pause mark, with a flourish, at the end—these are all characteristics that can be found in almost any Mozart manuscript. Taken in conjunction with the general style of the writing, they would prove this to be a facsimile of a genuine autograph, even if André had not signed it in his bold hand, and even if Nissen, Constanze Mozart's second husband, had not written his usual words on the top at the right: 'Von Mozart und seine Handschrift.' Two points, however, are not wholly characteristic—the treble clef coming up to the top line of the stave, or above it, though this exception to Mozart's usually low placing of the clef can also be seen in various entries in his own 'Verzeichnüss'. The style of the bracing is also rather unusual, but can be paralleled, e.g. in pl. 7 of the volume of facsimiles in the André Mozart auction of 1929. The designation 'Andantino fürs Clavier', however, is certainly not in Mozart's hand. The plain 'd' in the first word is enough to show that: from his earliest years, in indications of tempo, he favoured an open 'd' with a flourish. This facsimile, produced by lithography, is very probably the first of any Mozart work to appear in an English publication, though others had appeared abroad in the biographies by Nissen and Schlosser (both 1828), and in the periodical *Cæcilia* in 1824.

Examination of this facsimile reveals a nice problem in transmission, which may be briefly summarized thus: how, before 1830, did Cramer come to possess a Mozart autograph bearing both André's signature and a note in Nissen's handwriting? Obviously Cramer cannot have acquired it during his first visit to the Continent in 1788 to 1790, for there is no evidence, *pace* Barclay Squire's article in the *D.N.B.*, that he went near Vienna then (though he might possibly have met Mozart in Berlin in 1789), and, in any case, Nissen and André did not write on Mozart's autographs in his lifetime! Hence it follows that he never composed the piece specifically for an album of Cramer's, though such an album did in fact exist. Since we know that Cramer did not touch Vienna during his third visit to Europe in 1816–18,[1] it is probable that he acquired the autograph during his second tour of 1798 to 1800, when he did go to Vienna. But how he acquired it, or from whom, remains a mystery.

Nissen and André would hardly have written on it *after* it had been given to Cramer by, let us suppose, Constanze Mozart at some unrecorded meeting. She, or whoever else was the donor, must have met him late in 1799, or early in 1800, because he was definitely back in London by May 1800, and André did not begin his negotiations with Nissen and Constanze until about the middle of 1799. From the known facts and this hypothesis, it seems a certain deduction that it was a copy of the Andantino that she sent to André on 26 January 1801, and not the original.

Here it is appropriate to add a brief account of Cramer's little-known but enduring interest in Mozart. In 1806 he published an edition of the Clavier Concerto in D minor, adding a fine cadenza to the first movement; about 1825 he republished this with five more Mozart concertos, likewise supplying cadenzas; before 1822 he had arranged and published several songs from *Don Giovanni*, *Figaro*, *La Clemenza di Tito*, and *Die Zauberflöte*; in 1848 he arranged, as solo pianoforte pieces, for Brandus of Paris, Mozart's String Quintet in E flat and Quartet in D minor, and in 1849 and 1850 Novello issued similar arrangements of the 'Haydn' quartets in B flat and A major. In 1852, six years before his death, he arranged several airs from *Idomeneo*. We have a definite expression of his feelings for

[1] The evidence for these visits has been exhaustively studied by Thea Schlesinger in *Johann Baptist Cramer und seine Claviersonaten*, Munich, 1928.

Mozart in an unpublished letter[1] written to J. A. Stumpff in London. This document reads:

My dear Sir,

The object for which I now address a few lines to you is, for the purpose of your endeavouring (in your own name as also in mine) to promote and encourage a subscription in London for erecting a monument to the memory of the immortal W. A. Mozart in his native town of Salzbourg. I am fully persuaded that, should you be enabled to assist in the accomplishment of this truly meritorious undertaking, it would not only prove a source of infinite gratification to yourself, but also to yours.

Dear Sir,

Very truly,

J. B. CRAMER.

It would I conceive be very desirable for you to address the Philharmonic Society on this very interesting subject.

Salzbourg.   June 25, 1837.

The date and place of this letter are most interesting, because, in *A Musical Sketch Book* which he published in 1848, Cramer included a piece headed 'Alla waltz. A. W. Mozart fils. Salzbourg, 1837'. This suggests that the two men may have met at Salzburg in 1837. Is it not then possible that Cramer had his album with him, and let the younger Mozart take a copy of the Andantino? When he later told Czerny of this album, and gave him the copy, he may have left him with the impression that it was specifically written therein by his father. (After nearly forty years, any account Cramer gave Mozart in 1837 of the events of 1799 may have been rather vague.) This would at least account both for Czerny's statement to Cocks in 1852, and for the genesis of a second copy besides that sent by Constanze to André in 1801. (Without some such deduction, it has to be assumed that *two* copies of a trifling piece existed soon after Mozart's death—which is, to say the least, unlikely.) But there seems little doubt that Cramer's album of contemporary autographs did actually exist, for it is described—all too briefly—

---

[1] In the possession of C. B. Oldman.

in an article by August Gathy, 'Der Altmeister des Clavier-spiels'.[1] Unfortunately, inquiry of both the present firm of J. B. Cramer & Co. and the Secretary of the Royal Philharmonic Society has failed to produce any trace of it. It was not included in an auction of part of Cramer's library in 1819, for which there is a sale catalogue in the British Museum, and an entry in Wurzbach's *Mozart-Buch* of 1869 (p. 244) implicitly bears this out by mentioning one autograph in the possession of J. B. Cramer, by which presumably the firm was meant.

The uncertain and contradictory circumstances surrounding the history of this little Andantino add to the irony of the fact that it is not a wholly original composition by Mozart, a fact that eluded Cramer, Czerny, and Mozart's son!

Yet even in his smallest pieces there is almost always some point of interest which forms a link in the chain of his musical development, and this is no exception. Einstein in his supplementary notes to Köchel[2] quotes an observation of Dr. Hans Gál to the effect that this piece is actually a free adaptation of 'Non vi turbate, no' in Gluck's *Alceste*. This had in fact been mentioned as long ago as 1934 by Tovey in his monumental essay on Gluck[3] where he wrote conjecturally of this Andantino:

He (Mozart) copied it on pianoforte staves for some unknown purpose, possibly as a theme for a set of variations. Such a work would have made an agreeably serious counterpart to the excellent comic variations on Gluck's 'Unser dummer Pöbel meint' (K. 455).

Since the discovery of the facsimile autograph proves that the work is genuine Mozart, it would be most interesting to know whether this reminiscence of Gluck was conscious, as Einstein suggested in Köchel when he remarked that such an entry in an album might be a joke on Mozart's part. But this will not now square with the facts, and it is at least as likely that it was unconscious, for we know that he was steeped in Gluck. Apart

[1] In *Neue Zeitschrift für Musik*. Bd. 16, 1842, p. 49.
[2] p. 1037.
[3] In *The Heritage of Music*, ed. Hubert Foss (London), vol. ii, p. 94.

from such obvious imitations as the march and oracle scene in *Idomeneo*—both inspired by *Alceste*—resemblances between *Die Entführung* and *La Rencontre Imprévue*, and the echo of the ballet music *Don Juan* in the finale of the D minor String Quartet,[1] we find a close parallel to this reminiscent Andantino in Mozart's Divertimento K. 187 for flutes, trumpets, and drums. In an appendix note on this work, Wyzewa and Saint-Foix pointed out that its seventh movement, an allegro moderato, is a transcription of an aria in Gluck's *Paride ed Elena*.[2] That opera was produced in 1770, and the date of the Divertimento is, most probably, 1773. This proximity, however, proves little, since Mozart's borrowings, from other composers no less than from himself, at both long and short intervals, are very numerous. It is perhaps safest to assume that they were unconscious, because his store of musical ideas and associations must have been far larger and more complex than we can imagine from our imperfect knowledge of what he heard, studied, transcribed, and arranged, both from recollection and score. Nor can we hope to guess what it was that stirred in the depths of his memory and brought to the surface the melody of Gluck's 'Non vi turbate'. Abert does not appear to mention this Andantino at all, but it is worth remarking that Saint-Foix gives an interesting note[3] on its subsequent history. Though unaware of its affinity with Gluck, he observes that he has found it in a collection of religious music (published in Paris after 1852) in the guise of a hymn to the Virgin Mary, entitled 'Mater divinae gratiae'! Unfortunately, since he does not give the title of the collection, this adaptation of Gluck-Mozart can only be added anonymously to the curious tale of adaptations of Mozart's works made for ecclesiastical use.

In point of date, the evidence of the handwriting of this Andantino is inconclusive, because in the last few years of his

---

[1] Cf. Einstein, *Gluck* (London, 1936), pp. 61, 62, and Abert, 'Mozart and Gluck', *ML*, July 1939.

[2] Vol. ii, p. 432, where K. 188 is a misprint for 187. The air is actually no. 7 of act 1, 'Nell' idea ch'ei volge in mente'.

[3] Vol. v, p. 329.

life Mozart's autograph sometimes resembles his style of ten years earlier. But it is possible that Köchel's original conjecture of 1775—a point at which Mozart's interest in Gluck was nearing its zenith—may be nearer the mark than Einstein's 1790, for which, in any case, there is now, prima facie, no evidence. Yet he himself had doubts about 1790, as is implied by his suggestion that in the heading of C. A. André's copy—'Abschrift der Mozartschen Handschrift für J. B. Cramer'—the word 'für' should be 'bei'. Comparison of the Breitkopf text with the facsimile autograph shows that in three bars there are differences in notation, apart from discrepancies in phrase lengths, some of which Breitkopf makes too long. In the rising sequence of chords in bars 1 and 2 after the repeat, Mozart wrote E natural under the G, where Breitkopf has E flat; in the fifth bar from the end the three rising quavers run E flat, G, B flat according to Mozart and not F, G, A flat; and the chord at the beginning of the third bar from the end includes an A flat omitted by Breitkopf. Thus, this edition, having been based solely on C. A. André's copy, is patently inaccurate. But the Cocks printing of 1852 differs only from the autograph in phrasing and expression marks, both probably of editorial origin, and furthermore is correct in the points of notation where Breitkopf is wrong. This lends considerable weight to the theory that Cramer did meet the younger Mozart in 1837, and gave him from the autograph an accurate copy which Czerny passed to Cocks.

7

Joseph Mainzer and the Mozart Family

A POSTSCRIPT TO THE CLAVIER DUET K. 381

IT is probable that the name of Joseph Mainzer (Pl. 7) was very little known in England until in 1947 Dr. Percy Scholes paid him a well-merited tribute at the very beginning of volume one of *The Mirror of Music*. Mainzer, who was born at Trèves in 1801, and died at Manchester in 1851, was one of the most influential musicians of his day, with a remarkably wide range of interests. Besides being the first architect of the sight-singing movement that swept England in the 1840's and 1850's, and the founder of the journal that was the direct precursor of *The Musical Times*, he was an active composer and a prolific writer, perhaps even more so than Dr. Scholes allowed. There exists an anonymous *Notice bibliographique sur les travaux de Joseph Mainzer* (Paris, 1848), consisting of eight closely printed pages. This productivity is all the more noteworthy, as much of Mainzer's adult life before he settled in England in 1841 was spent in travel. His wanderings began shortly after his ordination in 1826, when he began to visit many of the famous musical centres of France, Germany, Austria, and Belgium. It was during this time that he met Mozart's widow and sister.

His account of this meeting first appeared while he was in Paris as two articles of a series contributed to the *Gazette musicale*. These were substantially reprinted in translation in the *Musical Athenaeum*, a serial which Mainzer published in 1842 and devoted wholly to his travels. Extracts were then reprinted in 1843 in *Mainzer's Musical Times*. Although most of his narrative is bare of dates, the chronology of the parts quoted here can fortunately be fixed with some exactness. The author himself mentions that he visited Munich (where the following extract opens) early in 1827, and later refers to the recent publication of Nissen's *Biographie W. A. Mozarts*, of which the preface was dated July 1828. These points, taken in conjunction with the later course of Mainzer's travels, make it practically certain that he left Salzburg before the winter of that year. Considerable cuts in the narrative have been necessitated by his digressive and somewhat turgid style.

... Aiblinger[1] took me with him on one occasion into their chorus of singers [i.e. in the Chapel Royal], and put me in a seat opposite the one occupied by Poissl. The mass performed was one of Eibler's.[2] I kept my attention on the stretch, so as to enter into the spirit of the composition, and enable myself to judge of Eibler by his work. Although of Haydn's and Albrechtsberger's school, he seemed, singularly enough, to have in some sort yielded to that predominant genius of novelty it was his aim to combat; for instance, in the mass I am alluding to, he had borrowed from Michael Haydn's school that perpetual violin accompaniment, utterly out of keeping with the *Et incarnatus est*, set to four voices only, and reminded me most forcibly of the quatuor in Maestro Rossini's *Tancredi*. Whilst entirely engrossed with these observations, I fancied that the rest of the congregation, either from devotional motives, or from a wish to understand the spirit of the composition, would have paid some show of attention to the service; such, however, was far from being the case; Poissl, thanks to his bright uniform, as gaudy as a cardinal or a bird of Paradise, seemed more eyes than ears, for the former were exclusively employed in watching the motions of a lady kneeling near him; the band and choristers, influenced by the same object, sadly forgot the task they had to perform; Mesdames Sigl[3] and Schechner[3] and M. Pelegrini[4] kept up a continual whisper; in fact, this lady seemed to excite universal attention, although neither her personal

[1] J. C. Aiblinger, 1779–1867, Kapellmeister of the Italian Opera at Munich, and a prolific composer of church music.

[2] J. E. von Eybler, 1765–1846, composer of church music and a Kapellmeister in Vienna, who helped to nurse Mozart during his last illness. The task of completing the *Requiem* was first entrusted by Constanze to him, but he gave it up in favour of Süssmayer.

[3] Two singers, well known in Munich. Some details of them are given in Mendel, *Musikalisches Conversations-Lexicon*, Bd. 9.

[4] Probably J. Pellegrini, an opera singer in Munich, cf. Mendel, op. cit., Bd. 8.

appearance nor her dress bore aught worthy the curiosity of the male, or the jealousy of the female, portion of the congregation. She had long outlived even 'that uncertain age'. Her costume was neat, but without any pretensions beyond. I observed when she arose that she was slightly lame; why then should she be the focus of every eye, the observed of all observers? The mystery was soon cleared up: at the conclusion of the service, Aiblinger beckoned me to him; I left my seat and rejoined him, when, advancing towards this lady, he introduced me to her. She was—*Mozart's widow!* . . . Mozart being no more, the homage so well his due, was tendered to his widow. She was overpowered with the attentions paid her: balls and parties were given solely on her account. I cannot forbear calling to mind one party in particular, that was at once worthy of Mozart, and eminently characteristic of German domestic life. I refer to it with as much satisfaction as, I feel confident, his widow will experience at being thus reminded of it, should this work perchance ever reach her hands. She had been incited by M. von H.—, to hear Mozart's music, and begged me to accompany her: our party was joined by her sister, widow of Heibel,[1] composer of the opera *der Tirolerwastel* [*sic*], that had been extremely popular throughout Germany. . . .

This evening was specially devoted to Mozart. Words would be all inadequate to describe the effect produced on me by the performance of the great master's soul-stirring works in the presence of her who had marked their gradual development. It seemed as if the different instruments were actuated by one soul, as if the same thought was expressed by but one mouth. So it was when they sang together the *Ave, verum corpus*, and selections from Mozart's 'Requiem'. In Marcello's psalms, which closed the musical part of the evening's entertainments, the heaviness of a heart, overwhelmed with persecution and adversity, was most admirably represented; the singers seemed like unto the heaven-inspired minstrel, the king of Israel, to feel that the end of their woes and their anguish was at hand. . . .

Time passes all too quickly away where the discourse is seasoned with kindness and good feeling, and unluckily Mme. Mozart could

---

[1] Jakob Haibel, 1761–1826, husband of Constanze Mozart's sister Sophie Weber, was choirmaster at Diakovar. His opera *Der Tiroler Wastel*, first produced in 1796 at Vienna was very successful, and kept the stage at intervals all over Europe until 1850.

not prolong her stay, having merely left Salzburg to order some prints and portraits required for Mozart's biography[1] that she was then publishing; accordingly we were compelled to separate, though very unwilling to leave a house that recalled so many associations.

Before her departure for Salzburg Mme. Mozart wished to pay another visit to the galleries, glyptotheca, and theatre. I was her escort, and accompanied her to the 'Englischer Garten', a public lounge worthy of rendering Munich an object of envy to all other European capitals.

Salzburg

We began by calling on Mme. Mozart and her sister, the latter of whom craved a blessing from my companion.[2] These ladies received us in the most cordial manner possible. We next proceeded to visit Mozart's sister, Baroness Sonnenburg,[3] the same who, a thorough *virtuosa* whilst still a child, accompanied her little brother to Paris and London, and attracted as much notice as he did; and when some years older, she ripened into a graceful girl with long auburn hair, blue eyes and well turned shoulders, delighted every assembly not less by her beauty than by her talent.

We were much struck, on our entrance to her abode, by observing how every object around us recalled the past. The furniture, the grand piano, everything in short betrayed, notwithstanding its being rather old fashioned, a considerable degree of elegance. The grand picture of Mozart's family, such as is to be seen in the biography published of him by his widow, was hung over the door. This picture representing Mozart's father at the head of his little domestic concert, made our imagination wander far away from the present, by bringing before us in all the prime and glow of youth and beauty, her whom we were about to see, an old woman of seventy-seven. A heavy footstep aroused us from the reverie into which we had fallen, and Mozart's sister appeared supported by a servant; but what a change—her head drooped, as though too heavy for her shoulders to support; her chin rested on her chest, and although we were close

[1] The biography of Mozart by G. N. von Nissen, Constanze's second husband, was published in 1828.

[2] Mainzer's guide in Salzburg was a Capuchin friar named Father Edmund, who was very musical, but far from happy in holy orders, and anxious to escape from the town.

[3] Mozart's sister Marianne had married Baron J. B. von Berchtold zu Sonnenburg in 1784.

to her it was difficult to gain a view of her face; her aquiline nose was all we could manage to catch a glimpse of. The light of her bright blue eyes was dimmed for ever, for she was blind, and her sense of hearing was likewise much impaired. Gradually, however, as we talked over the past, her withered frame appeared reanimated, and when she became aware that it was no idle curiosity but a deep feeling of respect for her brother Amedeus [*sic*] that had led us there, her heart seemed to warm towards us; for it was but rarely now she received such marks of attention; her reign had long since ceased; she felt this, and was anxious to learn if the memory of her brother had likewise dwindled into a mere name, for but little reached her ears of what was passing in the busy world. She enquired if the present generation of pianists still played Mozart's sonatas, variations and concertos; if his cantatas and offertories were still performed, and whether his quatuors and symphonies were as great favourites as his operas? and as she dwelt on the themes of her youth, she seemed again a girl. She still remembered her brother's earliest work, composed when he was only seven years old. We led her to the piano, and she played us part of little Amedeus' first sonata.[1]

How ever fresh and present to her memory was each circumstance connected with the happy days she had passed with her brother! She perfectly remembered when, with the same ardour that subsequently made him scribble music on every scrap of paper he could find, he gave himself up entirely to arithmetic. 'He talked of nothing, thought of nothing but figures', she told us 'and he turned into slates the walls of the staircase and of every room in the house, aye and the walls of our neighbours' houses as well: and many a threat, and many a chastising did he receive before his zeal was checked.'

After travelling to Vienna, Paris, and London, whither she accompanied him, he went alone with his father to Italy, and afterwards returned to Paris, accompanied only by his mother. She almost lost sight of him now that he was seeking his fortune in the world, and was acquainted with but a very slight portion of his works; she had even never seen the *Nozze di Figaro* and *Don Juan* but once, and then heard it indifferently performed. His first sonata was the only one of his compositions that she remembered; we refreshed her memory by playing and singing several pieces from his operas. Father Edmund sung that beautiful air to her—'*Wenn die Lieb' aus deinen*

---

[1] Not identifiable for certain: possibly one of the group K. 7–9.

blauen, hellen Affnen [*sic*] *ougen* [*sic*] *schaut'*,[1] with which she was delighted, for she shed tears and gave way to her emotion in a manner one would little have expected from a frame so worn out and attenuated as her's. 'Perhaps', cried she, in the height of her gratification, 'you may find some piece of his that you never yet heard of, amongst papers in my possession.' She ordered some old portfolios to be brought to her, and begged us to examine them. The first thing we lighted on was the sketch of his first sonata for four hands.[2] We discovered from this sketch that Mozart, when he composed for four hands, did not write the different parts in scores, but on two distinct pages, which considerably enhances the difficulty of composition. Another circumstance about this sonata that very much interested me, was to find that even Mozart effaced and corrected as he went on, and substituted new ideas for those he had already written down; it was not only some consolation, but it was very encouraging to see several minor compositions written and re-written, with here and there passages struck out or interpolated. . . .

I obtained leave for him [i.e. Father Edmund] to accompany me for the last time to the imperial garden at Heilbrun [*sic*].[3] We saw there the theatre of stone (Das steinerne Theater), which is entirely hewed out of the solid rock, entrance, boxes, stage, orchestra, and all. It was within this giant work, that plays, operas, pastorals, and equestrian performances were formerly represented under the authority of the Archbishops of Salzburg, then reigning princes. Among the sights worthy of note at Heilbrun, the waterworks must not be omitted. In one corner is a number of figures all put in motion by water, some play the violin, the flute, or the clarionette, whilst others are dancing; some represent workmen in their shops or labourers at work in the fields, or miners in their mines, whilst birds are singing and hopping about the trees; and a hermit leaves his cell to preach the gospel whilst crowds are rushing to hear the holy man's pious doctrines. All on a sudden before I had recovered my surprise at the sight of this little world, I was still more astonished at hearing the deep tones

[1] Presumably the song 'An Chloe', K. 524, of which the first words are 'Wenn die Lieb' aus deinen blauen Augen'.

[2] K. 381 in D major. It seems fairly certain, from the last sentence of this passage that 'sketch' is used loosely for 'autograph'.

[3] i.e., Hellbrunn, about four miles from Salzburg. It is now a public pleasure resort, in which waterworks, musical and otherwise, similar to those seen by Mainzer, are among the chief attractions.

of an organ issuing from a chapel in the middle of the picture, and as its solemn strains fell upon the ear, we could almost have fancied ourselves kneeling before some cathedral altar. The day now drew to a close and that evening I had fixed upon for my departure. . . . I next paid a farewell visit to Mme. Mozart, she gave me some letters to Seyfried[1] and the venerable Stadler,[2] Mozart's friends at Vienna; I bade adieu to Mozart's paternal abode, and as I cast a parting look upon its walls I fancied I could even yet descry traces of the figures he had scrawled upon them. It was now night, and I was just stepping into the coach when I felt a trembling hand upon my shoulder, and turning round beheld Father Edmund in a layman's dress, with his beard concealed by his cravat. He would not suffer me to ask him any questions, but I easily guessed the real state of the case. 'My poor friend!' was my only observation. 'Here', said he, giving me a roll of papers, 'here is a token from the superior of St. Peter's, and another from Mozart's sister; they will both serve to recall to your memory your inconsolable friend, Father Edmund.' He turned away and the coach set off. The papers he had given me burnt my hand, so eager was I to examine their contents. As soon as we got among the mountains I unfolded them, and found that the superior of St. Peter's[3] token consisted of one of Haydn's[4] most popular masses in the original manuscript, whilst Mozart's sister had sent me that first sonata for four hands I have before alluded to.

These events appear to have entirely escaped the notice of those scholars who have studied the vicissitudes that befell Mozart's family in the early part of the nineteenth century. They are mentioned neither in Schurig's exhaustive work, *Konstanze Mozart, Briefe, Aufzeichnungen, Dokumente, 1782–1842* (Dresden, 1922), nor in the valuable preface written by Prof. O. E. Deutsch and B. Paumgartner to their *Leopold Mozart's Briefe an seine Tochter* (Salzburg, 1936). Most recently, in the

[1] I. X. Ritter von Seyfried, 1776–1841, a versatile composer, who was a central figure in the musical world of Vienna, and a friend of Beethoven.

[2] The Abbé Maximilian Stadler, 1748–1833, who completed several of Mozart's works for publication, and advised his widow during her negotiations with Breitkopf and Härtel about his autographs.

[3] Mainzer gives his name as 'Nagenzaun', and says he was better known as Father Albert, and in a passage not quoted here, mentions that he had a large collection of the autographs of Johann Michael Haydn, 1737–1806, brother of Franz Joseph.

[4] See note 3, supra.

Neues Mozart Jahrbuch for 1942, a long article by Erich Valentin, entitled 'Das Testament der Constanze Mozart-Nissen. Mit
biographischen Notizen über Constanze und Georg Nikolaus
Nissen', contains no trace of Mainzer's name. It is only fair to
add that it does not occur either in Constanze Mozart's diary,[1]
but she must have received a good many visitors, and in it was
concerned solely with recording her own progress in publishing
the Nissen biography.

   Interesting, however, as Mainzer's narrative is for its account
of the veneration felt for Mozart's widow, his visit to Baroness
Sonnenburg is the more important episode. For, besides shed-
ding light on the latter's character in connexion with some
earlier events, he actually published two facsimiles, comprising
bars 1–45, both *primo* (Pl. 8) and *secondo*, of the first movement from the autograph of the afore-mentioned duet sonata
given him in such haste by Father Edmund. Through this
publication Mainzer linked his name in print with that of Vincent Novello. For in the issue of *Mainzer's Musical Times* for
15 December 1842, the editor announced his intention to publish
the Mozart facsimiles in the next number, that for 2 January 1843,
thereby eliciting a long, complimentary letter from Novello
which was printed therein. The first part deserves quotation:

Dear Sir,
   I perceive that you intend to give some notices relative to the
biography of Mozart, in your musical journal: it was my intention,
some time since, to have attempted something of the kind myself,
but other professional avocations prevented my indulging in what
would have been so very pleasant a literary occupation for me. Out
of some materials which I had collected to assist me in the accomplishment of my proposed task, I have selected half a dozen little
books, which I have done myself the pleasure of sending for your
perusal, and I shall be very happy to find that you will be able to
make some use of them in the preparation of your intended praiseworthy object of giving some account that will be a tribute of
respect to the memory of Mozart.

[1] Published by H. Abert in the *Mozarteums-Mitteilungen* for Feb. 1920.

Novello then goes on to mention the visit which he had paid to Baroness Sonnenburg at Salzburg in the summer of 1829.[1]

Although Mainzer's style is highly coloured and romantic, there would, even without the facsimiles, be little reason to doubt the substantial truth of his narrative, with whatever caution some of its details should perhaps be regarded. But the intervention of Novello, with whom he must surely have been acquainted, sets the seal of genuineness on the matter. (Incidentally, neither Mainzer nor Novello ever wrote any more about Mozart, but the material was utilized by Edward Holmes, whose biography appeared in 1845.) Mainzer's visit to Salzburg took place about eight months earlier than that of Novello and his wife.

Though Baroness Sonnenburg was blind, and in her seventy-seventh year, Mainzer makes it clear that she was far from being bedridden and barely conscious, as when the Novellos visited her. She still possessed some of her faculties, and knew that she had some of her brother's autographs. Yet as long ago as 1801 she had written to Breitkopf & Härtel[2] that she had practically nothing left! In 1825 Constanze had written to André about her sister-in-law in these rather ambiguous terms: 'As was to be expected, she will not part with any original manuscripts. But I shall be pleased to get copies made for you of the transcripts that she has, and to send them . . . to any address you wish. There is nothing to be got from this quarter.'[3] There seems to have been no love lost between the two old ladies, and it looks as if Constanze did not really know what manuscripts her sister-in-law had. The latter may have been a prey to that fluctuating exactitude of mind which is one of the privileges of old age.

How many more of Mozart's autographs his sister gave away cannot now be exactly ascertained. But we know that the autograph of the other early duet Sonata K. 358 was given by her to a certain Winslow Young, from whom it ultimately passed to Vincent Novello, who, in turn, presented it to the British

---

[1] *A Mozart Pilgrimage*, pp. 66–119.
[2] Nottebohm, p. 139.   [3] Anderson, vol. iii, p. 1511.

Mozart's Duet Sonata in D major, K. 381. A facsimile of the autograph of the primo part

Museum (cf. p. 79). It is also probable that Baroness Sonnenburg gave away mementoes to other visitors whom she must
have received[1] during the time that Constanze was away from
Salzburg, first as a widow in Vienna from 1791 to 1809 and then
as Nissen's wife in Copenhagen from 1810–20. In 1801, for
instance, there had come a French collector, Louis Philippe-
Joseph Girod de Vienney, Baron de Trémont (1779–1852), on
whom she bestowed a leaf of K. 381, from the very autograph
of which Father Edmund gave the remainder to Mainzer in
1828! Köchel, unaware of the latter's visit, records[2] the full inscription of this leaf (owned in 1940 by E. Weyhe of New
York): 'Fragment d'une sonate olographe [*sic*] de W. A. Mozart
donnée par sa Sœur la Bar^{ne} de Sonnenbourg au b^{on} de
Trémont a St. Gilgen, en 1801.'

It is also curious that the Trémont leaf was published in facsimile in the *Gazette musicale*[3] (to which Mainzer was a regular
contributor) for 1836, only a few numbers earlier than that in
which he described the acquisition of the autograph! If, therefore, he ever examined it with any care, he can hardly have
failed to notice that it lacked a leaf. Mainzer died in 1851, a year
before the sale of the Baron's remarkable library, rich in musical
rareties. A copy of the sale catalogue in the British Museum,
bearing manuscript prices but, unfortunately, no names of purchasers, records that this leaf of K. 381 fetched 6f. 90c., i.e. less
than 10s. as the pound then stood: today it would probably
make not less than £100.

The larger part of the autograph has now vanished, for whatever library Mainzer possessed was dispersed without trace after

---

[1] Until her husband's death in 1801 she lived at St. Gilgen, a village some 20 miles
from Salzburg, to which she then returned for the rest of her life.

[2] p. 990 and *MR*, vol. i, no. 4, p. 320. There is, unfortunately, no account of the
Baron de Trémont's visit to St. Gilgen in the six volumes of his memoirs (mentioning
257 of his contemporaries) now in the Bibliothèque Nationale in Paris. Some details
of his life are given in an article 'The Baron de Trémont. Souvenirs of Beethoven and
other contemporaries', by J. G. Prod'homme in *MQ*, July 1920.

[3] The leaf had previously been issued with Frey's score of *La Clemenza di Tito*.
Whistling's *Handbuch der musikalischen Literatur*, 1828, p. 545, lists s.v. 'Mozart' in the
duet section, 'Sonate in D ornée d'une page du facsimile de la copie de l'auteur', also
published by Frey.

his death. Thus the discovery of these two facsimiles in *Mainzer's Musical Times* has more than a sentimental interest. Added to the facsimile of the Trémont leaf now in New York they provide a useful source for checking in part the current printed editions of the sonata, particularly in phrasing. Mainzer's facsimile also shows that as early as 1772 Mozart was correcting his manuscript *currente calamo*, and that he used a very compressed style of abbreviations for repeated figures.

One further interesting fact emerges—that the autographs of four of Mozart's duets have crossed the English Channel at various times. Though Mainzer's possession, K. 381, is now largely lost, K. 358 is in the British Museum, and the two great duets of 1786 and 1787, K. 497 and K. 521, are in the Fitzwilliam Museum at Cambridge. It is even possible that the duet K. 19d, of 1765, which we now know to have been Mozart's first work in this form, may also once have existed in London in a contemporary copy. But that is another story, in which likewise Baroness Sonnenburg had some part.[1]

[1] Cf. Chapter 5.

8

A Swiss Account of Mozart in 1766

In the autumn of 1766 the Mozart family were slowly making their way home to Salzburg from the third of the extended European tours on which Leopold took his children. The fact that they stayed at Lausanne from 7 to 11 September is mentioned in scores of books and articles on Mozart, but barely a dozen authors have referred even to the existence of a long and most interesting contemporary account of the composer, then a boy of ten years and eight months. This was printed as *Discours XVI* in a periodical (now so rare that only three or four copies appear to be known) entitled *Aristide ou le Citoyen*, published at Lausanne from 28 June 1766 to 20 July 1767.

This *Discours*, which is anonymous—as indeed is the whole periodical—was first mentioned by Nissen in 1828, but for nearly a century only a few sentences of it were quoted. Successive editions of Jahn alluded to it briefly, until the fifth edition of 1923 when Abert omitted the reference entirely. In 1926 Albert Leitzmann printed a complete translation of the *Discours* on pp. 34–41 of his *Wolfgang Amadeus Mozart. Berichte der Zeitgenossen*. Then in 1938 the full French text was printed for the first time by M. Morhardt, in the *Revue musicale*.[1] The *Discours* first appeared in English in December 1950 when a translation, accompanied by a complete but rather faint facsimile of the original French text, and a long, exhaustive bibliographical and critical commentary[2] by Richard S. Hill, was published in *Notes* under the title of 'Mozart and Dr. Tissot'. This article, published as a tribute to Alfred Einstein on his seventieth

---

[1] For Jan. 1938, in an article entitled 'Mozart, enfant prodige à Genève et Lausanne'.
[2] My debt to this commentary is considerable, but the translation printed here is my own. Rather curiously, Hill omitted to mention Leitzmann.

birthday, had been occasioned by a happy coincidence that brought a copy of *Aristide* into the hands of Otto Haas, the doyen of all dealers in rare music and musical literature. After serving, at Haas's suggestion, as the basis for Hill's article, this copy was sold to Paul Hirsch, and added by him to the many rarities of his former library in the British Museum.

The text of the *Discours*, in translation, is as follows:

DISCOURSE 16

October 11*th*, 1766.

'With ivy crown this youthful poet's brow.'—VIRGIL.

I have no doubt, Gentlemen, that you have heard young Mozart, and I am quite certain that he has made on you the same impression as on all those whom nature has provided with senses capable of appreciating the productions of the fine arts. You will have seen, with as much surprise as pleasure, a nine-year-old[1] child playing the harpsichord as well as any great master, and what will have astonished you more is to learn from most trustworthy persons that he played it exceptionally even three years ago; to know that nearly everything he plays is his own composition; to have found in all his pieces, even in his fantasias, that characteristic of strength which is the mark of genius, that variety which announces the fire of imagination, and that harmony which proves sureness of taste; it is, in fine, to have seen him performing the most difficult passages with an ease and a facility which would have been surprising even in a thirty-year-old musician, and you will perhaps have asked yourselves the same question that I have heard a great number of people ask: Do you understand it?

It seems to me that it is as foolish to be astonished at nothing as to be astonished at everything—to see prodigies without trying to understand them is a characteristic of stupidity. I have often seen our young musician: I have studied him attentively, and I venture to put forward here a few ideas which are not so alien to your own design (as I conceive it) as they seem at first. The explanation of young Mozart, if you allow me to use that expression, belongs to the general question of the connection between the moral and the physical natures of man, and it is the more interesting because it

[1] Mozart was, in fact, at this time ten years and eight months old.

serves to explain what is extraordinary in all the other children in whom we have admired precocious gifts in some branches either of science or of the fine arts, and at the same time it does explain those men, in whom a mere chance has developed, sometimes very late in life, a great talent hitherto dormant in them.

The same cause which did not allow Ovid, while still a child, to speak in prose to his father, asking his pardon for making too many verses, and which compelled Molière to write plays instead of up-holstering chairs—has formed young Mozart; they were born poets, he was born a musician. But why is it that one is born a poet, a musician or a painter? It would be for metaphysics to teach us that. But if, on the one hand, it leaves us in ignorance of how the action of external objects on our senses reaches our soul and imprints on our minds impressions which enable us to reproduce their images, in return it demonstrates several experimental truths, which, if accepted as principles, shed much light on the most interesting questions of the study of mankind.

One of the truths is that organic differences make a person more sensitive to the impressions received by one of his senses than to those received by the others. Of two men passing from a collection of pic-tures into a concert hall, one will have been delighted by some masterpiece of a great artist; he will go on thinking of it and will hear nothing of the music; the other, who had looked at the pictures without seeing them, makes up for this by feeling keenly all the beauties of the concert.

He who is carried away by an image set to music is affected very little by it if it is in verse, and a painting of Iphigenia at the altar may draw tears from another who has seen Racine played without being moved by it.

A second truth, which is perhaps only a consequence of the first, is that the greater or less degree of sensitiveness in a sense-organ and the greater or less degree of disposition in the brain to be affected by the ideas of which that sense is the organ, cause the same object to be seen quite differently by different persons. There are some who like pictures without noticing anything else in them but a variety of colours which pleases them, while the painter's eye seizes at once all the beauties; and, apart from the fine arts, the ordinary child, looking with pleasure at a carnation, sees only whether it is red or white; the child born to be a botanist perceives some of its characteristics; a greater number of them escape him, which Tournefort[1] at the age of seven could see at a glance.

Another important observation is that although it is not certain, nor even probable, that different classes of ideas have their particular cells in the brain, nature has, nevertheless, decreed that there should be a close connection between ideas of the same kind, between those that we owe to the same sense-organ, between those which have come to us at the same time, in the same place, in the same circumstances, so that if one is awakened, it reminds us of all the others.

Again, it is proved that, as one part of the body acquires by frequent repetition of certain movements the facility to execute them with a speed, strength and precision which are astonishing, so the organization (a word by which I designate all that guides to the faculty of thought), the organization, I repeat, which is almost entirely occupied by sensations and ideas of a certain kind, can draw from this an advantage which people less occupied by this object or in whom that part of the organization is less perfect cannot understand.

I shall add, as a fifth truth, that very strong impressions have on a sensitive brain simultaneous effects which cause involuntary, irrepressible reactions. The sight of a new machine whose mechanism has been hidden from him, troubles the great mathematician until he has discovered it. Why should not the idea of a sound, and indeed of any sound, force a brain strongly affected by sound, to fill it with music?

Finally, on the basis of several examples, I can establish here that in men endowed with a very superior talent it seems that that part of the brain which may be the cause of this talent is the key to all the others, which only show when it is developed. Corneille was a poor lawyer and was looked on as a man much below mediocrity; when he wrote his first verses, what a mind these verses revealed. Stone,[2] at twenty-eight, was a youthful gardener, who did not know how to read; he saw a mason make a calculation; he was a born mathematician, so three years later he became a very distinguished scholar, who enlightened the greatest geometricians on the most difficult

---

[1] J. P. de Tournefort, 1656–1708, one of the most eminent systematic botanists who prepared the way for Linnaeus.

[2] Edmund Stone, 17??–1768, son of a gardener employed by the second Duke of Argyll, did not, in fact, learn to read until he was eighteen, not twenty-eight. He was the author of several mathematical treatises.

mathematical questions. At the age of fifteen, the greatest mechanician of our day[1] was unskilled in everything; his mother took him with her to his principal; he was waiting for her in an ante-room near which there was a big clock; the noise of the pendulum attracted his attention—he had a glimpse of the works through the openings of the case and soon manufactured those masterpieces which astonished Europe, of which he is today one of the leading academicians. The father of one of Germany's favourite poets, in despair at not being able to teach this son anything, sent him as a last resort to the country, to a man celebrated for education of that kind. He was no more successful than previous teachers but by chance a book of poems fell into the young man's hands; the bark covering the poet bursts: he writes verses and swiftly acquires all the skill needed for this art. I will not quote any other examples, they would carry me too far from our little Orpheus, to whom it is quite time to return.

He was born with a marvellous ear and sensory organization disposed to be strongly affected by music: the son of a great musician and younger brother of a sister whose playing has shared your admiration; the first sounds he heard were harmonious ones; in him the sensitive string vibrated from childhood; at once it re-echoed sounds, and he must have composed music from the moment he heard any. That power which the mind has over everyone's vocal organs is exercised on the fingers of a musician and, we may say, on his whole body; the instrument is so well tuned to his needs that soon he knows all its uses. He received at birth such keenness and delicacy of the organs that the slightest false note is painful to him. It is thus that the poetic ear is first wounded by a bad line, while he who labours at verse-making and has no other inspiration than rules, wastes the greater part of his time discerning what is wrong. In young Mozart the sensitiveness and the precision of his ear are so great that discordant, shrill or too loud notes bring tears to his eyes. His imagination is as musical as his ear: it always hears many sounds together; one sound heard recalls instantaneously all those which can form a melodious sequence and a complete symphony. With people who possess some very superior talent, all ideas manifest themselves in those relationships which they may have with this talent. That is what was very noticeable in our young man; he was sometimes involuntarily attracted to his harpsichord as by a secret force, and drew

---

[1] No certain identification is possible.

from it sounds, which were the lively expression of the idea with which he had just been occupied. One might say that at these moments he is himself the instrument in the hands of music and one may imagine him as composed of strings harmoniously put together with such skill that it is impossible to touch one without all the others being also set in motion: he plays all the images, the poet versifies them, the painter colours them.

This child is very natural; he is lovable, he has knowledge outside music, yet, if he were not a musician he would perhaps be only a very ordinary child. If he had not been born the son of a musician his talent might perhaps not have had the chance to develop till later on and his other faculties would have remained buried until that time.

We can confidently predict that one day he will be one of the greatest masters of his art; but is it not to be feared that, developing so young, he may grow old prematurely? It is only too true that precocious children have often been worn out in the flower of their youth. If overworked, nerves become hardened and unable to work more. But experience sometimes shows that men born with a special talent for one of the fine arts have gone on for a very long time. The organism suited to that talent works with such ease that exercise hardly wears it at all, and we can see that toil does not tire young Mozart. The short-sighted eye fixed on the stars wastes its efforts; the long-sighted eye ruins its sight observing insects: each kind of sight is much better preserved if fixed on objects within its reach. Ch. Maratti[1] was a great painter from the age of eleven until he was ninety, and at seventy Corelli, who knew how to play the violin as soon as he could speak, still moved at will the soul of his hearers.

I have discoursed to you a long time, gentlemen, of the child-musician. I should fail in what I owe to your views if I did not remind you for one moment of the moral qualities of the child, which have much more claim to your interest. A well-balanced brain seems made for a virtuous soul and courteous manners; experience has proved this in several great artists, and young Mozart provides a new proof of it. His heart is as sensitive as his ear; he has a modesty rare at his age, rare with that superiority. We are indeed edified on hearing him ascribe his talents to the author of every gift,

---

[1] Carlo Maratti, 1625–1713, a baroque painter of the Roman school, was eighty-eight when he died.

and conclude, with amiable candour and the most persuasive air, that
it would be unpardonable for him to boast of them. We cannot see
without emotion all the marks of his affection for a father who
seems worthy of it, who has given still more care to the formation
of his character than to the cultivation of his talents and who speaks
of education as wisely as of music. How well he is rewarded by success: how delightful it is for him to see his two amiable children more
flattered by a look of approbation in his eyes which they seek
with tender anxiety than by the applause of a whole audience. This
trait seems to me to characterize all three of them most advantage-
ously and they provide us with two thoughts on education which are
new, I confess, only in practice. One is that many men who could
have excelled in one way are only mediocre because the art to which
they have been dedicated is alien to them; this consideration, the
first that should be dealt with in deciding on the choice of a vocation,
is what is hardly ever weighed: instead of testing a child in different
kinds of vocation, as metal is tried on a touchstone to know its
nature, parents generally suppose that their wish will be strong
enough to bestow ability. Results bear witness to the justness of this
principle. A second reflection is that it would be very desirable that
parents whose children have outstanding talents should imitate M.
Mozart, who, far from forcing his son, has always been careful to
moderate his ardour and so prevent him from abandoning himself
to it. Every day the opposite attitude stifles the most promising
genius and may nullify the most superior talents.

I have the honour to remain . . .

★   ★   ★   ★

The position of this essay in early Mozart literature is most
interesting. Considering its exceptional importance it seems
quite extraordinary that after 1766 the original French text
should never have been printed complete until 1938. The great
rarity of *Aristide* provides a partial but not wholly convincing
explanation. Yet, apart from concert notices it is one of the
earliest accounts of Mozart as a child that ever appeared in
print, and certainly the longest dating from the 1760's, from
which period only four others are known. An account in the
Ausgburger Intelligenzblätter for 1762,[1] entitled 'Ein Brief aus

---

[1] Mentioned by Nissen, appendix, p. 217.

Wien über Mozart's Kinder', does not seem ever to have been quoted in full. An account of 1764, 'Mozart als Knabe in Paris', printed on 30 March in that year, in the *Hochfürstlich bambergische wöchentliche Frag-und-Anzeige-Nachrichten*[1] was reprinted in 1835 in no. 46 of a Hamburg paper, *Der Freischütz*, and is unknown elsewhere.

Two other short pieces, one printed at Hamburg in 1765, the second taken from Hiller's *Wöchentliche Nachrichten* for 1766, page 174, were reprinted in Jahn.[2] It is true that in December 1763, when the Mozarts were in Paris, Baron Friedrich Melchior Grimm had assumed the role of their protector and gave two accounts of them in letters of 1 December 1763 and 15 July 1766. But these were not printed until 1812, when they were included in Grimm's *Correspondance littéraire*. Similarly, during the Mozart's sojourn in London, the Hon. Daines Barrington conducted his famous examination of Wolfgang in June 1765, but nothing appeared in print until 1771, when Barrington published his account in vol. 60 of the *Philosophical Transactions* of the Royal Society. Pride of place and importance may thus be fairly accorded to *Discours XVI* of *Aristide*.

When we come to the question of authorship we are confronted with that tantalizing mixture of fact and conjecture which obscures many points in the history of Mozart's childhood. The few relevant facts are these. From Leopold Mozart's letter of 10 November 1766, we know that he had not intended to remain more than half a day in Lausanne, but was persuaded to make a stay of almost five days by several prominent persons, including Prince Ludwig of Württemberg. The catalogue of Wolfgang's works which Leopold kept up to 1768 mentions a flute solo (now unfortunately lost) composed in Lausanne for the Prince, who, like his brother, Prince Carl Eugen, was a keen amateur of music. Prince Ludwig had apparently settled on the outskirts of Lausanne, near which J. J. Rousseau himself was living, because he was attracted by the city's fame as a centre for the study and dissemination of rational and humanitarian

---

[1] Keller, no. 854.   [2] Vol. i, 1856, pp. 163–5.

ideas, particularly in relation to the moral betterment of mankind. Among those with similar interests to Prince Ludwig's
was his close friend, S. A. D. Tissot, one of the most eminent
of all European physicians at that time, who had made a special
study of public health and of the nervous system in relation to
genius, particularly in children. In the twentieth century he
would probably have been called a psychiatrist.

The whole tone of *Aristide*, and particularly the fact that its
issue for 6 September 1766, actually contained laws 'for a com-
munal society of men desirous of becoming more virtuous', led
Morhardt[1] to suggest that the journal was founded by Prince
Ludwig, and probably edited by him in collaboration with
Tissot. That the latter definitely did write in *Aristide* is proved
by another *Discours*—'Sur la mollesse', which was later reprinted among his works. Although these do not include
Discours XVI[2] it is reasonable to suggest that some credit for it
is due to Tissot, who was on the spot and known to have
specialized interests which correspond to the tone of the essay.
At least no more suitable claimant is known at present, but it is
also possible that Tissot had a collaborator in the Prince himself,
who was, after all, partly responsible for the Mozart family's
stay in Lausanne, being anxious, doubtless, to hear the child
play. But to ascribe the authorship unequivocally to Tissot
alone, as some writers[3] have done, is surely unjustified.

Fortunately this problem does not affect our estimate of the
merits and value of the *Discours*. In reading it we should accept
the awkward terminology and somewhat verbose, digressive
style as characteristic of the age. These defects are more than
outweighed by the kindly humanitarian tone of the essay, by
its penetrating psychology and insight into the nature of
Mozart's genius. Here, indeed, we find the qualities which

[1] Op. cit.
[2] No manuscript of it, whether autograph or copy, is in the Tissot Collection in the
Bibliothèque Cantonale at Lausanne.
[3] Max Fehr, *Die Mozart Familie in Zürich*, 1942, p. 10. Even Richard S. Hill says at
the beginning of his commentary that Tissot *was* the author, although he qualifie
this later.

make the *Discours* so instructive a complement to Barrington's equally valuable but colder and more scientific observations. The former deserves wide study for its prophetic quality no less than for its corroborative relation to other nearly contemporary accounts of Mozart in childhood.

The allusion to the 'strength' and 'variety' of his fantasias undoubtedly refers to the power of extemporization at the keyboard for which he was famous all his life, but particularly in later years. We may appropriately compare the description given in the *Discours* of Mozart's absorbed concentration at the keyboard with Barrington's words:[1] 'He had worked himself up to such a pitch that he beat his harpsichord like a person possessed, rising sometimes in his chair.' (We have later reports of his playing which indicate how in maturity, as in childhood, inspiration seemed to merge his whole being into the instrument.)[2] The description of Mozart's very keen sense of pitch and his reaction to a loud, discordant noise corresponds most interestingly to the well-known account given in Andreas Schachtner's oft-quoted letter of 24 April 1792. When the *Discours* writes of the child hearing many sounds together, it curiously anticipates a passage in the spurious letter to 'Baron von P.',[3] printed over Mozart's name, in which occurs the sentence: 'Nor do I hear in my imagination the parts successively, but I hear them, as it were, all at once.'

Whether or not Tissot and Prince Ludwig wrote the *Discours*, together or separately, they undoubtedly read it, and must have watched Mozart's later career with interest. When he died in 1791 the Prince had four years and Tissot six still to live. They were, therefore, able to have the melancholy satisfaction of knowing how truly prophetic had proved the observation: 'We can confidently predict that one day he will be one of the greatest masters of his art; but is it not to be feared that, developing so young, he may grow old prematurely?'

---

[1] *Philosophical Transactions*, vol. lx, 1771, p. 60.
[2] Cf. p. 251.
[3] Cf. p. 239, n. 1.

9

The Melodic Sources and Affinities of 'Die Zauberflöte'

IN the *Revue des deux mondes* for February 1913 there appeared a twelve-page review, written by T. de Wyzewa, of *Mozart's Operas* by E. J. Dent. As in so many of the best type of reviews, most of Wyzewa's space was devoted to a highly suggestive discussion of matters germane, but not strictly related to the book under consideration. Here, after two or three pages on Dent's work—a pioneer study that has since become a standard authority and gone into a second edition in 1947—Wyzewa plunged into an elaborate exposition of Mozartian aesthetic, with special reference to *Die Zauberflöte*. These pages constituted, in effect, an absorbing *parergon* to the *Biographie musicale* of Mozart, of which Wyzewa with Saint-Foix had published the first two volumes in the preceding year, 1912. In some ways this review was more than the mere *parergon* it might have seemed over forty years ago. We now see that its importance lay in the fact that Wyzewa there expressed himself at notable length on a number of points, which, as the event showed, were not to be treated nearly so fully or so cogently anywhere in the three later volumes of the *Biographie musicale*. The salient passage of Wyzewa's review (p. 945) runs as follows:

But above all, it was to his own earlier compositions that Mozart had recourse in order to gather material for such ideas as he had no time—or perhaps no longer the courage—to invent. Considered from this point of view, the score of *Die Zauberflöte* practically presents us with a 'pot-pourri'. Clearly, it is most desirable that musical writers should finally turn from enlightening us about the supposed 'Masonic' intentions of Mozart, and instead endeavour to set up for

us an inventory of those 'sources' from which he drew the varied
materials for his last opera.

Now of all musicologists who have ever studied this period,
Wyzewa undoubtedly possessed the most comprehensive
knowledge not only of Mozart's music, but also of that of his
contemporaries, famous and obscure. Thus it is a thousand
pities that he himself never, either in the *Biographie musicale* or
elsewhere, enlarged on the precise extent to which *Die Zauberflöte* is a 'pot-pourri'. Following up the suggestion quoted above,
the present chapter is an attempt to concentrate and throw
light on some of the important strands from which the marvellous melodic web of the opera is woven, and to suggest some
reasons why it is in the nature of a 'pot-pourri'.

The material for this study lies hidden in strange places.
Much of it lurks in the undergrowth of the footnotes to the
various editions of Jahn's biography of Mozart, overlaid by
accretions in the successive editions of that work prepared by
Deiters and Abert. Many hints, often of an exasperatingly
vague nature, reward patient perusal of the actual pages of
Wyzewa and Saint-Foix. Other points are made as the results
of personal observation, but they are such as lie within the scope
of anyone with a reasonably good memory who uses his ears
and eyes when listening to eighteenth-century music or reading
it in print. In order to avoid a plethora of footnotes, chapter
and page references cannot generally be given for facts taken
either from Jahn and his successive editors, or from Wyzewa
and Saint-Foix. (Indeed, it is not always easy to allot exact
priority for any particular observation.) One or two special
sources, however, must be mentioned as they occur, particularly
Chantavoine's unique book, *Mozart dans Mozart*.[1] It is probably
most convenient, even at the cost of a slight repetitiveness, to
examine the opera in the order of the score, and to enumerate

---

[1] Paris, 1948: hereafter referred to as C followed by the number therein of the relevant musical quotation. These references are confined here to points that have not
been made by any previous writer.

all melodic material *seriatim*, whether drawn from the works of
Mozart himself or from other sources.

The three groups of three chords with which the overture
begins and to which deep Masonic significance has been
attached, had been used before by Mozart to introduce the first
entr'acte of his music to *König Thamos*, that stiff but impressive
composition which had resulted from his meeting with Schikaneder in 1779. On a rather reduced scale, this chordal opening
bears a certain resemblance to the opening of Holzbauer's
Günther von Schwarzburg, an opera Mozart had heard and much
admired in 1777 at Mannheim. As to the famous fugal subject
of the overture to *Die Zauberflöte*, any musical schoolboy who
has read almost any book on Mozart has learned that he
'borrowed' it from a sonata in B flat that Clementi played at a
contest held in December 1781 between the two musicians in
the presence of the Emperor of Austria. This curious fiction of
a deliberate borrowing rests solely on a conjecture made in an
article written for the journal *Cäcilia* in 1829 by Clementi's
pupil Ludwig Berger, who had heard his master's account of
the contest in 1806!

The figure is basically little more than an Italianate cliché of
the period. A. della Corte has pointed out[1] its occurrence in a
quartet of *Il Barone di Torreforte*, an opera composed by Piccini
in 1765. It was used with sundry modifications in the violin
part to no. 5 of *Idomeneo* (Ex. 9), composed nearly a year *before*

Ex. 9.

Mozart's contest with Clementi, in the 'Prague' Symphony
(I: 37–42 *et passim*),[2] in the Allegro for Piano, K. 498a (I: 81),
and in the Sonata in B flat, K. 570 (I: 45, 46). As early as 1843
an anonymous writer in *Cäcilia*[3] pointed out the striking similarity between this figure and one in the fugal overture to *Die*

[1] *Piccini* (Bari, 1928), p. 54.
[2] A Roman figure in parentheses, followed by arabic, denote respectively the
movement of a work and the bar.   [3] Vol. xx, p. 132.

Auferstehung des Lazarus (1773) composed by J. H. Collo. This statement is repeated in all editions of Jahn—slightly varied in 1907 by Deiters, who made the name 'Kollo'—until Abert dropped it in 1923, probably finding, as has the present writer, that no such composer has ever appeared in any dictionary of music. Under a different title, however, the work itself does exist, for the 'Collo' of *Cäcilia's* contributor was a misprint for Rolle[1] in the overture of whose oratorio *Lazarus oder die Feyer der Auferstehung*, the phrase occurs:

Ex. 10.

This oratorio was printed by Breitkopf in 1779, but there is nothing to suggest that Mozart knew anything at all of Rolle's work, which, as its subscription list shows, was published entirely for towns in northern and central Germany. It is, however, noteworthy that this theme, as elaborated by Mozart, is closely akin to one that is prominent in the finale to Act I of Haydn's *Il Mondo della luna* (C. 418):

Ex. 11.

an opera that Mozart probably knew and remembered. One cannot help wondering what Clementi really thought when he heard Mozart's overture; for, being an honest man and knowing, as he must have known, that the theme was essentially common coin, he himself could scarcely have claimed priority of invention. Soon after the production of *Die Zauberflöte*, Cimarosa used it prominently in 'Io ti lascio', the second duet in Act I of *Il Matrimonio segreto* (Feb. 1792).

---

[1] I am indebted to O. E. Deutsch and the late Paul Hirsch for their joint divination of 'Collo's' real name, by which after 176 years Rolle is vindicated.

In the first number of the opera, the last part of the trio sung
by the Three Ladies is based, in its orchestral accompaniment,
on the vigorous repetition of a little phrase that had previously
appeared in 'Susanna or vià sortite', no. 13 of *Figaro* (C. 422, 423).
The haunting phrase to which in no. 3 Tamino sings 'Dies
Bildnis ist bezaubernd schön', repeating it a tone lower, is quite
an old favourite of Mozart's. He had used it, with different
note-values, to open his Violin Sonata in F (K. 377); it appears
with an additional third sequence, in the slow movement of the
G minor String Quintet (K. 516, III: 18–21), and also, much
earlier, in a clavier sonata (K. 279, I: 22). Yet however much
Mozart made the melody Tamino's own by pausing on the top
note of each descending scale, other composers had found it
useful. Einstein points out[1] the remarkable similarity in Gluck's
song 'Die frühen Gräber' (1773):

Ex. 12.

Will-kom-men, O sil-ber-ner Mond,

Moreover, the opening of Haydn's Clavier Sonata in B flat, of
1784, suggests that the figure was pretty widely current.

Even more emphatically can this be said of Tamino's next
utterance, his repetition of the words 'Ich fühl' es' and the two
following bars. Mozart had used this almost identically in
Idomeneo No. 11 [Ex. 13], and the melody of the first two bars

Ex. 13.

la pat-ria il ri-po-so, tu pa-dre___ mi se-i,

occurs at the very opening of the String Quartet in E flat
(K. 171, I: 1, 2), and in the Andante of the G minor Symphony
(K. 550, II: 77–79). Robert Haas pointed out[2] that the identical
melody, expressing sentiments similar to Tamino's, is found in

[1] *Gluck* (London, 1936), pp. 129–31.
[2] *W. A. Mozart* (Potsdam, 1933), p. 42.

Florian Gassmann's *I Viaggiatori ridicoli* (1776); Abert remarked on its use by C. P. E. Bach,[1] by Grétry and Paisiello; and a similar inflexion was favoured by Haydn in his G major Clavier Sonata of 1776 (II: 18–20). Finally, in this same no. 3, there is a broad similarity between the postlude and two other passages in Mozart: the ending of no. 4 of *Zaide*[2] and the conclusion of the Adagio of the 'Hunt' Quartet (K. 458).

In 1843 the aforesaid anonymous contributor to *Cäcilia* pointed out[3] the pronounced affinity between the introduction to no. 4, where the orchestra announces the coming of the Queen of the Night, and a passage in *Ariadne* by Georg Benda, whose music Mozart knew well and admired. We find the Queen's unhappy outburst, 'Ihr ängstliches Beben', occurring, almost note for note, at Ilia's words in *Idomeneo*, no. 11:

Ex. 14.

L'an‑gos‑cie,   gl'af‑fan‑ni,   gl'af‑fan — — ni,

Equally remarkable is the previous exact use (C. 436, 437) of the Queen's phrase 'Auf ewig dein' at the end of Constanze's aria, no. 6, in Act I of *Die Entführung aus dem Serail*. We may add, at the risk of repeating what is now a common-place of Mozartian criticism, that the coloratura of this aria, no. 4, is closely modelled on that in 'Dies ist des edlen Huon's Sprache', no. 6 of Wranitzky's *Oberon*.[4]

In the following quintet, no. 5 (composed, according to Nissen, during a game of billiards at Prague), the musical pivot of the first section consists of the opening figure—a trill on the tonic, followed by a descending arpeggio, which was in fact something of a favourite with Mozart. It dominates the vivid recitative of no. 23 of *Idomeneo* 'Volgi intorno lo sguardo', occurring as many as seventeen times in fewer than fifty bars,

---

[1] In a Trio Sonata edited by G. Schumann (Leuckart, 1910).

[2] Einstein, p. 454.

[3] Vol. xx, p. 133, whence the passage is quoted by Jahn.

[4] Other similarities between the characters of this opera and *Die Zauberflöte* were discussed by E. J. Dent in *Mozart's Operas* (London, 1913), pp. 359, 360.

and similarly permeates the whole of the Allegro of the Flute
Concerto in D (K. 314). In *Die Zauberflöte* itself, the figure
recurs in a nobler vein to lend tension to the great scene between Tamino and the Priest.[1] We should note the earlier
appearance of this figure in Gluck's *Alceste*, Act I, no. 4:

Ex. 15.

(High priest's recitative)

for this suggests a certain reminiscence on Mozart's part because
that opera made a great impression on him as a boy. This
observation was made by Jahn, but he omitted to point out that
the figure occurs no fewer than eight times, in varying keys,
and dominates the whole of the High Priest's recitative, exactly
as in Mozart. As to the 'Hm! Hm! Hm!' mumbled by Papageno from his padlocked lips, we find a clear ancestor of this
in Philidor's *Bucheron* (1763)[2] where Margot, struck dumb
earlier in the action, takes part in a septet, singing only 'Hi, hon,
hon' for several pages! Philidor's operas were not unknown to
Mozart.

It would appear that the brisk melody sung by Monostatos
in the first words of no. 6 'Du feines Täubchen' was running in
Mozart's mind in the last year of his life. He had used it in his
String Quintet in E flat (K. 614, IV: 27–30, 205–12) and we find
it, slightly modified in rhythm, as the beginning of the last of a
set of four German Dances (K. 602). But nine years earlier, this
lilting tune had served, in a more leisurely tempo and more
liberally spaced, as the opening theme of the Larghetto of the
Clavier Concerto in F (K. 413) [Ex. 16]. Its use in *Die Zauberflöte* on the lips of Monostatos is a pretty piece of dramatic irony,

---

[1] Though not strictly relevant to the present discussion, it is interesting to note that
Mozart used this figure again in an identical way in Vitellia's recitative 'Ecco il punto',
no. 22 of *La Clemenza di Tito*.

[2] Pp. 66 ff. of the full score.

for it exactly anticipates the despairing cry of Papageno and Pamina 'Ach nun ist's mit uns vorbei' in the first Finale (p. 93) where they are caught by him as they try to escape.

Ex. 16.

Of the incomparable duet no. 7 'Bei Männern welche Liebe fühlen', which Mozart improved greatly from his original draft by a simple yet brilliant change of rhythm, it is only to be remarked how nearly the opening melody corresponds to the first bars of the Minuet of the 'Linz' Symphony (K. 425).

Before we begin to examine the Finale of Act I, let us consider a further passage from Wyzewa's review. It follows immediately after that quoted above:

Mozart remembered that formerly he had spent his youth in creating, with juvenile prodigality, a glorious throng of melodies of wonderful freshness and grace, which later he alone knew to exist. Particularly at the age of twenty, during the entire year 1776, a veritable flood of beauty had poured forth from his heart, and this treasure now rested in the bottom of a desk drawer, in the unused manuscripts of his serenades, divertimentos, and all his instrumental works of this period, an incomparable treasure of melodies and rhythms, astonishingly suited to the lyrical atmosphere of his new opera [i.e. *Die Zauberflöte*].

Now it is a curious fact that nowhere in the *Biographie musicale*, whether in discussing the works of 1776 or *Die Zauberflöte* itself, did Wyzewa and Saint-Foix amass enough evidence to justify this remarkable statement, which applies, as examination of the score shows, to the Finale of Act I[1] and to Act II. But it is possible to find nearly a dozen figures or melodies that derive from, or at least are akin to, Mozart's music of 1776. There is a wealth of history in the very first melody that

---

[1] In order to facilitate reference to this loosely strung sequence of 10 or 11 numbers, page references are given where necessary: they are those of the Breitkopf & Härtel score, Ser. 5, No. 20.

floats from the lips of the Three Boys, 'Zum Ziele führt dich diese Bahn'. This calm, stately trio can be traced back to an old song

Ex. 17.

die Katz die last das   Mau - sen nit, die Gans fliegt ü - bers   Meer

which, as far as we know, first appears in print in Part 2 of the so-called *Augsburger Tafelkonfekt* of 1737.[1] It may also be found, slightly modified, in the final chorus of Bach's 'Coffee Cantata', and unmistakably adorns the Rondo of Beethoven's Pianoforte Concerto in C, op. 15. Wyzewa remarks that Mozart himself had used it—significantly in the key of E flat—as the main theme of the Finale of the Divertimento in E flat (K. 252): it also appears in a brisk version as the main subject of the Rondo of his Concerto for Two Claviers (K. 365, III: *passim*).

For the general flow of melody in Tamino's recitative (pp. 79–86), sung first by himself and then in dialogue with the priest, one need go no farther than the opening of Gluck's *Iphigénie en Aulide*, where Agamemnon's soliloquy offers some interesting resemblances. But it is Mozart himself who provides —rather unexpectedly—the original of the surpassingly lovely utterance of the priest 'Sobald dich führt der Freundschaft Hand' (p. 85). It is none other (C. 451, 452) than a passage of flowing bass in the Piano Sonata in A minor (K. 310, I: 129–32). When one examines Tamino's flute solo (p. 87) followed by his song 'Wie stark ist nicht dein Zauberton', it is not perhaps surprising to find that it is first cousin to the flute entry in the Andante for Flute and Orchestra in C (K. 315). Many of Mozart's melodies for wind instruments have a certain broad similarity common to each group, and this for the flute is no exception.

In the sprightly phrase, 'Schnelle Füsse, rascher Mut', with

[1] Friedländer, *Das Deutsche Lied im 18. Jahrhundert* (Stuttgart, 1902), vol. ii, p. 14. The melody actually appears only on p. 22 of the bass part of No. 7 in the original edition.

which Pamina and Papageno commence their escape (p. 90), Mozart reverted to a melody used (C. 457, 458) in his youthful opera *La Finta semplice*. [Ex. 18.] The entry of Monostatos to

Ex. 18.

Spo - sa ca - ra   Spo - sa bel - la

cut off the escaping pair (p. 93) is marked by the words 'He, ihr Sklaven, kommt herbei!' which introduce the sequence of identical fourths rising and falling emphatically that were to Mozart a means of expressing servitude or submission (C. 461, &c.). We find a very similar sequence at the last entry of the Queen of the Night (p. 209) with her servile crew. It can be traced back to Osmin in *Die Entführung*,

Ex. 19.

Marsch! fort, Marsch! fort, Marsch! fort,

and appears, most strikingly, in Leporello's 'Notte e giorno faticar' at the very rise of the curtain in *Don Giovanni*.

For the great choral salute 'Es lebe Sarastro, Sarastro lebe!' (p. 97) Mozart recreated this passage from the first chorus of *König Thamos*:

Ex. 20.

Er - hör - e die Wun - sche, die Wün - sche er - hör - e

At the repeat of the chorus's homage to Sarastro (pp. 106, 107) he altered the rhythm slightly *more suo*, and added a running figure in the violins, with the result that he nearly reproduced a passage from the Sonata in F for clavier duet (K. 497, I: 125):

Ex. 21.

When the chorus proclaim Sarastro's actual approach (p. 97) Papageno babbles in terror, 'O wär' ich eine Maus', &c., and the melodic line almost reproduces a theme from the Concerto for Two Claviers (K. 365, I: 269, 270) of 1780. To conclude the examination of this solemn Finale to Act I, Pamina's cry 'Mir klingt der Muttername süsse' (p. 102) is an actual echo of Tamino's phrase in no. 3 'Dies etwas kann ich zwar nicht nennen', and anticipates that which they sing together in no. 19 'Wie bitter sind der Trennung Leiden'. Undoubtedly this beautifully shaped melody was something of a favourite with Mozart, for he had used it, with sundry modifications, in a number of previous works—the Serenade for Wind Octet in E flat (K. 375, III: 26–32), the song 'Als Luise' (K. 520),

Ex. 22.

the Violin Sonata in E flat (K. 481, II: 19–21),

Ex. 23.

and Ilia's first entry 'M'avrai compagna al duolo' in the quartet in *Idomeneo*.

In studying the March of the Priests, we need to bear in mind the fact that, during the latter half of the eighteenth century, March rhythms and tunes had a certain broad similarity. This is sufficient to account for the basic resemblance between this March and those in Gluck's *Iphigénie en Tauride*, and that in Wranitzky's *Oberon*. But it is perhaps natural to find the sources for part of the March of the Priests in Mozart himself. When in *Così fan tutte*, no. 29, Ferrando sings Ex. 24 he anticipates,

Ex. 24.

pie - to___   so il ci - glio

note for note, bars 2–4 of the March. The phrase at its end occurs with emphatic frequency to punctuate several of the variations of the *Sinfonia Concertante* in E flat (K. 297 b, III); broadly, the march in *Idomeneo* adumbrates the shape of the March of the Priests, as does also a remarkable passage in the sketch-book known as *Mozarts Unterricht in der Composition, 1784*:[1]

Ex. 25.

Two divertimenti in F (K. 247, VI, and K. 253, I) both contain marchlike andantes, in which the germ of the Priests' March

---

[1] Cf. R. Lach, *Mozart als Theoretiker* (Vienna, 1919), where the complete transcription of the sketch-book is given.

can be discerned. But what are we to say of the opening of
Corelli's Op. 5, no. 6?

Ex. 26.

Since it is improbable that Mozart knew Corelli's music, even
though it was familiar to Padre Martini's circle, we can surely
ascribe this parallel to musical coincidence.[1]

After the repeat of the triple series of three chords, comes
Sarastro's 'O Isis und Osiris' in which he sings 'Stärkt mit
Geduld sie in Gefahr', a phrase that closely resembles a passage
in Haydn's symphony 'La Reine' (I: 93–95):

Ex. 27.

No. 12, 'Wie, wie, wie', opens with a very characteristic
melody which Mozart had previously used in his G major
String Quartet (K. 387, IV: 108–10). When he composed the
opening of Monostatos's aria 'Alles fühlt der Liebe Freuden', he
probably did not realize that he was repeating not only a phrase
from his own Clavier Concerto in E flat (K. 271, III: 35–39):

Ex. 28.

but also a striking and nearly identical rhythm from a symphony of his admired friend Myslivecek which he must have
known since Leopold Mozart quoted it in a letter of 22 December, 1770. [Ex. 29.] Abert remarked pertinently on the basic

Ex. 29.

[1] Many examples of such coincidences are given in Wilhelm Tappert's *Wandernde
Melodien* (Leipzig, 1890).

similarity between Mozart's Moorish creation in 'Alles fühlt'
and the air 'Grande, grande réjouissance' in Grétry's *Amitié à
l'épreuve*, where the African Amilcar sings a brisk melody
doubled throughout by the piccolo.

In the opening bars of 'In diesen heil'gen Hallen', Mozart
echoed two bars from 'Torna la pace' in *Idomeneo* (no. 31):

Ex. 30.

In the soaring figure on the violins that introduces and
dominates the trio 'Seid uns zum zweitenmal willkommen'
(no. 16) he repeated that which punctuates the Ladies' farewell
(in no. 5) to Tamino and Papageno. How well Mozart liked
these airily rising quavers we can see from their use in the last
bars of the Violin Concerto in A (K. 219), in those of the
Adagio of the String Trio in E flat (K. 563, II), and in the
Clavier Sonata in E flat (K. 281, III: 18–21).

While *Figaro* has obviously less common ground musically
with *Die Zauberflöte* than has *Idomeneo*, Pamina's words 'Nim-
mer kommt ihr, Wonnestunden', in her aria 'Ach, ich fühl's'
(no. 17) are a clear echo of Susanna's

Ex. 31

from 'Deh vieni non tardar'. Pamina's repetition of the words
'meinem Herzen mehr zurück' is an intensified form of the end
of Orpheus's first aria in Gluck's *Orfeo*.

In the trio (no. 19) Tamino's central utterance to 'Der
Götter Wille mag geschehen' emerges, on examination, as a
heightened form of an especially favourite phrase of Mozart's.
His nearest use of it, in time and similarity, was in the Clarinet
Quintet (K. 581, I: 42–44):

Ex. 32

in simpler form it appears in the following works—the Concerto for Three Claviers (K. 242, I: 74, 75); the Clavier Concertos in B flat (K. 450, I: 33–35) and in F (K. 459, III: 151–3); the Clavier Sonatas in G (K. 283, II: 10) and in C (K. 309, II: 67, 68); the Clavier Rondo in F (K. 494: 70, 71); and the 'Haffner' Serenade (K. 250, VIII: 1, 2). In this same trio, no. 19, we find yet another echo from *Idomeneo* no. 21: the cry 'Ach, gold'ne Ruhe' repeats Ilia's melody:[1]

Ex. 33

Peggio è   di   mor - te

Jahn remarked[2] that the melody

Ex. 34

of a chorale by Scandello (1517–80) was the counterpart, in long note values, of Papageno's 'Ein Mädchen oder Weibchen'. Chantavoine has noted an even more interesting parallel in Haydn's *Il Mondo della luna*:

Ex. 35

Wollt' die. Drei-stig-keit ent - schul- den

It hardly seems possible to ascribe both of these to mere coincidence.

Chantavoine has pointed out (512–14) that in the second scene of the Finale to Act II Pamina's emphatic utterance after her attempted suicide, 'Führt mich hin, ich möcht' ihn seh'n'

---

[1] See further István Barna, 'The Development of a Mozart Melody', *MR*, Nov. 1949.

[2] Vol. iv, 1859, p. 564. This curious piece of information, which was acknowledged by Jahn from a note of C. F. Becker's in *Neue Zeitschrift für Musik*, vol. xii, p. 112, was unaccountably omitted by Abert, vol. ii, p. 708.

(p. 171), is found twice in earlier works, in the Finale to Act IV of *Figaro*—Susanna's 'Che smania, che furor' (bars 203–305) —and in the Masonic Cantata *Die Maurerfreude* of 1785:

Ex. 36

wie dem Star - ren For - scher - aug - e

All three are in E flat, with identical notes. The fugal subject that introduces the beginning of the ordeal scene (p. 174) is shown by Abert to be identical with the Kyrie from a Mass of 1701 by Heinrich Biber, while the melody intoned by the Two Armed Men has been generally recognized as that of an old chorale 'Ach Gott von Himmel sieh' darein'.[1] When Pamina is at last reunited with Tamino, she actually repeats (pp. 179, 180) at the words

> Sie mag den Weg mit Rosen streu'n,
> Weil Rosen stets bei Dornen sein.

the opening phrases of Tamino's 'Bildnis' aria—a beautiful touch, whether deliberate or not.

When Mozart composed the music of the ordeal scene, with Tamino's flute-playing punctuated by chords on trumpets and drums, he was reproducing, in a heightened form, the spirit of his Divertimento K. 188 of 1776, for those instruments, combined with flutes. It is also instructive to glance at no. 3 of *Les Petits riens* which flutes and violins play alone in imitation. The actual music of Tamino's flute ends with a straight descending scale of tonic down to supertonic, followed by this little twisting phrase

Ex. 37

which Mozart used a good many times in his last years. It

[1] First known in 1524 in the *Erfurter Enchiridien*. Into this melody Mozart wove, after some previous experiment, a second one akin to Kirnberger's *Es wollt uns Gott gnädig sein*.

makes nearly a dozen appearances in *Così fan tutte*; it clinches
the end of the first minuet in the String Trio (K. 563, II: 54),
and has a similar effect in the String Quartet in B flat (K. 589,
III: 7, 36, &c.), in the A major Quartet (K. 464, I: 234), in the
Minuets (K. 585, no. 5, trio), and in the Armonica Quintet
(K. 617, rondo, 16, &c.).

The delectable duet sung by Papageno and Papagena will
always remind the Mozart-lover of certain earlier works,
particularly the Finales of the Clavier Concertos in F (K. 459)
and G (K. 453), but in addition to these the piquancy of their
music is heightened by melodic quotations from Tamino's
'Bildnis' aria.

In the final scene of all, the solemn notes of the words of wel-
come, 'Heil sei euch Geweihten', are repeated from a variety of
earlier works, most appropriately, perhaps, from the last chorus
of *König Thamos* [Ex. 38] but not inaptly from the Finale of
Figaro, where the Countess forgives the Count [Ex. 39]. We
also find this phrase in the Clavier Sonata in E flat (K. 282, I:
3–5), and in the final chorus of *Idomeneo* [Ex. 40]. Most interest-

Ex. 38

Höch - ste   Gott - heit,   mil - de___ Son - ne

Ex. 39

Con - tes - sa, per - do - no!   per - do - no, per - do - no!

Ex. 40

Scenda I - me - ne - o,   Scenda A - mor,   Scenda I - me - ne - o

ing of all, perhaps, is the fact that the identical progression
occurs in *Die Zauberflöte* itself, in the woodwind chords at the
very opening of the ordeal scene (p. 174). Finally we should
remark that the melody sung by the chorus at 'die Schönheit und
Weisheit' (p. 221) is an echo both of the very words of Tamino's

first utterance of 'Wir wandeln durch des Tones Macht' on p. 181 and of the melody in variation 3 of the Divertimento in F (K. 253, I):

Ex. 41

Their common ancestor is to be found in the final words of no. 16 of *Idomeneo*, 'Del ciel la clemenza'.

However impressive may be this array of musical evidence as far as it goes, it could certainly be strengthened and extended by a wider study of eighteenth-century music and by an exhaustive knowledge of the corpus of Mozart's own works. For in his short, intense life he undoubtedly heard far more music than is specifically mentioned in his letters and other sources. It is certain too that had his life been prolonged to a more normal span, and had some active critic of about 1810 drawn his attention to the melodic sources and affinities of *Die Zauberflöte*, no one would have been more surprised than he. This aspect of the opera was not divined by anyone writing at the time of the first production in 1791, or indeed for long afterwards. Mozartian literature of the nineteenth century casually noted a few parallels and possible sources, but it was left for Wyzewa, writing partly, perhaps, from instinct, and partly from knowledge that he did not live to co-ordinate and put into print, to formulate this bold theory of a 'pot-pourri'.

Seen in this light, *Die Zauberflöte* presents a paradox virtually without parallel in musical history—an opera universally admitted to be a work of genius, and seemingly one of striking originality, which is in part a synthesis of material drawn from a variety of sources. Here we have a supreme instance of the fact that, as Emerson wrote,[1] 'the greatest genius is the most indebted man'. It lies beyond the scope of our present inquiry to enumerate and analyse the exact means by which Mozart endowed this opera with its profound and enduring qualities. But it

---

[1] 'Shakespeare; or the Poet', in *English Traits. Representative Men* ('Everyman' Edition, 1908), p. 245.

remains for us to try to correlate and explain these 'parallels', 'borrowings', or 'sources'—whatever they may be called—by following one or two lines of investigation. This we can only do with the reservation that our conclusions, although they may seem attractive and reasonable, cannot be logically and absolutely proved. For we are drawn into speculation about the mental processes of genius, and this is at best hazardous.

To call Mozart a learned or scholarly musician, in the sense in which Brahms might be so described, would be inaccurate. But, in a more limited sense, it is certain that he, like Brahms, was steeped in a genuine feeling for tradition. The background of musical culture with which his mind was imbued was exceptionally wide, although covering a relatively short space of time—a century and a half at the most. From this period there flowed into his life many streams of musical thought and practice which he absorbed as easily and deeply as only true genius can, even as, for instance, Milton had nurtured his mind in the cumulative tradition of Homer, Vergil, and Dante.

We also know that Mozart had a remarkably retentive memory, which appears to have been of a strongly associational type, in that it was freely and powerfully influenced by similarities of emotion, dramatic situation, and the like. Although this fact has been clearly brought out by Chantavoine in his above-mentioned *Mozart dans Mozart*, he failed to make the most of his case because he concentrated almost entirely on the operas. A full study of the instrumental works also is indispensable, because repetitions from Mozart's own and other composers' music are quite as numerous as in the vocal works, and all the sonatas, symphonies, concertos, chamber music, and divertimenti must be examined if the picture is to be complete. Obviously the absence of words makes the exact association of musical ideas harder to define, but tonality (as in *Die Zauberflöte*) is a factor of great significance.

Let us turn from Mozart's sense of tradition and from his powers of memory and association to the circumstances in the last years of his life—an admittedly trite subject, but here very relevant. The pathetic series of letters to Puchberg[1] reveals Mozart's distressing condition—poverty-stricken, ill, and worried, having seen most of his hopes and dreams come to naught. Yet the stream of his genius flowed unquenched, although diverted at times into strange channels, and sometimes uncertain of its direction. Above all, his faith in Masonic ideals remained unshaken. Therefore, when in the spring of 1791 Schikaneder gave him the opportunity of realizing his long-cherished ambition to compose a serious German opera, especially one with a Masonic basis, the effect on a sensitive artist in Mozart's physical and mental state must have been overwhelming.

Moreover, we can see in his works from 1789 onwards many signs of the new style—limpid, homogeneous, closely knit with airy counterpoint, and buoyant with flowing melody—into which his art was to develop during its Indian summer of 1791. *Die Zauberflöte*, being conceived and written in such a conjunction of material and artistic circumstance, and under such urgent impulses, must be regarded as the supreme expression of Mozart's genius. Here, then, we find ample reason for the melodic stuff of this opera being so notably derivative. The need for hasty and intermittent work combined with an abnormal state of mind and body to heighten the powers of a retentive mind richly stored with tradition and habitually moved by subtle association of musical ideas. In *Die Zauberflöte* we can observe the last and deepest stirring of the pool of

[1] Some new light is shed on this matter by the discovery, kindly communicated to me by Emily Anderson, of a hitherto unknown letter of Mozart. The autograph has disappeared, but part of the text is quoted in catalogue 39 (*c.* 1910) of J. Halle Antiquariat, Munich, Ottostrasse 3a, Lot 122. The letter, dated 29 Sept. 1787, is written to Baron Berchtold zu Sonnenburg at St. Gilgen, Mozart's brother-in-law, otherwise unknown as one of his correspondents. The sentences quoted in the catalogue are these: 'Liebster H. Bruder! In aller Eyle; . . . wenn Sie mir den Wechsel übermachen, so bitte ich, ihn an Hr. Michael Puchberg . . . zu adressiren, denn dieser hat ordre das Geld zu übernehmen, da ich Montag in aller frühe nach Prag reise—Leben sie wohl; Küssen sie für uns beyde 1000 mal unsere liebe schwester. . . .' The earliest occurrence of Puchberg in Mozart's correspondence known till now was in a letter of June 1788. The composer's financial dealings with him may thus be advanced by about nine months. The date of the Mozarts' departure for Prague to attend the first performance of *Don Giovanni* can now be fixed as 1 October 1787.

memory and experience. What is old springs to new and radiant life: this opera is Mozart's *nuove musiche*.

While this hypothesis may reasonably serve to explain the clear facts of its melodic nature, we must admit the virtual impossibility of discovering how the music took shape as it did. From which layer or layers of consciousness it grew, we can only guess. Probably most of the 'borrowings' were unconscious and not the result of recollection, still less of a deliberate re-perusal of the autographs of 1775 and 1776, as Wyzewa seems to suggest. Even if the progress of composition was spasmodic, Mozart's inspiration must frequently have worked at white heat, for with him composition was analogous to a chemical process in which elements are dissolved and new combinations of 'hooked atoms'[1] come into being.

There is one further fact worth noting in this context. In his edition of Köchel, Einstein drew attention for the first time to the probability that the autographs of Mozart's String Quartets K. 575 and 589[2] consist in part of actual drafts for quartets made nearly seventeen years before. This strongly suggests that in 1789 Mozart sometimes found it hard to begin composition[3] and had recourse to earlier material for the initial impulse and idea. Since it is also a fact that his instrumental music of these three last years abounds in melodic repetitions from his own works both recent and remote, is it not possible that by 1791 he had almost formed a habit of drawing sub-consciously on memory and association? This suggestion can of course only be applied to a limited part of *Die Zauberflöte* and other works of 1791. In melody, as in harmony and structure, Mozart could and did produce music of unprecedented novelty and brilliance, as in the Concerto for Clarinet, adapted though the greater part

---

[1] I borrow the metaphor from John Livingston Lowes's study of Coleridge, *The Road to Xanadu*, wherein some striking analogies in creative effort are to be found.

[2] Now in the British Museum, with those of the other eight great quartets. Cf. Chapter 4.

[3] A parallel springs to mind of some of Handel's borrowings from other composers from about 1736 onwards. For details see Sedley Taylor, *The Indebtedness of Handel to Other Composers* (Cambridge, 1906), and E. J. Dent, *Handel* (London, 1934), pp. 106, 107.

M

of its first movement was from a discarded draft of a concerto for basset-horn written late in 1789.

An attempt to analyse the melodic material of *Die Zauber-flöte* is far from being mere indulgence in criticism as an end in itself, but is essential to our understanding of a wonderful opera. More detailed study than can be given here would show that besides the subtle remoulding of material from previous works, Mozart often actually let his characters catch up phrases from each other's lips, as it were, almost to the extent of parody. This and other unifying characteristics contribute much to the extraordinary homogeneity of the music albeit forged out of such diverse material, and suffuse it with a gentle irony, which compensates, to some extent, for the conspicuous lack of action, at least in the ordinary sense of the term. In addition, the tonal structure, carefully calculated in relation to character and situation,[1] enhances the power and directness of the melodic style.

Notwithstanding the *Requiem*, it is *Die Zauberflöte* that really embodies Mozart's testament of spiritual and musical faith, the finest qualities of nearly twenty years' creative effort. The true unity of life and art here shines revealed, calmly and unmistakably, as nowhere else in Mozart's music. Just as the alchemy of his genius transmutes and resolves so many of the discrepant elements of a 'pot-pourri'—stylistic as well as melodic—so is the complex pattern of selfish human passions, marvellously delineated in his earlier operas, finally exalted in *Die Zauberflöte* and purified into the fulness of divine love which embraces all mankind.

An eminent English Mozartian, W. Warde Fowler,[2] summed up the characteristics of Mozart's later works by quoting lines from Wordsworth's *Laodamia*:

> The gods approve
> The depth, and not the tumult, of the soul,
> A fervent, not ungovernable love,

---

[1] It is most instructive to listen to the opera on gramophone records, where the tonal sequences flow on unbroken by dialogue.
[2] Warde Fowler, p. 90.

which, incidentally, epitomizes perfectly the mutual feelings of
Tamino and Pamina. Between the spirit of Wordsworth's verse
and Mozart's music, there are obvious points of divergence, but
also notable affinities, and when in Book 3 of the *Excursion* the
poet praises

> The Universal instinct of repose,
> The longing for confirmed tranquillity,
> Inward and outward, humble, yet sublime,
> The life where hope and memory are as one,

does he not help us to gain insight into the intrinsic significance
of the melodic fabric of *Die Zauberflöte*?

10

The Growth and Significance of Mozart's Counterpoint

A GENERAL view of Mozart's career shows clearly that the contrapuntal elements in his music developed in four fairly distinct but natural stages. Juvenile apprenticeship, often of an academic kind, was followed by a period of intensive exploration and experiment, culminating in spasmodic efforts to assimilate new ideas. This led gradually to technical mastery, both in a selective, allusive manner, and in extended movements, but it was offset by rather erratic judgement. When, finally, Mozart had discovered a true relationship between texture and emotion, he combined taste in choosing a particular style of counterpoint with a fine instinct for using it most effectively and naturally.

Mozart's earliest known attempts at contrapuntal writing date from the time of the family's visit to London in 1764–5. When in June of 1765 the Hon. Daines Barrington undertook his thorough investigation into the boy's powers, he wrote: 'I have been informed by two or three able musicians, when Bach the celebrated composer had begun a fugue and left off abruptly, that little Mozart hath immediately taken it up, and worked it after a most masterly manner'.[1] About the same time Mozart composed the motet 'God is our Refuge' (K. 20)[2] which displays some rudimentary polyphonic skill. During his father's illness in July Mozart wrote also some short fugues for clavier.[3] A sketch-book dating from his return to Salzburg in

---

[1] *Philosophical Transactions*, vol. lx, 1771, pp. 61, 62. On p. 62 Barrington gives Mozart's age as '8 years and 5 months', a curious miscalculation, for on p. 54 the year and month of his birth are correct.

[2] Cf. p. 90.

[3] Published in *Mozart als achtjähriger Componist*, edited by Schünemann, Leipzig, 1909.

1767 contains lessons given by his father in thorough-bass and counterpoint, in addition to examples of *cantus firmus* taken from Fux's *Gradus*. After writing his first vocal fugue in a Mass in G major (K. 49) of 1768, he soon produced a quantity of other church music in the same vein. There is no lack of evidence to show that in early years he was assiduously studying polyphony, but neither this study nor its results need detain us long. He was like a small boy who masters sufficient Latin grammar for matriculation, learns all the rules and exceptions, so that he can write neat sentences to illustrate them, but has no grasp of the spirit of Latin as a living literature. Moreover, some of the teaching he received was uninspired. This was due partly to the fact that the subject was not in high esteem at Salzburg, where the court composers all wrote exercises in *cantus firmus*, fugues and canons, without feeling enthusiasm for a style then obsolescent, however much it was said to have flourished not so long ago, many miles away to the north, in the hands of a great organist named Bach. Furthermore, the archbishop himself was not devoted to counterpoint for liturgical purposes but preferred a style approximating to that of popular Italian opera which would give a service with plenty of brilliance and colour in it, but not lasting more than forty-five minutes![1]

Because of the indirect influence exercised by Mozart's early masses, litanies, and the like on his instrumental style, it is impossible to ignore them entirely. Both his letters and his father's give ample proof that he took this kind of composition seriously, even though, as part of a musician's vocation, it continued to be somewhat despised at Salzburg. After Mozart's death much of his ecclesiastical music was rated below his other works, more so, perhaps, abroad than in his own country.

---

[1] Cf. Mozart's letter to Padre Martini of 4 Sept. 1776. It was apparently due to the archbishop's radical taste that in Mozart's Masses of 1777 the Credo ended in a short chorus instead of in the more usual fugue. There is some interesting information on the official attitude to the older style of church music in the anonymous pamphlet *Biographische Skizze von Michael Haydn* (in fact by J. G. Schinn and J. Otter) published at Salzburg in 1808.

Consequently, its place in his stylistic growth and the importance of its contrapuntal element were mostly obscured and
neglected, though things might have been a little better in
England, where Victorian taste was fostered by Vincent
Novello's publication in 1819–24 of eighteen Masses, some of
which he discovered himself. Unfortunately this enthusiasm
concentrated on the superficial purity and grace of some of the
weakest Masses, to say nothing of others, notably the famous
'Twelfth', that were spurious. This was bound to produce an
indiscriminate reaction, which has been prolonged, in England
at any rate, by the antipathy of the twentieth century towards
the style of south German ecclesiastical music of the mid-
eighteenth. Hence, very largely, the eclipse of practically all
Mozart's Masses, except the 'Coronation' (K. 317), the C minor
(K. 427), and the *Requiem*. Yet there is great beauty and vitality
in some of the others, particularly in the F major (K. 192),
which clearly benefited from the two most potent influences on
his contrapuntal writing.

The first of these he encountered on his travels in 1770, when
he took lessons (of which the difficulty is attested by manuscript
sketches) in fugue, canon, and polyphony from Martini at
Bologna and the Marquis de Ligniville at Florence. These two
men, of European fame in their lifetime but now almost totally
forgotten, both actively adhered to the tradition of sixteenth-
century Italian polyphony and no less staunchly opposed the
new-fangled 'theatrical' tendency in church music. Here at last
the true spirit of polyphonic music was revealed to Mozart,
though he had little chance for nearly two years to show how
much he had learnt. Then came the second flash of illumination,
from contact with Haydn's Op. 20 Quartets, written in 1772,
shortly after those comprising his Op. 17. When Mozart had
studied these in the light of the new understanding given him
by Martini, he probably realized that a reorientation of the
musical universe, as he knew it, was sooner or later almost
unavoidable.

How great a stimulus Haydn's music gave to Mozart's quartets can be seen by comparing the six dating from 1772 and early in 1773 (K. 155–60) with those composed at Vienna in the late autumn of the latter year (K. 168–73). Mozart's addition of a fourth movement to each quartet—K. 155–60 were all in *three* movements only—was almost certainly due to his study of Haydn, and brought him up against new problems in balance which he did not finally solve until much later. Here, however, we are less concerned with the temporary shift of structural emphasis than with his first excursions of any length into purely instrumental counterpoint, inspired by the fugal finales of the second, fifth, and sixth quartets of Haydn's Op. 20. In Mozart's earlier quartets the counterpoint is negligible: but in K. 168–173, composed in August and September 1773, there are three movements of outstanding interest. The first quartet, in F major, has a most striking slow movement, in the tonic minor, whose subject is taken note for note (the key too is the same) from the Finale of Op. 20, no. 4, though its treatment as a kind of four-part canon is in the spirit of Martini. Because the tightness of the part-writing conveys an impression of suppressed anguish, we feel that neither here nor in the fugal Finale is Mozart completely at ease in his medium. Through tending to handle the instruments as if they were voices, he is led to distort or misinterpret their characteristic qualities and misses much of the contrast on which contrapuntal writing for strings depends for its success. But the theme of this fugue is genuinely instrumental in conception: though strictly organized, it is wonderfully fresh. It is a brave attempt to adapt and re-create the spirit as well as the matter of Haydn's Op. 20.

Within a month, however, Mozart had learnt much, and he concluded the last quartet of the set, K. 173 in D minor, with a vigorous fugue on a subject of a chromatic type uncommon in his music at any period, and quite outstanding among the works of the 1770's. It is not a perfect fugue, but there is little padding and much less awkwardness of transition than in the previous effort, while the treatment of the subject by inversion and the complete change of mood in the coda are most adroitly handled.

In the first movement of this same quartet the close-knit development of the second melody augurs many still finer contrapuntal touches to come. Another instructive movement from
the same period is the Finale of the Symphony in G major
(K. 199), which starts off famously in Haydnesque two-part
counterpoint, but digresses before long into a kind of Viennese
waltz melody. This juxtaposition of conflicting styles foreshadows such movements as those concluding the String Quartet in G and the Clavier Concerto in F major (K. 459). Much
less hesitant is the Finale of the Clavier Concerto in D major
(K. 175), in which Mozart made a notable attempt to stiffen
sonata form with polyphony. Though not a great work, its
rhythmical verve and the breadth of the part-writing (which
must have rejoiced Haydn's heart) undoubtedly helped it to
remain so long a favourite with both the public and its composer, who played it many times in the next ten years. In 1782
he substituted the somewhat arid Rondo K. 382 for his original
Finale, induced perhaps by a passing diffidence about risking
even such a mildly polyphonic piece before a Viennese audience.

The earnest and intensely personal tone of many of Mozart's
compositions in the early 1770's reflects the fact that he was
caught in the backwash of that flood of emotional subjectivity
comprehensively known as the *Sturm und Drang* period. After a
final outburst of passion in the 'little' G minor Symphony—
surely the most remarkable symphony ever penned by a youth
of seventeen—reaction set in, launching him, even as it did
Haydn, on the easily flowing tide of the courtly style, on which
he was, in the main, to lavish his talent for the next few years.
Nevertheless, beneath the surface stronger currents were running, which now and then surged up in powerful eddies, suggesting that the discipline of his all-too-brief contrapuntal effort
had been no mere passing phase. That impression, so far from
being obliterated by the writing of genial serenades and divertimenti, was growing all the time, though the moment and the
impulse for its decisive blending into his style were yet to
come. Meanwhile, Mozart's contrapuntal usage is as varied as

it is unpredictable, and herein lies much of the interest of his music during this period. To discuss it at full length is hardly possible here: therefore a few typical instances must suffice.

In the brilliant Clavier Sonata in D major (K. 284), what unexpected strength is won from the writing in octave canon for the ninth of the set of variations! But this gave only a glimpse of Mozart's growing power, displayed at greater length, though still discreetly, in the Finale of the 'Paris' Symphony, with its opening *fugato* and passages in elaborate imitation allotted to contrasting instrumental groups. In a work destined for the public ear he could not yet give much rein to his contrapuntal instinct, though in a chamber one such as the great E minor Violin Sonata, he clearly felt less inhibited. In its sombre first movement he revels in striking canonic effects, especially just before the development and again in the coda. Even the more elegiac minuet is enriched and strengthened by allusive part-writing. Not long after, in the beautifully wrought little Symphony in B flat major, Mozart gave a surprising display of erudition, by introducing into the first movement a favourite phrase[1] he was to immortalize in the Finale of the 'Jupiter' Symphony. Here it dominates the development for nearly forty bars of undulating counterpoint, passing smoothly from one group of instruments to another. In the Andante of the next symphony, that in C major (K.338), some delicate touches of part-writing emphasize the several restatements of the grupetto-embellished theme, but this, and indeed all else of the years 1778–80, is surpassed by the fine polyphony that diversifies many sections of the magnificent Wind Serenade in B flat major (K. 361).

Mozart was now gradually scaling the height whence there would spread before him new horizons of musical texture, and we can see how much the widening vista contributed to his rich and flexible handling of the older forms in the gloomy but massively scored 'Kyrie' in D minor.[2] Apart from the C minor

---

[1] See Appendix 2.

[2] It is perhaps worth pointing out that an unfinished orchestral Fugue in D major (K. 291) attributed to Mozart at this period in the first two editions of Köchel has been restored to Michael Haydn in the third edition. It was completed by Sechter.

Mass this was his last piece of church music until the *Requiem*; it was composed not later than March 1781, in which month we have a clear hint of the way Mozart's mind was moving. On the 18th he wrote to his father: 'I am absolutely determined that he (i.e. the emperor) shall get to know me; I should love to run through my opera for him, and then play a lot of fugues, for that is what he likes.' Mozart would hardly have thought of this, had he not loved fugues himself, and there is mention of fugue playing for private enjoyment in a letter of 27 June 1781. From now onwards, in consequence of various circumstances, this aspect of music was in the ascendant. There were three main influences.

First, Mozart's contact with Baron Gottfried van Swieten, a devotee of Bach and Handel who had brought back copies of many of their works when he returned to Vienna from his post as Austrian ambassador in Berlin; secondly, the peculiar fugal proclivity of Constanze Mozart, of whom her husband wrote on 20 April 1782:

> When Constanze heard the fugues she absolutely fell in love with them. Now she will listen to nothing but fugues, and particularly the works of Handel and Bach. Well, as she had often heard me play fugues out of my head, she asked me if I had written any down, and when I said I had not, she scolded me roundly for not recording some of my compositions in this most artistic and beautiful of all musical forms, and never ceased to entreat me till I had written down a fugue for her.

Thirdly, the less direct effect of the emperor's continued liking for fugues. Mozart played one by his special request at a concert on 29 March 1783, and we may surmise that if, as is likely, the musical taste of the court in these two years took some of its tone from the emperor, he continued to have an eye to the main chance. It has often been stated[1] that contact with Bach *caused* this momentous crisis in Mozart's creative life. It would be truer to say that it only precipitated it. Furthermore, we do not know exactly when Mozart first met van Swieten:

[1] As by Einstein in *Greatness in Music* (New York, 1941), p. 125.

his name does not appear in the letters until 10 April 1782, more than a year after the first mention of fugues, nor is there a shred of evidence that Mozart knew any of Bach's works before he finally settled in Vienna and was drawn into van Swieten's orbit.

Thus Mozart's inner compulsion towards counterpoint coincided with the impact of the full force of Bach's genius, and with the growing necessity of reconciling all that it had to teach him with the style of composition expected of him in Vienna. His efforts to find a compromise introduce an element of conflict into his style that is usually less pronounced in the chamber works than in those on a larger scale. In this period of second apprenticeship he composed, in just under three years, over thirty works either wholly contrapuntal in texture or at least predominantly so, representing numerically if not in actual bulk nearly a third of his total output during that period. Thanks to Einstein's masterly arrangement in the third edition of Köchel, incorporating the fragments into one chronological sequence with the completed works, we get a synoptic view of the astonishing variety of Mozart's efforts to master the north German style—vocal canons, fugues for two and four hands at the clavier, fugues for voices and for strings (including arrangements, with original preludes, of numbers from Bach's '48', *Art of Fugue*, and organ trios as well),[1] fantasias embodying free polyphony, and a suite in imitation of Handel. The fragmentary state of many of these seems to betray the spasmodic and anxious nature of his work. But his enthusiasm for Bach did not wane. Attwood, who was Mozart's pupil from mid-1785 until at least the end of 1786, told Holmes[2] that a volume of the '48' was always lying open on his master's clavier.

Mozart soon realized how lifeless by comparison with Bach

---

[1] This implies a fairly wide knowledge of Bach with which it is difficult to reconcile Mozart's remark 'Here's something one can learn from'—elicited by hearing the motet *Singet dem Herrn* at Leipzig in 1789. We may suspect that Rochlitz, who reported the occasion, exaggerated slightly, as there is not so much difference between *The Art of Fugue* and the motet as to imply that Mozart had learnt nothing from the former.

[2] p. 162. This must have been a MS. copy.

was the fugal style of Eberlin, a Salzburg composer taken as a model in his youth. The complete mastery he sought so earnestly was not easily won, if indeed he ever won it in the way he originally intended. By the beginning of 1783 he probably began to realize that it would profit him more to distil the essence of Bach's art and synthesize it with his own. But this too cost a great effort, and not for several years was he sure in his handling of the result. A detailed critical study of all Mozart's works from this fascinating period is still a desideratum, but cannot be attempted here. To illustrate the results of his self-tormenting on the contrapuntal rack—for that was what it often amounted to—a few examples must suffice.

In the remarkable Finale of the G major string Quartet an elaborate fugal structure alternates with a second thematic group of purely melodic interest. The fugal mood is generally untroubled, sometimes austere, but often verging on radiance, so that no contrast is really called for. Mozart apparently realized this, for the temper of the homophonic sections is almost complementary. The harmony and disposition of the fugue are perfectly clear, revealing him as complete master of his chosen form; had he wished, the whole movement could have been a brilliant, purely fugal *tour-de-force*. Did he evolve a compromise because he was dubious as to how the public might react to the first of a set of quartets so ending—even with an explanatory dedication to Haydn? The autograph of this movement is confused in parts, particularly in the working-out section. This may indicate some uncertainty of original intention, or even a change of plan from a sudden inspiration in writing out the work. Despite a parallel to this contrast of style in the Clavier Concerto in F major (K. 459), the Finale of the G major Quartet remains something of an enigma.

The ostensibly fugal opening of the contemporaneous Clavier Concerto in C major (K. 415) turns out to be an elaborate canon in disguise, but there are some fine polyphonic touches in the tuttis. The other movements, and the clavier part generally, are less daring, excepting the first cadenza, which is conspicuous for bold canons with both hands in octaves. The style of the whole Concerto is curiously uneven yet more complex than either its fellow in F major (K. 413) or that in A major (K. 414). They have few of these spasmodic outbursts of counterpoint, but embody much more of the *bel canto* so dear to the Viennese audience.

Mozart's desire for contrast in texture naturally varied from one work to another; sometimes he pursued it almost as an end in itself, sometimes it was bound up with the problem of mood, as in the C minor Wind Serenade, where the spirit of Bach contributed to the solution. What surer foil could there be to the gloomy and passionate tone of most of the work than the lucid and nicely balanced ingenuity of the minuet in canon and the trio in canon *al rovescio*? Erudition no less profound, but emotionally at the opposite pole, dominates the work in which Mozart bade farewell to his self-tormenting—the Fugue in C minor for two Claviers, which he completed on 29 December 1783, not long after his labours on the unfinished Mass in the same key. Here he seems to have reached the apparent turning-point of these years of artistic and domestic crisis. Within its turbulent career of 119 bars this fugue combines technical skill with a sustained ferocity that allows a mellower mood to displace the harshness in only a few bars, as when the subject first appears in inversion. Since this tense fugue was followed by a period of a more urbane temper, is it fanciful to suggest that its function was cathartic, in the Aristotelian sense? At any rate, it changed and set the tone for fourteen months, since the C minor Clavier Sonata is the only composition in a minor key to break the flow until the epoch-making D minor Concerto of February 1785.

Any division of the work of a genius into periods is bound to be arbitrary, but for the sake of convenience the next section of Mozart's contrapuntal development may be taken to end with the 'Jupiter' Symphony, in August 1788. From 1784 to 1787 were the years of his fame as a virtuoso during which his very virtuosity limited his use of counterpoint even more than in his first months in Vienna, when it had been a potential asset. Now,

as the strength of its incessant urge was not to be denied, indirect expression became more varied than the direct might
have been. Thus, in spite of his deeper instincts, Mozart became
a master of allusive and incidental counterpoint—*fugato* sections
with swift inversions and graceful canons, introduced with
kaleidoscopic suddenness, above all in the concertos, to the be-
wilderment of his contemporaries, but to the abounding delight
of posterity. Here again so many notable works call for attention that only a representative number can be mentioned.

In his variations Mozart is fond of giving any section in a
minor key a contrapuntal flavour that is made all the more
piquant by contrast with the chiefly melismatic and rhythmical
interest of the remainder. This can be seen in many of his
mature sets for clavier solo, no less than in more pretentious
works, most arrestingly perhaps in the minor section of the
Finale of the Clavier Concerto in G major. In bars 97 to 127 the
line of the tune is broken up into a continually shifting tissue
of fragments, treated in a kind of chromatic polyphony. Rondo
form being akin to variations in structure, it is not surprising
to find a noble contrapuntal episode in the minor section of the
Rondo in F major (K. 494). A similar usage, marking a definite
alteration of mood, occurs in the bold two-part writing at the
end of the Rondo in A minor. Likewise in the sixth and last variation of the A major Quartet Mozart emphasizes the change from
the minor of the fifth by passing from a lyrical, contrasting style
to a concentration in three parts moving over the confident and
stately march-rhythm of the bass. In many movements of the
great clavier concertos we find fugal episodes, but nowhere so
outspoken as in the astonishing Finale of that in F major (K.
459), whose style was anticipated by the G major String Quartet. Here, in a public work, Mozart affirms the doctrine stated
more timidly in the Concerto in D major of 1773, that of his
belief in the adaptable vitality of counterpoint. In few other
movements did he introduce such a strenuous contrast of interests—the purely homophonic and rhythmical against the purely
fugal. The exhilaration of the whole comes from the mutually

infectious verve of both these elements and the keyboard supplies a unifying force lacking in the Quartet. The overture to *Der Schauspieldirektor* contains a fascinating display of polyphony, especially on the woodwind, but for sheer contrapuntal virtuosity the Finale of K. 459 marks a climax in Mozart's development.

His more personal inspirations of this period contain some achievements of outstanding mastery and beauty. In the *Maurerische Trauermusik* the tradition inculcated by Martini is illumined by a mature command of orchestral colour, here including his beloved basset horns. The supposedly Gregorian plain chant forms the centre of a web of three- and four-part writing, poignant and solemn as befitted Mozart's Masonic sympathies. Another opportunity came in the Sonata for clavier duet in F major, in which the exuberance of the many polyphonic episodes in all three movements ranks among the marvels of his art. The style of this sonata leads up logically to the more austere beauty of the Clavier Concerto in C major (K. 503). Certain sections of its first movement, written in eight parts in triple canon, are of a complexity not unworthy of Palestrina or the Gabrielis. Pendant to this is the first movement of the 'Prague' symphony, which expounds one of the liveliest contrapuntal debates in all Mozart up to this time. An elaborate sketch for the intricate beginning of the 'allegro' has recently come to light.[1] With these two works he approached the final assertion of his contrapuntal mastery. Technically they mark the passing of a crisis (accentuated by his disappointment over *Figaro*) as surely as the Concerto in D minor proclaimed the triumph of his 'daemonic' compulsion over the tradition of *Gesellschaftsmusik*.

Passing over Mozart's application of instrumental polyphony to *Figaro* and *Don Giovanni* (a highly relevant topic, but too complex for fair treatment here), we come to the Finale of the 'Jupiter'[2] Symphony. *What did it mean to Mozart and why was it*

[1] Einstein, p. 155.
[2] For some account of the possible origin of the epithet, see Appendix 3.

composed at the time and in the style that it was? This movement
has been generally accepted *in vacuo* as just another manifestation of his genius, but it is really far more than that. Its archaistic
style, so different from all else in the last three symphonies, was
an amazing choice, and deserves to be acclaimed as the gesture
it surely is. The history of art has known many feats of genius,
but few to equal that of the five years 1784 to 1788 in which
Mozart composed one work after another, at an average inter-
val of about eighteen days. About eighty out of some 105 may
be reckoned as masterpieces, culminating in the 'Jupiter'. The
Finale consists of 423 bars of cool, pure thinking in sound, cast
in the style of a polyphonic essay in sonata form. The note of
quiet exultation in its five-part climax is unmistakable. He chose
this medium not only because its disciplined purity atoned for
his past uncertainties of style, but also because through it he
could cast off for ever the slough of compromise. It was the
triumphant proclamation of a new simplicity of purpose, to
compose, regardless of criticism,[1] for the full satisfaction of his
own artistic instincts. This Finale must have cost him a stupen-
dous effort, and he probably foresaw the temporary exhaustion
that would follow on this climax to his labours. His certainty of
mind is reflected in the clarity of the autograph which, throughout, has practically no corrections. (He may, of course, have
made sketches which have not survived.)

We know little about the genesis of the 'Jupiter' Symphony
or its companions, but two facts are clear from Mozart's letters
to Puchberg: first, that he was arranging some subscription concerts at the 'Casino'[2] for the summer of 1788, for which we
may conjecture that these symphonies were intended; second,
that later, for lack of subscriptions, he decided to postpone
them for a few months. The date of the letter containing the
second fact is 17 June. The E flat Symphony was entered in his
own catalogue on 26 June, the 'Jupiter' on 10 August. This post-

---

[1] The *Musik Real-Zeitung* for this very year 1788 published on p. 50 some harsh
criticism of the contrapuntal method of Mozart's Violin Sonata in E flat (K. 481),
which included the opening subject of the 'Jupiter' finale.

[2] Cf. Pohl, *Joseph Haydn* (Leipzig, 1878), vol. ii, p. 131.

ponement makes it likely that he knew, even before he began to put the former on paper, how slender were the chances of the three works being performed in his lifetime;[1] yet he must have gone on hoping. It was a most courageous decision, however long it took to form in his mind, to sum up and declare his contrapuntal faith in a movement which might have served still further to blight his waning prospects of material security. It is true that Micha, Dittersdorf, Monn, and Michael Haydn had all concluded a symphony in like manner, but they attempted nothing so bold as this and probably had relatively little at stake.

We can see something of the trend of Mozart's mind in the contrapuntal style of the Clavier Sonata in F major (K. 533) (for which he did not, or could not, compose a third movement in the same vein), and in the rescoring for strings (K. 546) of his two-clavier Fugue in C minor. Is it merely a coincidence that the opening notes of the 'Jupiter' Finale occur in the bass of the immediately preceding minuet and in the Andante of the G minor Symphony? If hints they are, they should not provoke surprise, for he had used this sequence of notes a dozen times before.[2] (In his church music, they are usually associated with strongly affirmative words, such as 'credo'.) Their apotheosis in the 'Jupiter' Symphony seems to symbolize the triumph of his conviction, born of a six-year struggle, that he must now let strength and unity of form govern invention and sensuous expression. Such at least is part of their message in the light of what he subsequently composed; but no less clearly does the overwhelming emphasis laid on the Finale of this Symphony suggest that henceforth in a work in several movements the interest was to be concentrated in the last, which was no longer to contain the resolution of the contrasts in the preceding three

---

[1] Had they been played before 1792, the Viennese press would undoubtedly have mentioned them. The earliest known performance of the 'Jupiter' came soon after the turn of the century: this Symphony had, however, been published in parts as early as 1793.

[2] These are listed in Appendix 2, together with some earlier and later uses of the sequence.

or four, but would form the logical climax of style, mood, and matter.

In the String Trio in E flat, the last three string quartets, and the last two quintets, the importance of the finales reflects this reorientation of structural outlook. In temper and texture alike they derive from that momentous climax of 10 August 1788. Besides the beauty of new contrapuntal resource, they express a spirit of serenity and self-confidence that Mozart too rarely found compatible with the restless brilliance of 1784 to 1787. These qualities can only have been distilled from the spiritual ferment of which the Finale of the 'Jupiter' was born; assuredly they do not reflect any aspect of his material circumstances from 1789 to 1791. The variety of the contrapuntal energy that he displays is almost bewildering, yet generally light and effortless, as typified in the Finales of the Quartet in F (K. 590) and the Quintet in D major (K. 593). The perfect little Gigue in G major, the Sonata in D major (K. 576), the two 'Fantasias' for mechanical organ,[1] and, above all, *Die Zauberflöte* crown the tale of the chamber music.

When Mozart expressed the mystical vision of the Two Armed Men in a solemn chorale with its sublime quasi-fugal accompaniment, he forged one of the last links in the long chain stretching back, through the 'Jupiter' Finale, through the *Maurerische Trauermusik*, the F major Clavier Concerto, the C minor Fugue for two claviers, and the G major String Quartet (K. 387) to the hesitant contrapuntal utterances of his boyhood. This chain truly symbolizes one of the fundamental differences between Mozart and the Kozeluchs, the Wanhals, and the Wenzel Müllers of his day. He had both the knowledge and the integrity to recognize the greatness of Bach's genius. By measuring his own powers against it and absorbing it[2] he forced a crisis to which he found a solution that, so far from checking the consistency of his own development, ultimately identified

[1] These are analysed and discussed on pp. 205 ff.
[2] It is perhaps significant that when Cantor Doles, a pupil of J. S. Bach, heard Mozart playing the organ in St. Thomas's Church at Leipzig in April 1789 he was reminded irresistibly of his great master's style. Cf. p. 235.

itself with the highest endeavour of his art. His fashionable contemporaries ignored Bach or, if they even knew him, failed utterly to comprehend him or reinterpret the vitality of his music. Hence their works lacked the supple contrapuntal strength which, though contributing to Mozart's failure in his lifetime, was to be one of the cornerstones of his immortality.

11

Creative Contrast in Mozart

IN great works of art, whether in paint, stone, or sound, contrast plays so vital and varied a part that it is all the more remarkable how often its presence is taken for granted or else almost ignored. In music especially it repays detailed study, for in some ways its possibilities are greatest in an art that exists in time and not in space. Contrast in music may lie in form or in harmony, in tone-colour or in rhythm, it may be gradual or sharply defined, limited to a single piece or movement, or even dependent for its effect on the subtle relation which a whole work may bear to another. The last is, broadly speaking, only an extension of the other kinds on a large scale, so let us glance at a few examples of these others before considering this special form of contrast as it evolved in Mozart's hands.

Here an analogy from painting may be of assistance. Put Brueghel's landscape 'Summer' (one of his 'Four Seasons') beside Rembrandt's 'Night Watch'. It needs no expert knowledge of art to appreciate how easily and subtly Brueghel leads the eye gradually from the bright foreground of peasants away over fields and valleys with their softer colouring, to the almost unreal blueness of the mountains and rivers merging with the far horizon. There are no bold stages between the distant background and the foreground. Rembrandt, working on a comparatively shallow plane, delights the eye by a series of sudden plunges from darkness and shadow into brilliant light, across the whole canvas. With its easy transitions from powerful chords to pearly scale-passages, its clever gradations of mood and rhythm, Chopin's 'Barcarolle' may be compared to Brueghel's landscape. But when Haydn, in his great E flat Sonata (no. 52), ends the first movement on sonorous chords and fiery

progressions, and then follows with an Adagio in the sweetness
of an unrelated E major, he is exploiting a technique similar to
Rembrandt's. So too does Beethoven all through the first
movement of his Pianoforte Sonata in D minor.

In Mozart the iridescent ebb and flow of the Rondo in A
minor for clavier is truly Brueghelesque, but the slow movement of the Violin Sonata in B flat (K. 454) is full of violent
transitions in Rembrandt's manner, in which rhythm and key,
light and shadow alternate powerfully, as after the double bar
where F minor rises from a pause on B flat. Plainly, in their instinctive feeling for this and other kinds of contrast, Mozart and
Haydn owed much to the generation of composers who had
rebelled against the domination of fugal uniformity and developed first-movement form, which is based essentially on the
setting-off of two groups of contrasting themes. Two far-
reaching conventions sprang from this artistic revolution. The
various movements required contrast among themselves—even
more than had the sections of the older suite form—and since
sonatas and even symphonies were very often written in groups
of six, for reasons of patronage or publicity, one was often
differentiated sharply from the next. However a musician developed in the eighteenth century, the force of this method of
production remained, if only as a natural economy of effort.
With Mozart it may have contributed to the habit of composing one work in contrast to its immediate or near neighbour,
though the primary forces were different and more complex.
There are others among the great masters who shared this
tendency, but it is Mozart's music that can be studied with most
profit, for we must know the dates of the several pairs with some
exactitude, and his own thematic catalogue, which he kept from
1784 onwards, fulfils this need with particular completeness.

In discussing these works we tread undeniably on rather delicate ground. As Jahn well remarked:[1]

The springs of artistic production flow too deep to be awakened
by any of the accidents of life. The artist, indeed, can only give what

[1] Vol. iv, 1859, p. 104.

is in him and what he has himself experienced; but Goethe's saying holds good of the musician as well as of the poet or painter; he reveals nothing that he has not felt, but nothing *as* he felt it.

It is only rarely that we can ascribe a piece of instrumental music to a definite external happening which aroused a stream of creative emotion. Such, probably, was Chopin's study in C minor, the 'Revolutionary'. With a composer of so mercurial and ambiguous a personality as Mozart we cannot say that a work, still less a pair of contrasting works, is related to any transient event, even when his letters tell us he was in a certain mood on a certain day. But it may be possible to find some connexion between the conflicting contrast in adjacent compositions and the forces more permanently at work in his mind. That there were such forces we cannot doubt, though it may be hard, and perhaps seem impertinent, to try to analyse them.

For much of Mozart's music written prior to 1784 we lack precise dates; too often the exact month is not known, let alone the day. It would be interesting to speculate on the reason for the great gulf between the Sonata for Clavier in A minor, that for Violin in E minor, and the comparatively trivial works composed during his visit to Paris in 1778; likewise on the great difference between the two Serenades for Wind Octet in C minor and E flat major of 1781–2. But the absence of precise chronology would forbid any definite conclusion. In February 1784, however, Mozart began to keep his *Verzeichnüß*. The first half-dozen or so of the masterpieces that streamed from his pen in the spring and summer of that year reflect on the whole a steady gaze towards the brighter side of life. We may note, however, that on 14 October came the stormy Sonata in C minor with two fresh and tender works in B flat[1] (the Clavier Concerto K. 456 and the Quartet K. 458) less than three weeks away on either side of it. In January 1785 Mozart crowned the set of quartets which he was dedicating to Haydn with the

---

[1] This contrast of key cannot, of course, be applied to movements not in the particular key in question. Thus the slow movement of the concerto, being in G minor, is irrelevant.

A major on the 10th and the C major on the 14th. Obviously they were in his mind at the same time, yet the distinction between them is most pronounced. The mood of the A major is wistful and disconcerting; chromatic melody prevails and produces the effect of quiet shading; throughout the method is allusive, and there is little differentiation between the movements. The Quartet in C is one of the most brilliant, exulting, and, in its Andante especially, exalted works Mozart ever wrote. Only in the minuet and trio does the flame sink and burn more darkly. It is a triumph of externalization, just as its fellow gives masterly expression to a spirit of reflection that is profound but not gloomy.

Within seven weeks Mozart had repeated this feat of contrast even more intensely in his very next compositions. On 10 February he finished the Clavier Concerto in D minor, and on 9 March that in C major (K. 467). From the febrile tumult of the first, with its sensuous Romanza, it is a far cry to the second, so stately and square in its military rhythms and so delicately poetical in its Andante. A similarly contrasting sequence came in the autumn. Hard on the heels of the sublime *Maurerische Trauermusik* in C minor and the Clavier Quartet in G minor came two works in the confident serenity of E flat major—the Violin Sonata, K. 481, and the Clavier Concerto, K. 482. In the spring of the next year came one of the most remarkable of all Mozart's creative efforts, the completion within three weeks of two clavier concertos while he was also fully occupied with *Figaro*. Even more striking than the contrast between the concertos in D minor and C major is that between those in A major (K. 488) and C minor. Both are powerful works, but this quality is not so obvious in the A major because of the sweetness of its melodies and the flowing grace of its outlines. But in the C minor Mozart laid bare all the starkness of conflict as never before, even in the sonata and fantasia in this key.

After *Figaro* Mozart fell, like the runner from Marathon, exhausted in the moment of his triumph, for the opera's greatness was lost on the public, and its very brief success must have

disappointed him bitterly. Until December 1786 he devoted
himself rather spasmodically to chamber works, some very
beautiful, but, except for the noble Duet Sonata in F major,
introspective and mostly lacking the freshness of his earlier
music. In the late autumn he began to prepare for the winter
concerts in Vienna and completed the Clavier Concerto in C
major (K. 503) and the 'Prague' Symphony in D major on 4
and 6 December respectively. Despite its major key, the concerto is often gloomy and always austere, even in the Andante;
the lilting rhythms and sunny geniality of the symphony are
quite alien to it. The concerto is Olympian in its uncompromis-
ing aloofness, and makes deliberate parade of strength and
sonority. The symphony too has strength, but it is more concealed and only prominent here and there beneath the gaiety
of the music. Undeniably these two masterpieces, so opposite
in structure and mood, were maturing simultaneously in
Mozart's brain.

The same can be said of the two String Quintets, in C major
and G minor, between which there is a bare three and a half
weeks. The difference in the mood of each is too well known
to be described here. On 4 June 1787 Mozart finished two exquisite miniatures, the songs *Abendempfindung* and *An Chloe*.
The first glows with passion and reveals a sustained depth of
feeling unparalleled in his other songs. The second is by comparison a pretty trifle, for all its formal perfection. There are
several similarly contrasting pairs in the lesser works of this
time, but the accepted miracle comes later, in 1788, with the
three symphonies. Can we doubt that the plan of all three
germinated in one creative impulse? The E flat Symphony,
however, was finished first on 26 June, while those in G minor
and C major (the repetition of the tonal contrast of the great
quintets is significant) came over a month later, on 25 July and
10 August. Hence these symphonies may perhaps be regarded
less as a triad than as one plus a pair. In any case the contrast
between the first and the last two is as remarkable as that between the last two themselves.

This sequence of widely differing pairs in Mozart's music between 1784 and 1788 is too regular to be dismissed simply as a series of coincidences. But was it a conscious attempt either to maintain emotional balance through recourse to extremes, or to relieve inner tension through deliberate change of mood? It seems unlikely in Mozart's case, though perhaps others may have worked in this way. Thus may be interpreted the varying curve of both scope and spirit that runs through Beethoven's symphonies from the third to the ninth. There is likewise little doubt that Brahms, one of the most self-conscious of all the great masters, often planned contrasting pairs of large-scale works, for instance the two groups of his symphonies, the 'Tragic' and 'Academic Festival' overtures, and the Violin Sonatas in D minor and A major. But we must also take into account the instinct, common in all creative artists, to avoid monotony and staleness which might come from too long a concentration on one particular mood. Milton studied English history deeply while writing *Paradise Lost*. Ben Jonson wrote his lyrics to Celia as soon as he had finished *Volpone*, if not while actually working on it; Titian liked to be engaged on both secular and religious paintings simultaneously, ranging from a love scene in Greek mythology to a Holy Family. Mozart shared this instinct, but it was not preponderant, partly because of his unique, almost cynical power of detachment, and partly because of his fecundity of sustained invention.

We should therefore look deeper for the cause of this sequence of contrasting pairs, in the known facts of his life and character. May it not be that there were two elements continually at war within his mind? The one was rooted in the contemplative, lyrical side of his nature, his gaiety of heart and wide human sympathies. The other sprang from the long-drawn material failure and frustration, and the consequent unhappiness which made him rebel passionately against the darkness of his fate. But because he was so fundamentally sane and endowed with so resilient a spirit, he could not allow one or other of these elements to be in the ascendant for long, and thus unconsciously kept the balance through the outlet of these contrasted pairs. There can of course be no final proof of this, but it seems probable that the crowning humiliation and despair of 1789 purified his soul of this conflict and brought him some measure of calmness and resignation. For after this date[1] those works which fall into pairs—namely, the Quartets in B flat (K. 589) and F major, the two Fantasias for mechanical organ with their strongly parallel tonal structure (cf. p. 205), and the two last String Quintets—are complementary in a most satisfying way. This impression is confirmed by the absence of violent contrast within them and their separate movements, as indeed is the case in other compositions of these years, such as the B flat Clavier Concerto (K. 595). This at least is an indisputable musical fact and plain to see in print. The reason for it may be that at last, in spite of himself, Mozart had attained something of that inner harmony so long desired, to which he was to give supreme expression in *Die Zauberflöte*.

We cannot listen satisfactorily to two pieces of music at once, but we can study and compare them in score, and so be able to refer subconsciously to the one when hearing the other played. Thus, when we hear the massive scoring in eight parts in the 'Allegro maestoso' of Mozart's C major Clavier Concerto (K. 503) we should not, if we accept the thesis of this chapter, be astonished by the thought that such music evolved in his brain at the same time as the simple melodies and flexible rhythms of the first movement of the 'Prague' symphony. Yet we can also see, if we recall the sombre style of the slow introduction of the latter, that Mozart's mind was not working in watertight compartments during the creation of these masterpieces. To discern such features as this, which are to be found in all the pairs of works mentioned here, and to grasp the significance of their inter-relationship, needs a greater effort of comprehension than we usually expend on one work *in vacuo*.

---

[1] Henceforth Mozart did not enter in his catalogue the actual day on which he finished a piece, as he had done sedulously up till now. The fact that he was often content to put just the month is surely a reflection of his apathetic frame of mind.

But is it not well worth while? For our reward is nothing less than a glimpse of the vital forces which, after long striving, Mozart succeeded in holding nicely balanced. So fascinating

> Is the conjunction of the mind
> And opposition of the stars.

12

The Nature of Mozart's Genius

SOME ANALOGIES AND REFLECTIONS

ANALYSIS of any music in formal or scientific terms rarely helps to explain its attraction, for it is fundamentally 'l'art de penser avec les sons', and a succession of sounds does not often have the same meaning for any two hearers. But when we know something of the character of the composer and of his place in the history of music and civilization it is possible that analogies from other arts may be of help. Let us try to discover why Mozart's best works give such high and lasting pleasure. A rather vague attempt to explain it has sometimes been made by saying that his music represents the consummate union of form and feeling. There may be some truth in this if we consider music in comparison with architecture. It has been said[1] that 'architecture is frozen music'; conversely, may not music be described as architecture in a state of fluidity or movement? Here some words of Roger Fry[2] may be quoted: 'In a work of art', he wrote, 'what gives us the special aesthetic pleasure is the recognition that the matter of which the work is made has been, as it were, penetrated and impregnated by an idea with which we associate ourselves. We see something akin to ourselves penetrating and moulding the matter. The fullest pleasure occurs when, having realized the general idea, the main relations of the members of a building, the main composition of a picture, we are able to consider the interior relations of the parts, without finding any point at which the

[1] The phrase is frequently, though incorrectly, ascribed to Goethe. The author is probably F. W. J. von Schelling: cf. *MMR*, May 1950, pp. 86, 87.
[2] 'The Arts of Painting and Sculpture', in *The Outline of Modern Knowledge*, ed. William Rose (London, 1931), pp. 914, 915.

informing idea breaks down.' For the moment let us consider the bearing of the last sentence.

There are three principles of traditional architectural design which are generally recognized as being indispensable for any building which is to be 'good' in the highest sense of the word. These, *mutatis mutandis*, are equally applicable to music. The first is *unity*, which implies a dominant feature and consistency of inspiration which binds the whole together, and gives it beauty and dignity. If there are two dominant features, they must avoid producing an 'unresolved duality', which connotes the bad effect of an exact and emphasized balance largely unrelated to any less prominent feature in the work as a whole. The second principle is *punctuation*, which gives to every element not serving as a link between others a clearly defined but not exaggerated termination. The third is the *canon of inflection*, which governs the satisfactory relation of all the parts to the whole and their surroundings. (With this are combined matters of proportion which are to a certain extent a question of taste, but less so in music than in architecture.)

Applied to the music of the years 1740–1800 and to Mozart in particular, these principles offer an interesting analogy. Thus, each of his last three symphonies (those in E flat, G minor, and C major) is cast in one definite mood whose unity is revealed as convincingly to the ear as it is by analysis or technical study. While each one is informed by a strain of noble and logical thought, it contains enough contrast to avoid monotony; repeated and balanced phrases are subtly varied, but not overemphasized; the end of any sequence of ideas, whether at a double bar or at the conclusion of a movement, is so perfectly turned and shaped as to be of a most satisfying brevity; and each movement is as intimately related to the whole as are the parts within it to one another. It does not need much study to see that in the music of many of Mozart's contemporaries, apart from Haydn, it is often the lack of one or more of these apparently simple qualities which has prevented most of their work from being of lasting value. Yet it is these very qualities that give homogeneous perfection to such buildings as the Parthenon, or a flawless Byzantine church like San Vitale at Ravenna, or to the chapel of King's College at Cambridge. Their details, too, offer musical analogies. In Mozart's symphonies (and in scores of his other works) the ornaments and figuration are wrought with as much artistry and poise as the frieze of the Parthenon, as the mosaics of San Vitale, or the Tudor roses on the walls of King's Chapel. Even nearer is their analogy to the flowery arabesques in the ornamentation of the best European Baroque art of the seventeenth and eighteenth centuries, such as decorates the palace at Würzburg, the great monastery at Ottobeuren, the pilgrimage church of 'Vierzehnheiligen' in Franconia, the University Church in Salzburg, and many other public buildings in south Germany and Austria.

Comparisons with architecture can undoubtedly help us to appreciate the beauty of Mozart's craftsmanship and richness of invention. These are related to less strictly analogous qualities, such as his insight into the effect of timbre and the tonal balance of various instruments, and his effortless mastery in writing for difficult and unusual combinations of them. Even when this technical brilliance approaches virtuosity, it is never pursued as an end in itself. Unity of form and feeling is still preserved, and we cannot find 'any point at which the informing idea breaks down', in his String Quintet in C major, for example. Throughout all its movements we find the same perfect proportions, beauty and dignity of line, sureness of purpose, and feeling for subtle contrast which combine to make it an edifice of sound as grand and inspiring as the austere yet mellow dignity of a great Norman building like Romsey Abbey. Both are infused with a sense of restraint and a quality of repose which make them wholly satisfying. With what insight did Busoni remark: 'Architecture is the art most akin to his'! (cf. p. 44).

If we would understand more of the spirit that gives the finest of Mozart's compositions their peculiar beauty, we shall find a close analogy in the spirit of the ancient Greeks, with whose art and life Mozart has greater affinities than any other composer. Now this does not mean that to appreciate these things one must be a learned Hellenist; for on them are based many of the most precious moral and artistic values of that European civilization in which everyone can share, whatever his educational background. It is curious that this analogy has been appreciated only by very few writers—Warde Fowler,[1] for example, H. F. Amiel, and Schumann. The last, however, was right only in a limited sense when he remarked how Greek was the G minor Symphony, and it is not really helpful to restrict the parallel to this and similar compositions. For there are many other works written by Mozart (particularly his chamber music) in which we meet a far wider range of emotions corresponding more nearly than this symphony to those expressed in the art and literature of Athens in the fifth century B.C. Their two chief qualities were restraint and proportion, which dominate all branches of Greek art, whether a tragedy of Sophocles, the designs of Ictinus for the Parthenon, an epigram of Simonides, or vases by masters such as Epictetus or Sotades. All have the same purity of line and thought. Greek art at its flowering was the product of a people fully conscious of their own genius, yet until the time of their decline quite free from overbearing egoism; of a people constantly searching after the true values of human life, with a happy serenity born of self-knowledge, and tempered by a just sense of the sadness and inscrutability of man's brief destiny. Are not these qualities prominent in Mozart's personality, as revealed in his letters and his music, as they are in no other composer?

'You Greeks', said the Egyptian priest in Plato's *Timaeus* (22b), 'are always children; no Greek is ever old.' By which he meant that they were instinct with the generous frankness, the simple yet ardent seriousness, the sense of wonder and pleasure in experiment which mark the child. Such were certain aspects of Mozart's character. To the end of his life, moreover, he retained a childlike freshness of vision, unclouded by disappoint-

[1] Warde Fowler, pp. 61, 76; for Amiel, see pp. 29, 30, *supra*.

ment and worry, which imbues many of his works—for instance, the Finale of the String Trio in E flat, K. 563, and the
three songs, K. 596, 597, 598, composed for a children's album
in January 1791—with a simplicity quite free from affectation.
At the same time, Mozart developed as a man who, in the
phrase of Simonides, stood 'four-square without a flaw', which
does not, however, necessarily imply that his character was
faultless, for even genius is human. Rather should these words
be referred to the balance of mind and to the perfect control of
emotion that find expression in his music, the embodiment of
the 'golden mean' to which the Greeks attached so much
importance. Far from being passionless, untroubled creatures,
they craved an artistic expression that quivered with controlled
excitement. It was because they were susceptible to extremes of
emotion that they valued the mean so highly, and strove incessantly for restraint and balance. So with Mozart.

Of these qualities there is no finer example than his Quintet
for clavier and wind instruments (K. 452). It is significant that
he himself expressed a high opinion of it, one of the few pieces
of his self-criticism that have come down to us. All through it
he achieved a triumphant solution of one of the hardest problems in musical construction, that of giving full scope to elements of contrast without sacrificing the essential unity of the
work. This profound quintet is serene, unrhetorical music, full
of confidence, with spacious but not grandiose melodies, and
the ornamentations are a marvellous blend of grace and dignity.
But behind its strength and continuity lies a transcendental
quality, which never fails to arouse in us emotions that may
vary greatly each time we hear it, but are always equally satisfying. This is so with many of his best works. The more limpid
and simple they seem, the more subtle and charged with meaning do they reveal themselves on close study. Yet revelation in
any complete sense is impossible, for this music, though profoundly lovable, remains utterly impersonal and aloof.

Perhaps it is in Mozart's blending of passion with purity that
we may find one of the sources of this paradoxical quality—a

blending which, as Warde Fowler pointed out, is so truly Greek. It is most interesting that Brahms, a romantic composer if ever there was one, should have highly praised this purity of Mozart in a letter to Dvořák.[1] It seems to come partly from the formal precision and economy of the music, and from the ingeniously varied spacing of the parts, but even more from the absence of false or exaggerated sentiment. This is connected with the restraint described above, but different elements enter into this question. Naturally it is most readily to be discerned in the operas. A song like Susanna's 'Deh, vieni non tardar' in *Figaro* is the incarnation of this purity, with its buoyancy, its tenderness, and delicate truth.

Another aspect of Mozart's genius, and one that lifts him above all other musicians, lies in the universality of his music. It was Plato who first enunciated the truth of the matter in that passage of his Symposium (223d) where Socrates maintains that it is the essence of a truly great poet to be able to write both tragedy and comedy, types which, for the Greeks, included a wide variety of lyrical verse. To whom, beside Mozart and Shakespeare, can this canon be applied? The intensity and style of their dramatic power may differ, but they are at one in their unique ability to move us profoundly over the whole gamut of human emotions. In Mozart the dividing line between tragedy and comedy is unusually fine. It must also be remembered that all his life he cherished a passionate enthusiasm for *opera seria* (in which he achieved his greatest success at the age of twenty-three with *Idomeneo*, despite an almost impossible libretto), and when writing *opera buffa* or a *dramma giocoso* he was often carried away by the momentarily tragic aspects of a character or situation. There are scenes in which we feel Don Giovanni to be a truly tragic figure, despite their proximity to the buffoonery of Leporello. So, too, in *Die Zauberflöte* the intense pity aroused by Pamina's despairing attempt at suicide is not made incongruous by the antics, just past or to come, of Papageno or Monostatos. Mozart sweeps us along on a flood of emotion which derives

---

[1] Cf. Warde Fowler, p. 75.

much of its strength from implied contrast, just as the fool in *King Lear* makes his master's sufferings all the more poignant by his ironical jesting.

In instrumental music Mozart is one of the few spontaneous humorists who also wrote works of tragic intensity. The wit and charm of the divertimenti of his twentieth year are coeval with the sombre power of his Violin Sonata in E minor. In the gay Divertimento in D (K. 334) the element of contrast consists of a profound and gloomy set of variations in the tonic minor. The tragic vein of the String Quintet in G minor is followed very shortly by the riotous parody of contemporary clichés in his *Musikalischer Spaß* for horns and string quartet. We feel that Mozart plays with notes quizzically, weaving them into patterns of fantastic grace and elegance, just as in his letters he revels in the swift play of words. Yet it must be emphasized that with Mozart laughter is never far removed from tears and the most moving pathos; it is impossible to foretell exactly what the whole mood of a movement is going to be, though there is rarely any feeling of incongruity.

In this he resembles the Greek dramatist Aristophanes, whose comedies combine a unique blend of airy, ribald wit with moments of affecting sadness, when the grotesque figures suddenly become human, and excite our pity by identifying themselves with the dark fate and suffering of mankind. In his *Lysistrata* there is no feeling of false sentiment when the heroine suddenly turns from scenes of unrestrained licence to deliver a great speech on the agony of women in time of war. Mozart was gifted with this power to raise fantasy to the plane of great poetry, increasing his effect by means of that swiftness of thought which has all the elusive qualities to be expected in such impersonal music as his. Shakespeare, too, often contrives the same kind of transition from the ridiculous to the sublime. It would, of course, be absurd to maintain that no artists besides Mozart and Shakespeare have possessed this range of qualities. Many have had two or three of them, but no others have had them all together, or combined deep insight into the emotions of the human heart with the ability to interpret them with truth and conviction in so many forms.

Mozart is sometimes denied a place among the very greatest composers on the ground that he is inferior to Beethoven and others in his capacity for the expression of suffering. It has been maintained that in his G minor Quintet, where the poignant intensity of the earlier movements finds release in a light-hearted finale, he should rather have transformed his emotion into something more noble. But we cannot say dogmatically that this movement was an error or a makeshift. He had no difficulty in solving the same problem most successfully in the Finale of his Clavier Concerto in C minor, written just before, and in that of the G minor Symphony, written not long after this Quintet. Until 1787, in his thirty-second year, he had not drained the cup of sorrow to the full; only in the next two years did he plumb the depths of suffering and disappointment, and his emotions found their transcendental expression in *Die Zauberflöte*. Here and in some of his late chamber works we meet much of that same tranquillity and spirituality that Beethoven expressed in his late quartets and sonatas, but with the difference that Mozart had achieved his end without passing through any stage of exaggerated heroics.

Mozart's artistic instinct was never led astray by his emotions. The truest capacity for suffering is not that which flaunts it before the world, or that which represses all sorrow. Rather does a really great man avail himself of the natural right of humanity to obtain some alleviation from his sorrow through his art, but without obtruding it on the world with exaggerated or egotistical sentiment. He will rise superior in the end; he will not make capital out of his emotions or debase them, but will bequeath to posterity a legacy of beauty and inspiration born of his own adversity. Bigness in music is far from being synonymous with greatness, but universality, the power to create both comic and tragic opera, to write religious works whose deep sincerity still moves us, and to enrich in form and feeling the whole range of chamber and orchestral music, is the hallmark of one type of the greatest genius. Mozart achieved all this without ever allowing bitterness to betray his sense of artistic proportion.

Perhaps we may now attempt to define the way in which his manifold qualities give him his unique place among musicians. The focusing point of them all is his personality, about which his letters and the trustworthy evidence of contemporaries leave us in no doubt. Besides being endowed with exceptional powers of detachment and concentration, in his self-confidence and self-knowledge Mozart must have been an extraordinarily lovable person. Fully conscious of his genius, yet wholly free from arrogance and from condescension towards his friends, he was generous and always ready to help others, though desperately poor himself. He hated humbug and was outspoken, sometimes to the point of truculence, but was free from any touch of boorishness and thoroughly enjoyed the good things of life. The wit and grace of his music and his letters are not incompatible with the brand of coarse schoolboy humour that we find in the latter, for it was common to many people of his time, and probably represented a reaction to the ban placed on most forms of sexual humour by the strong moral influence of the Church. He retained the mind of a poet, never stultified by his brilliant technical gifts or fecundity of invention, and with it a marvellous insight into the human heart, which is the source of the idealization in his music of such fundamentally ordinary people as Susanna, Zerlina, and Cherubino. How he detested mere prettiness, and how he reacted to the morally ugly and terrifying things of life, we can tell from the grandeur and controlled ferocity of much of his music in minor keys, such as the Clavier Concertos in D minor and C minor, and from the savage utterances of Figaro.

Mozart's range of emotional sympathies did not preclude him from remaining a normal man in his daily life and behaviour. For many, the satisfying excellence of his music lies in its essential humanity, because we can feel that 'the matter of which the work is made has been, as it were, penetrated and impregnated by an idea with which we associate ourselves. We see something akin to ourselves penetrating and moulding the matter.' As a complement to Roger Fry's words, we may quote a sentence which Gounod[1] wrote about Mozart: 'In very truth, he touches and moves us, we all recognize ourselves in him, and we proclaim that in this he knows human nature well and truly, not only in its different passions, but in the variety of form and character which they may affect.'

[1] *Le Don Juan de Mozart*, 3rd ed. (Paris, 1890), pp. 20, 21.

13

Mozart's Compositions for Mechanical Organ

THE background of the pieces that Mozart composed for mechanical organ is as remarkable for the nature and history of the instrument as for the life and work of Josef, Count Deym, who was directly connected with them. It is true that the quality of the music is so good that it can be enjoyed in its own right, but some account of both the machine and the man may add to the general interest. The instrument which Mozart himself described as an organ in a clock was in fact but one form of a genus that had enjoyed a long and varied existence, and was extant in his own time in numerous guises. If, then, we wish to understand how he could, without demeaning himself, compose some profound music for what may seem to us today little more than an ingenious toy, we must needs see the mechanical organ in historical perspective as a means of music-making that had begun nearly two centuries before Mozart was born, and lasted long after his death.

From the sixteenth century onwards, when the marvellous mechanical skill of the clockmakers was extended to other fields, music-making machines delighted human ears all over Europe, exercising on all ranks of society the fascination that is always associated with unseen processes. The outward form and size of the instruments varied amazingly, from small pieces of exquisite craftsmanship to large, grotesque objects; but in all, and at all stages of their evolution, the basic principle remained much the same. A cylinder, usually of wood but sometimes of metal, was made to revolve slowly by clockwork mechanism. In it were inserted pins, or pegs, spaced out in a certain order corresponding to the notes of the music which the machine was to play. As the cylinder revolved, the pins either came into contact with a row of metal strings (or the teeth of a metal comb), or opened valves attached to small organ pipes into which air was forced by bellows, likewise mechanically worked. All the sound-producing media were carefully graded so as to approximate to the notes of the chromatic scale. The one disadvantage of this mechanism was that the cylinder could only give a relatively small number of tunes specially arranged or written to suit the limited timbre of the machine; the compass obviously depended on the size of the object into which the whole contrivance was built.[1]

The vogue for music of this kind was most widespread in the eighteenth century when the earnest rationalism of the age seems to have craved some kind of counterpart in things bordering on the realms of supernatural magic. It must not be forgotten that the followers of Mesmer and Cagliostro were as flourishing as those of Kant and Voltaire. As time went on, the whimsical fancy of inventors and craftsmen introduced mechanical music into an astonishing range of objects. In addition to human and animal figures,[2] some of the devices which gave forth delicate jangling tunes were decanters and jugs, when lifted off their bases; portrait albums, when their leaves were turned; snuff-boxes, when their lids sprang open; seal-rings, when pressed on paper; the *nef* (one of the earliest of all), a model in precious metal of a fully rigged ship, laden with wine and spices, which played tunes as it was pushed round the dining-table; and, last but not least, the Victorian bustle that played 'God save the Queen' when the wearer sat down! But to mention the bustle is to stray rather beyond our period.

For a long time the comb principle was the one generally

---

[1] Some fine illustrations of instruments, together with descriptions of their mechanism, will be found in *The Curious History of Music Boxes*, by Roy Mosoriak (Lightner Publishing Co.: Chicago, 1943). See also *Musical Boxes*, by John E. T. Clark (2nd edn., Fountain Press: London, 1952); and Hugo Leichtentritt, 'Mechanical Music in Olden Times', *MQ*, Jan. 1934. A large mechanical organ, with automata, still plays regularly in the grounds at Hellbrunn, cf. p. 125, n. 3.

[2] Cf. A. Chapuis and E. Droz, *Les Automates. Figures artificielles d'hommes et d' animaux* (Neuchâtel, 1949).

preferred as being easily adaptable to small objects. But it co-
existed, from at least the beginning of the eighteenth century,
with the small pipe-organ, as for instance in the 'serinette'
which enjoyed long popularity in France for the training of
song-birds. Its notes were few and shrill, but gradually the
organ was incorporated in larger objects, until the mechanism
ceased to be built into the object, as with clocks, but the clock
itself became a mere appendage to the larger machine. By
1800 mechanical pipe-organs existed in their own right, and
grew to large dimensions. It is perhaps not generally remembered that Beethoven's *Battle Symphony* was originally written
for a powerful mechanical orchestra called the Panharmonicon,
made by the same Mälzel who supplied the composer with
his ear-trumpet. Instruments of this type could command
remarkable effects of rubato and crescendo, so that some
contemporary critics maintained that their performance of
complicated works such as Haydn's 'Military' symphony and
the overture to *Die Zauberflöte* was superior in accuracy and
clarity to that of a living orchestra. These *Orgelwälzer*, or
cylinder organs, were very popular in Viennese restaurants, in
one of which Beethoven used to ask for the overture to Cherubini's *Medea* to be played to him. If Beethoven was not averse
from hearing a mechanical instrument and composing for it, it
need hardly surprise us that many of his predecessors and contemporaries felt likewise. Some of their names may be mentioned, without giving a detailed list of works by each: C. P. E.
Bach, Quantz, Kirnberger, Michael and Joseph Haydn, and
Handel[1] were among those who enriched the repertory of
mechanical music. In the case of Joseph Haydn three of the
musical clocks for which he composed have been preserved.
Containing about 112 pipes each, and dating from 1772, 1792,
and 1793, they were the handiwork of Father Niemecz (friend
and pupil of Haydn, and the librarian of Prince Esterhazy) and
have been the means of securing for posterity thirty-one charm-

---

[1] Cf. W. Barclay Squire, 'Handel's Clock Music', in *MQ*, Oct. 1919; and Edward
Croft-Murray, 'Musical Clocks by Charles Clay', in *Country Life*, 21 Apr. 1950.

ing pieces, of which the majority are otherwise entirely un-known.[1]

Wide popularity created a continual demand, and it was, after all, almost as efficient a form of diffusion as the gramophone of our own day, and, aesthetically at least, a much more pleasing one. Besides original compositions, much music was arranged for mechanical reproduction, very often, we may guess, without the composer's knowledge or consent. In this line, tunes by Grétry, Gluck, and Martini were great favourites. One interesting consequence of the fame of the musicians concerned and of the rare beauty of the clocks and other objects that played their music was that the instruments themselves became much prized by aristocratic collectors, among whom were Richelieu, Marie Antoinette,[2] Frederick the Great, and Napoleon.

It was in the last decades of the eighteenth century that there came upon the scene Count Deym, concerning whom all the information known has been gathered by Prof. O. E. Deutsch, and published in two articles[3] to which this part of the present chapter is much indebted. Born in Bohemia in 1750, Josef Count Deym von Střítež (to give him his full name) ultimately entered the military service of Austria, but after a duel he fled to Holland and assumed the name of Müller. His skill as a modeller in wax brought him fame and wealth, first at Naples, then from about 1785 onwards at Vienna where he exhibited a collection of over 100 copies of statues, busts, and vases, mostly classical in style, and copies of famous pictures. His premises were first at the Stock-im-Eisen Platz; later, in 1795, he moved to the Kohlmarkt, calling his exhibition the 'Müller'sche Kunstgalerie'. Finally he transferred his collection, which had grown considerably, to a handsome specially

---

[1] They have been edited by E. F. Schmid, *Joseph Haydn: Werke für das Laufwerk* (*Flötenuhr*), Nagel (Hanover, 1931).

[2] Cf. Julien Tiersot, 'The Musical Clock of Marie-Antoinette', *MQ*, July 1932.

[3] 'Count Deym and his Mechanical Organs', in *ML*, April 1948, and 'Mozarts Musik in Graf Deyms Kunstgalerie', in *Konzertblatt der Gesellschaft der Musikfreunde*, 1 Dec. 1948.

constructed building, in Palladian style, known as the
'Müller'sche Gebäude,' near the Rotenturmtor, on the Danube
Canal.[1]

In 1799 Deym married Josephine, the younger daughter of
Beethoven's friend Countess Brunsvik. When Deym died in
1804 the gallery was managed by his widow until 1819. Some
of its contents had been sold in 1814 and it was partly destroyed
after Josephine's death in 1821. All trace has vanished of the
mechanical organs, although the Müller'sche Gebäude was not
demolished until 1889, up to which year its hall had served for
concerts and dances.

Fortunately the contents of the gallery are fairly well known
from contemporary descriptions and advertisements. By far the
most important is an announcement in the *Wiener Zeitung* on
17 August 1791, describing at length 'Laudon's Mausoleum'.
This exhibit consisted of a monument, in classical style, to the
memory of the Emperor Joseph and Field-Marshal Laudon[2] and
showed them in 'Elysian colloquy'. 'Each hour', the announcement ended, 'a suitable funeral music, especially written for the
purpose by the unforgettable composer Mozart, is to be heard,
which lasts eight minutes and in precision and purity surpasses
anything that was ever attempted to be suitably applied to this
kind of artistic work.' This 'funeral music' can only be the so-
called Fantasy in F minor-major, K. 594, which Mozart entered
in his catalogue late in 1790 as 'A Piece for an Organ in a Clock'.
We know from a letter of 3 October 1790 that he was composing it during his stay at Frankfurt. Since, however, the entry
bears no exact date (such as Mozart generally gave to the earlier
entries), some delay in the completion of the exhibit may be
presumed.

The other musical exhibits in that section of the gallery

---

[1] It is illustrated in O. E. Deutsch's *Franz Schubert, sein Leben in Bildern* (Munich,
1913), vol. iii, pl. 138.

[2] The dates of their deaths were, respectively, 20 Feb. 1790 and 14 July 1790.
Laudon, who became a national hero during the Seven Years War, and to whom
Haydn dedicated his Symphony No. 69, is mentioned several times in Mozart's
letters.

containing 'mechanical clocks' are given by Deutsch as follows:

1. . . . a bracket-clock [*Pendile*, i.e. *pendule*], eight feet high, running uninterruptedly for eight days and playing on steel rods twelve different pieces;

2. . . . a lady *en négligée* [*sic*] and modelled life-size, seated at the pianoforte, on which lies the apparatus required for playing; she touches the keys with her fingers, and one is frequently deceived with the more certainty when the adjoining magnificent clock, which is in a well-gilt case, announces the quarter-hours with its chimes, but the hours with the pianoforte itself;

3. . . . an ingenious apparatus representing Pan with goats' feet and horns and distinctly blowing sundry merry shepherd's ditties on its nine-note Pan's pipes;

4. . . . a pyramid nine feet high . . . with a precious clock, which plays the flute most deceptively;

5. . . . another elaborate clock . . . with two boys in Spanish clothing seated on either side and at each hour blowing a different duet on their flutes;

6. . . . an automaton dressed as a Spaniard, blowing the flageolet; . . . the Bedroom of the Graces . . . flutes and a pianoforte play, now by turns, now together, and again both mingling their unadulterated sounds with other musical instruments and representing a full concert;

7. . . . a mechanical canary bird . . . pipes several neat pieces very clearly and distinctly;

8. . . . a mechanical art clock . . . which strikes quarters as well as hours and accompanies them each time with chimes . . . two choirs of trumpets and drums parade in the background.

In addition, Deutsch, quoting from a different source,[1] mentions as an appurtenance of the Bedroom of the Graces 'A glorious flute music, as though inspired by the breath of love, resounds, without its being possible to tell whence the magic notes come. It is an Adagio by the unforgettable Mozart.'

While the advertisement of 17 August 1791, coupled with Mozart's letter of 3 October 1790, makes the connexion of

---

[1] *Neuestes Sittengemählde von Wien* (Vienna, 1801), vol. i, pp. 38 ff.

K. 594 with Deym unmistakable, the link connecting the two men personally is tenuous. O. E. Deutsch suggested that they were brought together by Leonhard Posch, a sculptor who had made the famous wax relief of Mozart in 1788, and is known to have worked for Deym. We also know that the latter took Mozart's death-mask. But there is no direct evidence that the other two pieces, K. 608 and K. 616, were commissioned by Deym. What has been often stated as a fact is really only an inference from the nature of the music in the light of the knowledge that Deym's gallery was the sole place of its kind in Vienna. The identification of the two later pieces with the eight exhibits described above remains similarly conjectural. Deutsch convincingly suggests that K. 616 may have been played by exhibit no. 2—the lady *en négligé*, but K. 608 is much harder to place, as its very nature is not suited to any of the other seven items. Can it possibly have been composed as an alternative piece for use in the 'Laudon Mausoleum' itself? As to the 'Bedroom of the Graces', Einstein conjectured that this music was none other than the Armonica Quintet (K. 617). If so, the work must have been arranged for the purpose.

It is instructive to consider briefly K. 594, 608, and 616 as a musical group. While it can hardly be a coincidence that all three are largely in the keys of F major or minor, it is not easy to adduce reasons for this. The key of F, whether major or minor, was used but infrequently by Mozart, although in it he composed some notable works. It seems unlikely that this choice here bore any relation to the nature of the cylinder-mechanism. But the fact that the playing time of all three pieces is of nearly the same duration, namely $8\frac{1}{2}$ to 10 minutes, is obviously related to mechanical limitations. Possibly, however, the sorrowful, commemorative mood evoked by K. 594 was sustained when, some two months later, Mozart came to compose K. 608.

Is it unreasonable to suggest that he deliberately used F major again for K. 616 in order to round off this remarkable little trilogy in a complementary way, and give it tonal coherence?

The description of the pieces, taken from the entries in Mozart's *Verzeichnüß*, with their respective lengths, is as follows:

K. 594. 'Ein Stück für ein Orgelwerk in einer Uhr.' ('A piece for an organ in a clock.') Begun in October 1790, and entered in December. 153 bars (Adagio, F minor, 39 bars; allegro, F major, 77 bars; adagio, F minor, 37 bars).

K. 608. 'Ein Orgel-Stück für eine Uhr.' ('An organ piece for a clock.') Entered on 3 March 1791. 222 bars (Allegro, F minor, 74 bars; adagio, A flat major, 84 bars; allegro, F minor, 64 bars).

K. 616. 'Andante für eine Walze in eine kleine Orgel.' ('Andante for a Cylinder in a small Organ.') Entered 4 May 1791. F major. 144 bars.

Structurally, K. 594 and K. 608 are extremely interesting, being obviously complementary, yet also sufficiently different to serve as a paradigm of Mozart's 'creative duality' which is discussed in Chapter 11. In texture and in mood they stand apart from K. 616, which has its own distinctive excellence.

Only one of the three pieces has been preserved in Mozart's autograph—namely K. 616. This is written on three staves, all in the G clef. The manuscript sources of K. 594 and K. 608 consist of transcriptions,[1] on four staves, made during the early nineteenth century. (Both were once in Beethoven's possession, presumably by virtue of his friendship with the Brunsviks.) The misleading and totally unsuitable title 'fantasie' is also of nineteenth-century origin. It was applied to K. 608 as early as 1800 by Breitkopf & Härtel in cahier 8 of their 'Oeuvres complettes' of Mozart. K. 594 was similarly described in an arrangement for string quartet issued *c.* 1835 by Diabelli.

Mozart's attitude to K. 594 is informative and characteristic. The salient passage in the above-mentioned letter of 3 October 1790, written from Frankfurt to his wife, is as follows:

I have now made up my mind to compose at once the Adagio for

---

[1] A two-hand arrangement of K. 608 is mentioned by Köchel as having belonged in 1936 to the Viennese firm of Hinterberger. In 1951 Hinterberger offered this manuscript for sale, repeating the statement in Köchel that it might have been made under Mozart's supervision by Süssmayr or Stadler, and adding the opinion of Robert Haas that some corrections might be in Mozart's autograph.

the clockmaker and then to slip a few ducats into the hand of my dear little wife. And this I have done; but as it is a kind of composition which I detest, I have unfortunately not been able to finish it. I compose a bit of it every day—but I have to break off now and then, as I get bored. And indeed I would give the whole thing up, if I had not such an important *reason to go on with it*. But I still hope that I shall be able to force myself gradually to finish it. If it were for a large instrument and the work would sound like an organ piece, then I might get some fun out of it. But, as it is, the works consist solely of little pipes, which sound too high-pitched and too childish for my taste.

In spite, however, of the distasteful nature of the task, Mozart's integrity rose superior to the artificial medium, thus achieving in both this piece and K. 608, a notable triumph of mind over matter. As ever, he subjected his personal feelings to the highest principle of his art—to compose great music.

From the first bar to the last, K. 594 contains nothing forced or unnatural. It is deeply charged with spontaneous emotion. In balance, it broadly resembles the first movement of the String Quintet in D (K. 593), composed only a few weeks earlier, for in both the slow opening, subtly varied in harmony and form, is repeated after the allegro middle section. The solemn, melancholy Adagio of K. 594 is fully consonant with the general character of F minor as previously, though infrequently, used by Mozart. Generally it was enhanced by a marked contrapuntal tendency, as for instance in the Andante of the early String Quartet in F (K. 168), the middle section of the Rondo for Clavier in F (K. 494), and no. 6 of the clavier variations on 'Ein Weib ist das herrlichste Ding' (K. 613). In K. 594 the stately chromatic progressions of the opening bars (Ex. 42) lead to a melody (Ex. 43) which he had already used as a subsidiary theme in the Adagio of K. 593. These first thirty-nine bars serve as a curtain-raiser to the vigorous Allegro, in the tonic major, of which the dramatic opening theme (Ex. 44) is developed with some splendid part-writing into a terse sonata movement. The style is not unlike that of the organ

concertos of Handel, a composer for whom Mozart had a deep
admiration, and reminds us that between November 1788
and July 1790 he had re-scored *Acis and Galatea, Messiah,
Alexander's Feast,* and *The Ode on St. Cecilia's Day* for the
concerts sponsored by Baron van Swieten. The end of the
second part of the Allegro, through which the rhythm of
the phrase marked 'a' in Ex. 44 pounds away in the bass like
the strokes of a hammer, leads quietly to a resumption of the
F minor Adagio but with even deeper feeling, enriched by a
passing allusion to A flat major. Exquisite indeed is this use
of the gruppetti (Ex. 45) that are such a prominent feature of
K. 594, 608, and 616, and indeed of Mozart's late style gener-

Ex. 45

ally. There are few passages in all his music that surpass the
power and pathos of these thirty-seven bars. Their sustained
chromaticism, to which no parallel can be found in his own
works, is remarkably advanced for 1790.

Mention should be made here of a nine-bar fragment,[1] K. 593a in D minor,

Ex. 46

which has been assigned by Einstein to this period as a draft for K. 594. This conjecture is supported by the chromatic

[1] Kindly supplied to me by Fritz Spiegl from the original in the Mozarteum.

style of the music, an impressive Adagio, and by the fact that
it is written on three staves as was K. 616. Here, too, gruppetti
are prominent. If we assume that this supposition is correct,
the fragment provides additional evidence that Mozart took
his task seriously enough to discard an *incipit* which, for some
reason, failed to satisfy him. There is some further evidence
of this in connexion with K. 616.

In K. 608 he reversed the form adopted in K. 594 by devising
a scheme of two allegro sections, flanking one in slower tempo.
Here the opening carries an exceptional momentum, and consists of twelve bars of introduction, based on repetition of this
incisive phrase

Ex. 47   Allegro

after which there arises a fugue that is packed with all manner of contrapuntal ingenuity, on the following subject, in
rising positions:

Ex. 48

A repetition of the introduction in a sequence passing up the
scale through harsh modulations brings a quiet transition to
the meditative Andante in A flat. The following few bars, being
the recapitulation of the opening melody, will serve as a sample
of its quality and harmonic richness. [Ex. 49.] When the F
minor section returns, it is not a mere repetition; it is elaborated
as in K. 594, the grandeur of the fugue being enhanced by a
counter-subject that contributes to a great outburst of emotional
and intellectual energy. This is one of the culminations of

Mozart's writing in the 'strict' style, into which he had initiated himself nine years before by intensive study of J. S. Bach. Indeed, it is hard to imagine how such complex music as K. 594 and

Ex. 49

K. 608 could possibly have pleased the taste of casual visitors to the Müller'sche Gebäude. They probably expected mechanical music to be of short duration, simple, and cheerful in mood, like most of the Haydn pieces mentioned above. In all likelihood, Mozart wrote K. 594 and K. 608 as he did in order to satisfy himself alone. On this hypothesis, the music falls naturally into place in the evolution of his contrapuntal style as outlined in Chapter 10.

When, some seven weeks later, Mozart came to compose K. 616, the resultant music was as different in mood and style from the two earlier pieces as could possibly be imagined. Indeed, it is difficult to point to such a sharp contrast in any other comparable group of his works. Possibly the change was due to a suggestion from Count Deym himself. Gone, completely, were the characteristics common to K. 594 and K. 608—rhythmical and contrapuntal intensity; poignant chromaticism, forceful modulations, and tripartite scheme. In their stead,

Mozart had recourse to that blend of disarming simplicity and understatement which give such unfailing pleasure and recall his style of the late 1770's. This limpid music, so unusually high in register, conceived in May 1791, marked a stage in his spiritual progress towards the 'far serener clime' of *Die Zauber-flöte*, and indeed anticipated the singing of the 'Three Boys'.

In structure K. 616, though clear-cut, is not rigid, being a type of rondo with two principal melodies, contrasted in line and rhythm. But the subtlety of the figuration, combined with variety in modulation, produces an effect of suspended hovering, delicate yet unerring as the flight of a lark. The first theme

Ex. 50

has some affinity with the opening of the Larghetto of the Clavier Concerto in B flat (K. 595) of the preceding year. A subsidiary melody in the dominant

Ex. 51

has a much smoother line, but is not used prominently. The structure is built chiefly round Ex. 50, which is most resourcefully handled, as in such an ingeniously delayed return as this (here compressed on to two staves):

Ex. 52

All these 144 bars are packed with echo-effects, imitations and trills, and blossom into sprays of melody reminiscent of the Andante of the String Quintet in E flat (K. 614) written barely three weeks earlier. The result is a limpidity of texture well suited to make the most of a leisurely tempo imposed upon a mechanical instrument that could boast little or no sustaining power.

There exists a four-bar sketch (Köchel, p. 1040):

Ex. 53

which can be regarded with some certainty as a preliminary to K. 616. It is to be found on the back of a leaf bearing sketches for *Die Zauberflöte* (which was probably begun in April 1791) now in Uppsala University Library.[1] This fortunate conjunction, combined with the use of four staves, three in the G clef, leaves no doubt as to the date and nature of the sketch. The key, again, is F major.

K. 616 alone of these three pieces has come down to modern times in approximately its original medium. Köchel records the fact that the collection of instruments in the University of Leipzig possessed a mechanical organ, formerly no. 2052 in the Heyer Collection,[2] with a cylinder preserving K. 616 in a shortened form, lacking the development section.

For all three pieces, there is no doubt that the timbre of the original mechanical organ can be effectively simulated by a group of five or six wind instruments, perhaps including a piccolo and basset-horn. But as this combination might not suit the taste or resources of all would-be performers, other media call for mention. K. 594 and K. 608 are often heard on the organ, K. 616 less frequently. But this may be unsatisfactory unless governed by the utmost care in registration and restraint in interpretation. Mozart's own words, 'if it were for a large instrument and the work might sound like an organ piece, then I might get some fun out of it', cannot be taken as an open licence to justify the performance of these pieces in the heavy

[1] It is reproduced in Richard Engländer's article 'The Sketches for *The Magic Flute* at Upsala', *MQ*, July 1941.

[2] This collection is now in the Musikwissenschaftliches Institut und Musik-instrumentensammlung der Karl-Marx-Universität, Leipzig. The organ is described thus in G. Kinsky's *Musikhistorisches Museum von Wilhelm Heyer in Cöln, Kleiner Katalog der Sammlung alter Musikinstrumente* (Cöln, 1913), p. 208: 'A flute clock in Empire-style, *c.* 1810, with charming gilt woodcarvings; the panel shows the hall of a temple flanked with two corner towers.' The clock is illustrated in H. Dennerlein, *Der unbekannte Mozart* (Leipzig, 1951), at p. 278. The cylinder, however, cannot be earlier than *c.* 1830, because, besides K. 616 and Haydn's so-called serenade from the quartet op. 3, no. 5, it contained the overture to Auber's *La Muette de Portici*, composed 1828. Fritz Spiegl possesses a recording of K. 616 made from this cylinder: his arrangement of K. 594 for wind quintet was published by the Oxford University Press in 1953.

style of organ playing to which twentieth-century registration is sometimes prone. If the modern organ be used, the registration should be restricted to the reasonable limits suggested by our considerable knowledge of the instruments available to Mozart in Austria and south Germany (cf. pp. 238–41). For performance in England a Snetzler organ has much to recommend it.

Although K. 616 seems in some ways more suited to the keyboard than its fellows, the timbre and touch of the modern grand pianoforte are really quite unsuited to its delicate velocity, with which, however, the clean, percussive quality of the 'forte-piano'[1] of Mozart's own day is more in keeping. For K. 594 and K. 608, the commonly heard duet-version for four hands is far from satisfactory, because the tone colour is too thick to bring out the elaborate part-writing. There is thus some virtue in an arrangement made for string quartet or a small string orchestra. But obviously no final solution can be found to the problem of arranging for modern performance the music of an obsolete instrument such as Deym's mechanical organ. Successive generations are bound to have different ideas about the best method of keeping alive these three pieces by Mozart. The variety of editorial thought and care expended on them at intervals during the past century and a half testifies to the attractive vitality of the music.

[1] Artaria published what was probably the first two-hand arrangement of K. 608, c. 1805, as *Fantaisie . . . mise pour le forte piano par Muzio Clementi* (copy in my collection).

14

Mozart's Lost and Fragmentary Compositions

WHEN Ludwig Ritter von Köchel affixed the number 626 to
the *Requiem*, he could not have foreseen the emphatic finality
which that number would come to impose upon the general
conception of Mozart's output. So persuasive is the tyranny of
habitually used and widely accepted numbers that probably few
people realize that the total of works which he actually composed falls not far short of 700, if those now lost are taken
into account. A comprehensive survey of them appears to be
a desideratum in Mozart literature. This attempt to fill the gap
may perhaps add something to our knowledge of the range
of his genius, and will certainly enhance our appreciation of
his personal and musical sympathies. In this connexion, it
may not be wholly irrelevant to include some mention of
compositions which he planned but probably never executed,
and, lastly, some remarks on the relation of the fragments to
the corpus of his work.

The sources for our knowledge of the lost pieces are fourfold
—the catalogue[1] which Leopold Mozart compiled in September
1768, summarizing all his son's compositions up to that date;
Mozart's own *Verzeichnüß*, covering the period from 9 February
1784 to his death; the letters of Mozart and his family; Einstein's
edition of Köchel, to which, in its bearing on this topic, an
especial tribute should be paid. To avoid repetition of dates, let
us weave the lost and intended pieces into one chronological
sequence, which will be found to cover nearly the whole thirty
years of Mozart's productive life.

[1] First published in Nissen: reprinted in all editions of Holmes, and, most recently,
with incipits and annotations, in E. H. Müller von Asow's edition of Mozart's *Verzeichnis* (Vienna, 1943).

It was under the year 1765 that Einstein made the first insertion of a lost or fragmentary work, in the manner which made his edition of Köchel so distinctive. In the course of its pages, he placed over 200 such pieces, of which those that were lost presented less difficult problems. Although this *tour de force* was widely commented on at the time of publication (1937), it was not perhaps then seen in its true perspective. Einstein was not, however, quite the first in the field, for in 1926 Mena Blaschitz had produced a dissertation at Bonn *Die Salzburger Mozart-fragmente*, which has, unfortunately, remained in typescript. (This collection of fragments is by far the largest in any one place, and each leaf is effectively cased in a transparent cover for easy handling in the library of the Mozarteum.) Although Einstein differed, sometimes categorically, sometimes tentatively, from a good many of Mena Blaschitz's datings, he made acknowledgement to her pioneer work. The resultant conspectus represented a feat of scholarship, without parallel in the annals of musical learning, which could only have been achieved by a mind keenly attuned to Mozart's style. Einstein's work may justly be compared, particularly in its uncannily accurate placings of fragments, to that of Sir J. D. Beazley in identifying widely scattered fragments of Attic pottery as belonging to the same vase or a particular painter, or that of the late Humfry Payne who could tell almost at a glance whether a head of a Greek statue in the Louvre belonged to a torso preserved in a museum in Athens.

Starting, then, in Mozart's ninth year, Einstein enumerated four lost symphonies (K. 16a, 16b, 19a, 19b), which can be attributed with fair certainty to the boy's sojourn in London. The chief source of the incipits is an early manuscript catalogue formerly in the possession of Breitkopf & Härtel. From the same source comes K. 21a, a lost set of clavier variations described as 'comp. à Londres'. From the time of the family's stay in Holland during the winter 1765–6 there dates a sketch-book entitled 'Capricci' (K. 32a). Although these clavier pieces have not survived, the collection was still in existence

in 1799 and 1800 when it was mentioned in letters written
by Constanze Mozart to Breitkopf and to André. Leopold
Mozart mentioned in his 1768 catalogue two manuscript
books, containing clavier pieces, written from time to time in
London, Holland, &c. One of these was the London notebook
published by G. Schünemann in 1909 as *Mozart als achtjähriger
Componist*; the other comprised the 'Capricci'. Einstein points
out that an announcement of a concert in Amsterdam by Mozart
on 26 February 1766 read, 'Finally, the boy will play, on the
organ, his own capricci'.

Leopold Mozart's catalogue also mentions 'Various solos for
transverse flute [K. 33a] composed for Duke Louis of Wirtenberg in Lausanne' where the family stayed in August 1766;
pieces for violin; for the violoncello 'for the Prince of Fürstenberg'; the latter (K. 33b) can be dated to October 1766, when the
Mozart family was in Donaueschingen. Einstein assigns to
some time in the autumn of 1766 four harpsichord sonatas (K.
33d–g). The incipits of three are quoted by Mozart's sister
when writing to Breitkopf in February 1800: the fourth is
known from the Breitkopf MS. catalogue. Conjecturally, to the
same period belongs a piece for French horn which is mentioned retrospectively in a letter of 16 February 1778. The dis-
appearance of this, apparently Mozart's earliest work for a solo
wind instrument, is much to be regretted. So too are a number
of miscellaneous pieces listed, rather vaguely, in Leopold's
catalogue (K 41a–d): six divertimenti 'for various instruments
such as violin, trumpet, horn, flute, bassoon, trombone, viola,
violoncello, etc'; 'many pieces—for two trumpets, for two
horns, for two basset-horns'; 'various marches, for two violins,
two horns, two oboes, bass, etc'; 'military marches with two
oboes, two horns and bassoon—for two violins and bass'; 'many
minuets with various instruments'. This variety of instruments
shows that these works cannot be earlier than the time of the
family's return to Salzburg in November 1766, for neither were
such pieces called for during his travels, nor were the resources
easily available.

To the same period probably belong a fugue for clavier, a four-part fugue (K. 41e, f), and a 'Nachtmusik' for two violins and bass (K. 41g). Valuable as all these pieces would be, especially as evidence for the growth of Mozart's instrumental technique, they were, as far as can be inferred from the titles, mostly short and probably simple in form. Much more important is the lost Trumpet Concerto (K. 47a), written, according to Leopold's letter of 12 November 1768, to be played by a boy at the consecration of 'the new church in Father Parhammer's orphanage' in Vienna. How interesting if we could have compared this with Leopold's own Trumpet Concerto![1] The sum of all these works of Mozart's infancy which have not survived, when added to those that have, proves how incessant and varied was his creative impulse from his eighth to his twelfth year. The technical imperfections of the 'London notebook' have given rise to the reasonable assumption that Leopold must have improved many of his son's contemporary larger pieces, because they are mostly free from such blemishes. We should remember that Leopold most probably had a hand in the lost works.

To the end of 1769 there may belong, according to a conjecture of Einstein, three symphonies now known only from incipits in the Breitkopf MS. catalogue. The survival of these would have helped to fill a gap of nearly two years in Mozart's symphonic development. From a letter of 26 January 1770 we know that he had composed an aria 'Misero tu non sei' from Metastasio's *Demetrio*, but this has not come down to us. For the next four years, 1770–4, Mozart's output appears to have been preserved almost complete, excepting 'a little cassation in C' mentioned in a letter of 18 August 1771 for an unspecified medium, and apparently not placed by Einstein. Another cassation (K. 62), of which the incipit is quoted by Mozart himself in a letter of 4 August 1770, has also disappeared. Einstein assigns to the beginning of 1775 a Bassoon Concerto of which the incipit is given in the Breitkopf MS. catalogue, and con-

---

[1] Published in the *Denkmäler der Tonkunst in Bayern*, vol. ix, pt. 2.

jectures that it was not one of the three written a little earlier for Baron Dürnitz. The well-known Concerto K. 191 is to be regarded as distinct from all these, so that we have now but one out of five works of this type. Another regrettable loss is that of a Violoncello Concerto (K. 206a), written in March 1775.

During his sojourn in Munich in October 1777 Mozart composed four preludes for clavier which his father described as 'supremely beautiful' and 'incomparable' (K. 284a). These were doubtless in the same free style so cleverly used in the later clavier pieces. But none of these preludes nor a rondo (K. 284f) written at the same period for Countess Savioli have been preserved. We find mentioned in letters of 6–7 December, and 15 December 1777 some dance music composed for Cannabich, or perhaps arranged by Mozart for clavier from the latter's works. But the passages are not very clear; there is no mention of these in Köchel.

On moving to Paris in the spring of 1778 Mozart was commissioned by Le Gros, Director of the Concert Spirituel, to compose eight pieces (K. 297a) supplementary to a 'Miserere' by Ignaz Holzbauer. Although described in a letter of 5 April as 'hack work', these pieces, one of which contained obbligato passages for bassoon and oboe, are probably much to be regretted. So too is a scena (K. 315b), written for the eminent castrato Giusto Ferdinando Tenducci, for which Mozart devised, probably in imitation of a similarly destined work by J. C. Bach, the remarkable accompaniment of clavier, oboe, chromatic horn, bassoon, two clarinets, two horns, two violins, two violas, and bass. The combination of keyboard and woodwind in what may well have been a concertante style makes an interesting anticipation of the later Quintet for clavier and wind K. 452. In a letter of 11 September 1778 Mozart mentions his intention to compose 'six trios': it is not known whether he finished them or for what instruments they were. In this same period, so rich in vain hopes and unfinished projects, he began a duodrama *Semiramis* to words by a Mannheim poet, Baron

Otto von Gemmingen. It would have been very interesting to see how Mozart treated a 'declaimed opera', as he called it, with only two characters and the minimum of singing. But this piece, probably never finished, has vanished. Another dramatic piece that has not survived was a recitative and aria (K. 365a) composed in November 1780 for Schikaneder's production of the German translation by F. A. C. Werthes of Gozzi's *Le Due notte affannose*. Nothing is known of its orchestration.

After his removal to Vienna, Mozart was continually seeking opportunities to earn money and repute by composing. On 16 June 1781 he told his father that he was looking about for a short Italian cantata suitable for Advent, when he could expect two performances. Whether he ever composed such a work is not known, but from a letter of 1 August we know he chose a text by a poet named Rossi. So, too, in November of the same year, when the Grand Duke Paul Petrovich of Russia visited Vienna, Mozart wrote to his father saying that he intended to 'look about for Russian popular songs, so as to be able to play variations on them'. No such variations are extant, even if they were committed to paper.

This period was rich in music written for personal friends and pupils. In a letter of 21 July 1784 Mozart expressed the hope of composing an aria for Marguerite Marchand, a singer who had been trained by Leopold, but no such work has survived. There is a similar allusion, on 15 October 1787, to an aria written for Baron Gottfried von Jacquin. Another song, apparently now lost, is mentioned in an interesting passage in the autobiography of Mozart's contemporary Gyrowetz:[1]

It happened one evening that Mozart was late in arriving [at the house of Franz Bernard von Kees, a privy councillor and well-known patron of music], and they waited for him to begin, because he had promised to bring with him a song for the lady of the house. One servant after another was sent to find him, and at last he was discovered in a tavern; the messenger begged him to come at once, as all the company was waiting to hear the new song. Mozart there-

---

[1] *Biographie des Adalbert Gyrowetz* (Vienna, 1848), p. 10.

upon recollected that he had not written a note of it. He sent the messenger for a sheet of music paper, and set to work in the tavern to compose the song. When it was finished he went his way to the concert, where the company was waiting for him with great impatience. After a little gentle reproach for his delay he was most affectionately received; the lady of the house sang the new song, a little nervously, it is true, but it was enthusiastically received and applauded.

The period referred to is about 1785. It is possible, of course, that the story relates to one of Mozart's known songs, but it would be remarkable if the link between so unusual an episode and one of the fine songs of that time had been entirely lost. We may not unreasonably assume that the song has not come down to us. For his friend Michael Kelly, the Irish tenor who sang Basilio in the first production of *Figaro*, he wrote variations on a setting of Metastasio's 'Grazie agl' inganni tuoi',[1] but these have not, unfortunately, been preserved. Köchel refers to them in the notes on K. 532.

A rather similar anecdote is given by Parke under the year 1823 in his *Musical Memoirs*:[2]

I dined by invitation with an old gentleman, (Mr. Z——n, a German,) who had been intimate with Mozart, and had lately come from Vienna to England. In the course of our conversation Mozart being spoken of, he produced from his music room the copy of a minuet and trio on a quarto sheet, composed by that extraordinary musician in his best style, under the following curious circumstances: Mozart was one day accosted in the streets of Vienna by a beggar, who not only solicited alms of him, but by strong circumstances endeavoured to make it appear that he was distantly related to him. Mozart's feelings were excited; but being unprovided with money, (as is frequently the case with men of genius) he desired the beggar to follow him to the next coffee-house, where, taking writing-paper, and drawing lines on it with his pen, he in a few minutes composed the minuet and trio alluded to. This, and a letter, Mozart directed him to take to Mr. ——, his publisher, of whom the mendicant re-

---

[1] Kelly, vol. i, p. 226.
[2] London, 1830, vol. ii, pp. 179, 180.

ceived a sum equal to five guineas! The copy, I believe the only one in England, was presented to me, and was afterwards given by me to Mr. Shield.

Such an incident is quite consistent with Mozart's impulsive nature, but, as in the episode related by Gyrowetz, the work cannot now be identified. Nor is any mention of it to be found in the sale catalogue of Shield's library. But this is not in itself proof that this minuet may not have existed: the catalogue, printed shortly after Shield's death in 1829, is such a slovenly piece of work that a small sheet of manuscript could easily have slipped into the many undescribed lots.

Several other late lost works are known to us from Mozart's own catalogue. They are:

K. 470. An Andante in A major for a violin concerto of April 1785, probably written either for his Salzburg friend Heinrich Marchand or for Anton Janiewicz, both virtuosi. Einstein conjectures this Andante to have been an alternative for the second movement of K. 218, which concerto Mozart may have revived in Vienna.

K. 544. A short March in D major for violin, viola, flute, horn, and violoncello. Nothing is known of its purpose, and even the exact date of composition is uncertain, as Mozart entered three pieces in his catalogue on the same day—K. 543, K. 544, and K. 545.

K. 569. An aria 'Ohne Zwang, aus eignem Triebe', with orchestral accompaniment, composed in January 1789. Nothing is known of the occasion which prompted it.

K. 615. A final chorus 'Viviamo felici in dolce contento' with orchestral accompaniment, composed in April 1791 as an addition to Sarti's opera *Le Gelosie villane*.

Besides these, there remain two interesting occasional pieces. In September 1785 Mozart collaborated with two other Kapellmeisters, Salieri and Cornetti,[1] in providing music for a

[1] Who was Cornetti? No composer of this name and period is known to any dictionary, nor to Köchel's *Die kaiserliche Hofmusikkapelle in Wien*. In Gugitz's edition of Da Ponte's memoirs, vol. iii, p. 356, Cornetti has been identified with A. Cornet, but there seems to be no evidence for this. Gerber (2) states that this

Cantata (K. 477a), *Per la ricuperata salute di Ophelia,* of which the text was by Da Ponte. Einstein quotes a notice of it in the contemporary press. It was written to celebrate the recovery of Anna Storace from an illness. The manuscript is lost, nor have any printed copies survived, although they were on sale at Artaria's.[1] This is one of the very few instances of a printed work of Mozart's having disappeared.

A slight digression may be permitted to shed some light on the nature of Anna Storace's illness. The information comes from Michael Kelly:[2]

> His Royal Highness's (i.e. the Duke of York's) first visit to the theatre attracted a crowded and brilliant assemblage. The Emperor, accompanied by his brother Maximilian, the Archbishop of Cologne, was present. A new opera, composed by Stephen Storace, was pro-duced on the occasion: Signora Storace and myself had the two prin-cipal parts in it. In the middle of the first act, Storace all at once lost her voice, and could not utter a sound during the whole of the per-formance; this naturally threw a damp over the audience as well as the performers. The loss of the first female singer, who was a great and deserved favourite, was to the composer, her brother, a severe blow. I never shall forget her despair and disappointment, but she was not then prepared for the extent of her misfortune, for she did not recover her voice sufficiently to appear on the stage for five months.

The opera was *Gli Sposi malcontenti*, first produced on 1 June 1785. We may guess that Mozart, as a close friend of both com-poser and prima donna, was in the house that night. No copy of the libretto can now be traced, even if it was printed, but *Ophelia* was presumably the character sung by Anna Storace.[3]

Finally there is a double canon, K. 572a, written by Mozart

composer, who wrote some duets published by Artaria and reissued by Longman & Broderip, was a popular singing-master, but does not mention him as a Kapellmeister.

[1] The advertisement says 'wird angekauft', but the cantata never appeared in Artaria's lists. I am indebted to O. E. Deutsch for this information as also for the sug-gestion that the work was sold on commission.

[2] Vol. i, p. 231.

[3] The theatrical collection of the *Österreichische Nationalbibliothek* contains a playbill dated 1 June 1785, but it does not give the names of the singers.

at a convivial occasion in Leipzig, presumably on 22 April 1789. The sole authority for this is Rochlitz, whose testimony[1] is perhaps less dubious here than elsewhere. Each canon was in three parts, and the contrasting words—'Lebet wohl, wir sehn uns wieder' and 'Heult noch gar, wie alte Weiber'—combined with a most comical effect. It is most regrettable that Cantor Doles, the host of the evening, neither preserved Mozart's auto-graph nor, apparently, took a copy.

Substantially as we see that this conspectus of lost pieces aug-ments Mozart's output, it still does not represent the full sum of his life's work. We must also take into account the fragments, to the number of well over a hundred. They vary in length from a dozen or twenty bars to extensive movements completed up to or near the development to a span of a hundred bars or more. To these may be added about thirty discarded incipits which Mozart wrote out not on separate leaves but in the actual quire containing the finished work. These are mostly a dozen bars or less, but sometimes much longer, as in the Finale of the E major Clavier Trio (K. 542), where the sketch runs to sixty-five bars. Formerly the fragments on separate sheets were re-garded as pieces rejected because Mozart lost interest in them for various reasons. The truth was demonstrated by Einstein,[2] who proved that the majority of them are 'springboards' used regularly as a step towards the finer realization of a composition as a balanced whole.

But in studying the details and in demonstrating the psycho-logical import of the fragments, Einstein omitted to give a statistical picture of them as a group. If we may assume that the survival rate of instrumental and vocal pieces has been fairly equal, it is most interesting to note that the former outnumber the latter by more than four to one. The discrepancy is partly accounted for by the fact that more than two-thirds of the vocal

---

[1] *AMZ*, vol. iii, 1800–1, coll. 450 ff.

[2] Chapter 8. Works such as the Concerto for clavier and violin (K. 315f) or the *Sinfonia concertante* for violin, viola, and violoncello (K. 320e) are not 'spring-boards', but belong to the far smaller group of pieces which were, for sundry reasons, never finished.

fragments consist of church music, of which Mozart wrote very little after 1781. But even so, it is obvious that instrumental music cost him much more pains than vocal. We possess, unfortunately, very few of the drafts which he must have made for his operas, but even if these had survived complete they would probably not have altered the proportion to less than three to one.

Within the instrumental group itself the proportions are equally striking. The most numerous fragments from any one period of composition are those of 1781 to 1783—a dozen in all—forming the experiments leading to his final contrapuntal mastery. In types, fragments of chamber pieces exceed those of concertos and orchestral works by thirty-six to thirty. Within the chamber group, quintets come first with fourteen fragments, and quartets second with nine. This is particularly interesting in view of the fact that Mozart wrote thirty-two quartets but only nine quintets. But the greater effort which chamber music in general called forth is consonant with his own statement in the famous letter of 1 September 1785, dedicating his six quartets to Haydn, that these were the fruit of 'long and laborious toil'.

The particulars of many of the lost works, especially as to the size of the various groups composed in 1766 and 1767, are lamentably vague, making difficult an exact computation of the total which could be added to the canon of 626. Even at a conservative estimate, it is not less than sixty, covering almost every class of music then current. Yet they may not all be irretrievably lost. Intensive and systematic search in continental libraries, especially if promoted by the new complete edition of Mozart now in progress, might well bring to light some of these and perhaps other unknown works also. Such, at least, is the hope encouraged by the analogous discoveries made during the course of research for the new Haydn edition.

How greatly would the corpus of Mozart's work have been expanded and enriched had all his lost compositions survived! What light would have been shed on certain dark places in the growth of his style! But it is something to have the sources to measure, however imperfectly, the extent of our loss. For if we add the sum of the lost works to that of the fragments, in terms both of variety and creative labour, the result must increase our respect for the inexhaustible fertility of Mozart's genius, no less than for the tirelessness of his search for perfection.

15

Mozart and the Organ

FROM many contemporary accounts of Mozart, we know that his fame rested quite as much on his skill as a virtuoso of the 'fortepiano' as on his pre-eminence as a composer. He himself, however, as described in Chapter 16, regarded this instrument with mixed feelings, pride in his own technical accomplishment being offset by a strong distaste for the drudgery of giving lessons on it as a means of supplementing his uncertain income. Yet there was another instrument, the organ, for which his enthusiasm burned all his life with a steady flame. Considering how much the organ meant to Mozart, it is strange that its full significance should have been missed by his biographers, for his connexion with it is well worth recording in detail, if only to restore the balance, and to show that his favour as an executant was not bestowed upon one instrument alone. As befitted the son of the author of the most famous violin method of his day, Mozart acquired proficiency on the violin, so that he was fully equal to playing his own youthful concertos in public. After leaving Salzburg he restricted his activity as a violinist to participation in string quartets, in which he also sometimes took the viola. But his predilection was undoubtedly for clavier and for organ. Our knowledge of Mozart's experience of the latter comes mainly from his own and his father's letters.

We know that Leopold began to give his son clavier lessons soon after he was four, and we may fairly assume that he introduced him to the organ not more than a year later. For during the family's second journey to Vienna in October 1762, when Wolfgang was nearly seven, we find him at Ipps, where he amazed some Franciscan monks by the way in which he

strummed on their organ. Barely a year later, in June 1763, at
the beginning of the third European journey, the coach convey-
ing Leopold Mozart and his two children broke down at
Wasserburg, about thirty miles from Munich. In order to while
away the time, he took his son to the church and at the organ
explained the use of the pedal. To everyone's astonishment the
child thrust away the stool and played standing up, working
manuals and pedals together, 'doing it all', the pious Leopold
wrote, 'as if he had been practising it for several months', and
added, 'this is a fresh act of God's grace, which many a one
receives only after much labour'. At Mainz in August the child
played in the church of the Holy Ghost, and so amazed everyone that the town magistrate ordered his name to be inscribed
on the instrument, with full particulars. This inscription was
taken away when the organ was later removed to the church of
the Jesuits.

There is no mention of organ-playing while the family was
in Paris, but in May 1764, after their arrival in London, the
'invincible Wolfgang' performed famously on King George
III's private instrument in St. James's Palace, and Leopold wrote
that his organ-playing was more esteemed than his clavier-
playing. In June Wolfgang played an organ concerto at a concert in Ranelagh Gardens in aid of the Lying-in Hospital, but
though the *Public Advertiser* announced that he would play
works of his own composition on the harpsichord and organ,
nothing written specially for the latter has been preserved from
this period. At the beginning of the return journey through the
Low Countries, Leopold records that his son played in the
church of the Bernardines at Ghent, and later in the cathedral
at Antwerp. This occurred sometime during September, and
on 26 February 1766 it was announced in the *Amsterdamsche
Courant*[1] that he would play on the organ capriccios of his own
composition. These have unfortunately not come down to us
(cf. p. 218). Three months later, Wolfgang performed for an

[1] The full announcement is quoted in Scheurleer's *Het Musikleven in Nederland* ('s Gravenhage, 1909), p. 327.

hour on the great organ at Haarlem, concerning which his father noted the interesting facts that it had sixty-eight stops, and was made entirely of pewter which resisted the damp climate better than wood.[1] Finally, at Bibernach, near Ulm, towards the end of October 1766, an organ competition took place between Mozart and another prodigy, twelve-year-old Sixtus Bachmann.[2]

During the fourth journey, on the way from Salzburg to Vienna in September 1767, Leopold took his son to the famous abbey of Melk. By this time Wolfgang appears to have developed a distinctive style of organ-playing, for his father says that here they purposely concealed their identity, in order to give the organist of the abbey a chance of guessing who the performer was. For the next three years we hear nothing of the boy's progress, until January 1770, when he stayed with his father at Roveredo on their way down to Italy. Here he played in the principal church (probably St. Mark's) before a great throng that had quickly assembled as soon as his presence in the town became known. Later in the year, on the way back from Rome to Bologna, they stopped at Città Castellana, about thirty-three miles north of the capital, and there Wolfgang played one Sunday after mass, presumably in the cathedral of Santa Maria. In March 1771 the church of San Giustino in Padua was the scene of another performance on an instrument described by Leopold as excellent.

In October 1772, while on his seventh and last journey with his father, the boy stopped at Innsbruck, whence they drove to the quaint old town of Hall, and tried the organ in the church of the Royal Convent. On this occasion they were escorted by Countess Lodron, for whose family Mozart soon afterwards wrote three of his most charming works, the Concerto for Three Claviers and the Divertimenti in F and B flat (K. 247 and 287). Most probably the number of European towns in which

[1] An illustration of this fine instrument is given in Scheurleer, op. cit., p. 393.
[2] The sole authority for this incident is Nissen, p. 122. Unfortunately no details are given.

Mozart tested his youthful powers as an organist actually exceeds those so far enumerated. This is suggested by some entries in Leopold Mozart's own diary of his travels with his children.[1] Among the names of people noted as being important in Calais, Dunkirk, Bergues, Ulm, and Naples are those of organists of whom we now unfortunately know nothing. Yet Leopold would hardly have entered their names without some practical recollection.

Most of Mozart's playing hitherto had been avowedly in the nature of diversion or done with the aim of extending his own reputation and acquaintance. In October 1778 he toyed with the idea of trying for an appointment in Nancy, and his father, urging him to think and act realistically, wrote: 'As I feel sure that in such an important town you will have called on some Kapellmeister, conductor, or organist and tried one of the organs, I am hoping you will have made acquaintances. . . . You will remember that on our travels long ago we used to do this and at least went to see the organs in the churches.'

For Mozart, to see an organ was only a preliminary to playing on it, and with full manhood this erstwhile habit had changed into something approaching a passion. Moreover, this instrument became closely identified with his search for a lucrative post away from Salzburg, and his style of playing undoubtedly reflected his musical development in other fields, notably the all-important mastery of fugal forms. At Augsburg in October 1777 Mozart declared to Stein, the famous maker of organs and 'fortepianos': 'In my eyes and ears the organ is the king of instruments.' Stein, however, could not understand how a great clavier-player could have such a passion for an instrument that was deficient in sweetness, variety, and delicacy of expression and was amazed by the style in which Mozart improvised and played a fugue on one of his instruments. He found the pedal strange, because, as he wrote to his father, 'it was not divided. It started with C, and then D and E followed in the same row. But with us D and E are above, as E and F are here. But I soon got the hang of it.'

Shortly afterwards he astonished the monks in the monastery of the Holy Cross by the smoothness of his fugal execution both on the organ and on the clavichord which he says he played in the style of an organ. Writing from Mannheim in November he severely criticized the two court organists, Nicolaus Bayer and Anton Marxfelder. Leopold Mozart, too, was aware of their incompetence, for he described them as 'wretched' later in the same month when he wrote urging his son to try to show the Elector how proficient he was as an organist in order to secure an appointment. Although his purpose was now mainly serious, Mozart still gave way occasionally to his sense of humour, as on 13 November when just for fun he tried the organ during a service in the Elector's chapel,[1] beginning during the Kyrie and startling everyone (including Holzbauer) by playing a cadenza when the priest had finished intoning the Gloria. At the end of the service he caused further surprise by developing the theme of the Sanctus as a fugue. He had yet to learn that correct behaviour was a social as well as a musical asset, and it is not altogether surprising that he was not offered the post of court organist at Mannheim.

He remained in this city for some time, and in December 1777 performed on the new instrument in the Lutheran church, to an audience including all the Kapellmeisters then in the city, among them Holzbauer and Cannabich. His famous contemporary, the Abbé Vogler, played on the same occasion, but as an organist he only confirmed the low opinion that Mozart had of him in all branches of music. A few days after this Mozart went to the Reformed church, and played there for a full hour and a half, putting his whole heart into it, as he wrote to his father. In this same letter he said he was looking forward to performing again in the Lutheran church: he regarded his

---

[1] Here, as on Stein's instrument, he found the arrangement of the pedals unfamiliar, but he gave no details.

former visit as a mere preliminary to testing the full powers of the instrument, which he thought excellent both as a whole and in individual stops. Early in 1778 the post of organist at the Salzburg court fell vacant, but Mozart, despite hints from his father, was hardly anxious to apply for it.

While in Paris in May he was offered the position of organist at Versailles with a salary of about £90 a year. At first he considered this idea favourably, because only six months of the year were actually to be spent at Versailles. His father urged him strongly to accept, in view both of the security and the important social contacts and opportunities such an appointment entailed. But in July, shortly before the death of his mother, Mozart's brief enthusiasm faded, and he wrote to his father rejecting the idea with scorn, professedly on the advice of Baron Grimm. The truth was that at this time he did not really know what kind of a post he wanted, and the organ attracted him mainly as a sublime instrument for the casual making of music. His devotion to it as such was not a whit quenched by his prolonged failure to secure a good appointment anywhere. Even while proceeding slowly and reluctantly homewards he played in public in Strasbourg on two of Silbermann's best organs, those in the Thomaskirche and the Neukirche.

Thus in January 1779 Mozart found himself back in uncouth Salzburg, with the court appointment of Konzertmeister and organist. Such was the anti-climax to his two years of travel and lost opportunities. It must have been a bitter pill for him who had written scornfully from Paris, the most brilliant capital of Europe, 'and then, to be an organist!' It appears from a letter of his father's dated 31 December 1778 that a provisional certificate of appointment had been issued by the archbishop in September of that year, so we may guess that Mozart had been fearing the worst for some time. Moreover, when in a letter of 18 December he recommended to his father J. M. Demmler, the organist of Augsburg Cathedral, as a man who would benefit by an appointment in Salzburg, it looks as if he was trying to suggest a substitute for himself. A player from such an important place as Augsburg Cathedral would hardly have been satisfied with anything less than the best Salzburg could offer—a post in the archbishop's court. The actual certificate of Mozart's appointment was dated 17 January 1779[1] and it carried a salary of £45.

It is worth noting that Leopold Mozart, in a letter to his son written in June 1778, reported a conversation he had had with Countess Lodron, the archbishop's sister, on the duties of the court organist. The countess pointed out that as Mozart had resigned from the prince's service he could not be appointed Kapellmeister but he could, she went on, 'be appointed Konzertmeister and organist at fifty gulden a month', i.e. at £60 a year. As Leopold does not correct the statement, possibly both he and his son thought that the salary might be higher than it proved in the event.

During the rest of Mozart's life in Salzburg, and indeed during all his years in Vienna, we know but little of his activity as an organist. In October 1783, when he was on his way to Linz, we find him, true to his juvenile habit, entering the church at Lambach. He arrived just in time to accompany the Agnus Dei on the organ, and he played again later in the day. Apart from one important episode at Prague in 1787, which can best be described separately below, the curtain falls again, nor is it lifted until April 1789 when he visited Dresden. From there he wrote to his wife describing how he met Johann Hässler, a famous organist of Erfurt, and a pupil of J. C. Kittel, who had learned from Bach. Mozart played himself, he does not say specifically in what church, and was very critical of Hässler's style, for he thought he had simply absorbed Bach's harmony and modulations, but lacked the foundations of a solid technique. From Dresden Mozart went to Leipzig, where he threw himself into varied music-making with much of his old zest. On page 132 of Reichardt's *Berlinische Musikalische Zeitung* for 1805 there is a most interesting account by an anonymous ear-

---

[1] It is given in full by Abert, vol. ii, p. 906.

witness of his visit to the famous Thomaskirche, which deserves to be quoted in full:

On April 22[1789] he played the organ of the Thomaskirche, without previous notice and gratuitously. He played very finely for an hour to a large audience. The then organist, Görner,[1] and the cantor, Doles, sat near him and pulled the stops. I saw him clearly; a young, well-dressed man of middle height. Doles was quite delighted with the performance and declared that his old master, Sebastian Bach, had risen again. Mozart brought to bear all the arts of harmony with the greatest ease and discrimination, and improvised magnificently on the chorale 'Jesu meine Zuversicht'.

In the year 1790, when Mozart's fortunes and spirits were at their lowest ebb, we may conjecture that his interest in the organ remained constant, though our knowledge is still regrettably scanty. One piece of information comes from C. F. Pohl's article in *Grove* (fifth edition) on F. X. Chrismann, an Austrian organ-builder: 'Mozart and Albrechtsberger were present in 1790 at the opening of an organ built by Chrismann in the church of Schottenfeld, one of the suburbs of Vienna, and both pronounced it the best organ in Vienna.' This incident (probably taken from one of the Viennese newspapers, in his knowledge of which Pohl was almost unrivalled) does not appear to be mentioned anywhere else, and is of value as it helps to fill the gap in the time before Mozart set out on his journey to Germany in October.

From the various anecdotes about these months Jahn has preserved two that are worthy of mention here. The first tells of a visit to the church of St. Katharine in Frankfurt:

One Sunday, after service, Mozart came into the choir at St. Katharine's and begged the old organist to allow him to play something. He seated himself on the stool, and gave rein to his fancy, when the organist suddenly pushed him off the stool in the rudest manner and said to the pupil standing by: 'Mark that last modulation which Herr Mozart made: how can he profess to be a musician, and commit such grave offences against correct composition?'

[1] Identified by Abert with J. G. Görner (1697–1778). Perhaps the wrong name was given by Reichardt.

(Here, incidentally, is another link in the chain of evidence which shows how far Mozart's ideas were above the heads of the ordinary run of professional musicians.) The second anecdote tells how he visited Mannheim on his way home, and played in the church of the Trinity; this is of special interest as having been his last connexion with the town in which he had lingered so long thirteen years before.

Such, then, is the extent of our knowledge of Mozart's active connexion with the organ. It is not, perhaps, too much to say that it held an attraction for him which the clavier never exercised, for plainly he was drawn towards it at every possible opportunity. From the accounts in his own letters, and from an understanding of his musical temperament, we can hazard a reconstruction of his style as an organist. Besides being a clear and vigorous exponent of fugues (using, however, deliberate tempi), Mozart undoubtedly excelled in the art of extemporization, for which the peculiar qualities of the organ offered immense scope. The power of the instrument must have stimulated his imagination to a degree that the 'fortepiano' could never have done, although he was also renowned as an extemporizer thereon. We may be sure that he was judicious in his registrations, for while he loved a volume of sound, it had to be tempered with precision and clarity.

Fortunately, we can supplement this somewhat slender reconstruction from a valuable document which unaccountably escaped the notice of Abert and does not appear to have been translated into English hitherto. This is a letter[1] which was found among the papers of Franz Niemetschek, Mozart's first biographer, among the material he had collected for a second edition of his work. It was written to Niemetschek in 1818 by Norbert Lehmann, choirmaster of the Strahof church of the Premonstratensians in Prague, and describes Mozart's playing in that church during his visit to the city in the autumn of 1787. The relevant part of it runs as follows:

He took his seat on the stool, and for nearly four minutes played masterly chords on the full organ, thus making it clear to every

---

[1] It was first published by A. Ebert in *Die Musik* for 1910.

knowledgeable hearer that he was no ordinary organist. Next, he wished to play on the manual without swell or choir. All four reed stops were too overpowering for him. In addition to the usual pedal he chose the 8-ft. trombone without mixture. Then he began a four-part fugue which was all the more difficult to develop because it and its continuation consisted of nothing but mordants which are extraordinarily hard to bring out on an organ with such a heavy action. But in both his left hand and his right the fourth and fifth fingers were as strong as the first (the thumb) second and third, and everyone was amazed at this. I devoted my whole attention to the development of the theme, and should have been in a position to note this down right to the end. But then Father Lohelius came into the choir, and disturbed me so much with his questions that I lost the thread just when I needed to give my closest attention. Mozart had worked up with the pedals and bass from G minor so high that he could continue in B minor, but then Father Lohelius distracted me so much that I could not tell how he passed so quickly into E flat. Now wishing to end in this key, he held a pedal-point. Keeping B flat as the fifth on the pedals, he ran with both hands up to the two highest octaves of the keyboard, and there kept so many notes going with a plethora of ligatures and resolutions, that he played in B minor as if it were F sharp he was sustaining on the pedal. Partly because of the mordants, partly because of the middle voices, all his fingers were being used so that not one could rest for a moment. This was done in order that nothing should be heard from the pedals. Scarcely had I replied to Father Lohelius's first question when a spate of others had to be answered. He said: 'Brother'—'What is it?' —'He's holding a B flat'—'Yes, he is'—'He wants to get into E flat' —'Certainly, he does'—'But now he's playing in B'—'Yes, I know' —'How can that sound right?'—'Well, it does!' (because, in fact, so many notes in the higher octaves made such a terrible noise that even all the four reeds would not have been heard).

The ten fingers hopped about as busily in those two octaves as ants scurry around when their nest is destroyed. Through those many questions I lost the best and most artistic passages in which Mozart evinced his skill in composition. He then developed the theme of a fugue from Brixi's Requiem in C minor[1] so artistically

---

[1] Four composers of this name were working in Prague at this time. This Requiem may be one of the five composed, according to *Grove*, by F. X. Brixi (1732-71).

that the hearers stood petrified. He gave every part its full effect when it repeated the theme in a different key, and this was specially admirable in the tenor. If the bass was too low, and the tenor could not be compassed with the left hand, the right had to help it out with some notes and fingers.

Interruptions notwithstanding, Lehmann managed to write down a large part of what Mozart played, and this fugue has been printed in Ebert's article in *Die Musik*.

It is unfortunate that the quality of Mozart's compositions for the organ proper bear little or no relation to his fame as an executant. His sonatas for organ, strings, and bass, intended to be played during Mass between the Epistle and the Gospel were all composed before 1780, thus dating from the period of his service at Salzburg, the effect of whose uninspiring atmosphere is sadly evident in lack of power and originality. Even the best of these sonatas, the last two, both in C major (K. 329, with added woodwind, brass, and drums, and K. 336) are only second-rate Mozart. It has recently been suggested[1] that the interesting Capriccio in C (K. 395) may have been written not for the clavier but for the organ.

Discussion of the sonatas is hardly called for here because there is little to be added to the comprehensive study written by Orlando A. Mansfield.[2] These sonatas differ totally in style, purpose, and medium from the three 'organ' works of 1790 and 1791—two so-called fantasias and a rondo—which, though often played in arrangement on a modern organ, were composed for a small mechanical instrument (cf. Chapter 12). It is worth mentioning that Mozart's last reference to the organ proper is found in a letter of 3 October 1790, from which the relevant passage is quoted on p. 205.

The instruments on which the composer himself played offer a multifarious topic, on which very little has been written in

---

[1] H. Dennerlein, *Der unbekannte Mozart* (Leipzig, 1951), pp. 92–95.

[2] 'Mozart's Organ Sonatas', *MQ*, Oct. 1922. These works are also briefly discussed by Einstein in *Mozart*, pp. 267, 268, 332, 333: cf. also his article 'Two Missing Sonatas by Mozart', *ML*, Jan. 1940.

English.[1] Indeed, even in continental Mozart literature, the only considerable study appears to be one by Joseph Wörsching entitled 'Wolfgang Amadeus Mozart und die Orgel'.[2] Wörsching's researches have revealed that over a dozen of the organs on which Mozart played still survive in a form which is substantially that of his time. Some have been rebuilt, but the majority preserve manuals, pedals, and stops much as they were in the latter part of the eighteenth century. The three following typical specifications show clearly that Mozart had at his disposal, both for accompaniment of services and for extemporization, instruments of considerable power and tonal variety, a fact which modern performers might bear in mind.

The first is of the organ in the church of St. Peter, Salzburg, which was rebuilt in 1762–3.

Hauptmanual	*Rückpositif*	*Pedal*
Principal 8	Coppel 8	Grossbass 16
Coppel 8	Principal 4	Subbass 16
Octav 4	Flöte 4	Gambenbass 16
Flöte 4	Octav 2	Principal 8
Quinte 3	Quinte $1\frac{1}{2}$	Octav 4
Octav 2	Zimbel $1\frac{1}{2}$ (iv)	Octav 2
Kornett 4		Mixtur 4 (iv)
Mixtur 2 (viii)		Posaune 8
Zimbel 1 (iv)		

The second specification is of the great organ in the cathedral at Salzburg, which was built in 1702–3, enlarged four years later, and again in 1718. Some small changes were made in 1753.

---

[1] A series of articles on Austrian organs by Andrew Freeman appeared in *The Organ* from July 1932 to Apr. 1939, with a final article in Oct. 1946. That in the issue for Jan. 1937 dealt with 'Mozart Organs in Salzburg'.

[2] In *Augsburger Mozartbuch*, ed. H. F. Deininger (Augsburg, 1942–3): this volume formed Bd. 55/56 of the *Zeitschrift des historischen Vereins für Schwaben*. Wörsching's facts appear to be generally trustworthy, but it must be pointed out that he quotes as authentic an account of Mozart's organ-playing at Dresden given in the notorious letter to 'Baron von P.' of which the falsity was forcibly argued by Jahn as long ago as 1858 (in Appendix 21, vol. iii, of his first edition). Although Jahn's conclusions have been generally accepted by responsible critics, one may be permitted to wonder what was the original point of writing a fictitious account of an organ performance by Mozart, and whether this part of the letter may not possibly have had some basis in fact.

Hauptwerk	*Nebenmanual*
Prästant 8	Gamba (Holzprincipal?) 8
Viola 8	Coppel 8
Salicional 8	Principal 4
Quintaden 8	Octav 4
Nachthorn 8	Quint 3
Fleten 4	Waldfleten 2
Rohrfleten 4	Mixtur $1\frac{1}{2}$
Quint 3	Harpa 8 (1706, 16)
Sedecima 2	
Rauschwerk 2 (viii)	
Superoctav 2 (viii)	
Horn Sesquialtra $1\frac{3}{4}$ (iv)	
Cymbal 1 (iv)	

3. *Manual* (1706)	*Pedal*
Principal 8	Der grosse Agges/Infrabass 32
Flauten 4	Bourdon 16 (Zinn)
Flett duss 4 (36 Töne)	Contrabass 16 (ii)
Piffara 4	Gambabass 16
Flaschalet 2	Principalbass 8
Swegl 2	Octav 4
Cornetti 2 (ii)	Suboctav 4
Scarpa 4 (25 Töne)	Rauschwerk 8 (x)
Schalmei/Obona 4 (25 Töne)	Mixtur 3
Fagott 8 (22 Töne)	Bombardon 16 (Zinn)
Trombona 8 (22 Töne)	Sordunen 8 (ii)
Posaun 8 (22 Töne)	

Sonstiges

Heerpauken	Voglsang
Sperrventile	12 Bälge

The third specification is of the Barfüsser organ in Augsburg, which was built in 1755–7 by Stein, under the influence of Silbermann:

Hauptwerk	*Oberwerk*
Bourdon 16	Gamba 8
Principal 8	Waldflöte 8
Quintatön 8	Coppel 8
Viola 8	Echo douce 8

Coppel 8
Nazard 6
Octav 4
Hohlflöte 4
Spitzflöte 4
Quinte 3
Superoctav 2
Sesquialtera (iii)
   (replaced, *c.* 1760, by Grand
   Cornett (v))
Mixtur crescendo (iv–viii)
Cimbel (iii)
Trompete Diskant 8
Trompete Bass 8
Clarinette 4

Flaut. trav. 8
Octav 8
Spitzflöte 4
Superoctava 2
Flageolet 1
Mixtur crescendo (iii–v)
Krummhorn 8
Carillon (not given in Stein's
   specification-book)

Brustwerk

Never completed. Provision
   was made for '6 special
   stops suited for "affekt"
   playing'.

Pedal

Principalbass 16
Violon 16
Bourdon 16 (according to the
   specification-book)
Violoncello 8
Hohlflötenbass 4
Bombarde 16
Fagottbass 8
Zinkbass 2

For nearly thirty years Mozart found in 'the king of instruments' an intermittent centre of interest, without which his musical career might have been even more erratic than it was, and his sum of happiness certainly less. His instinctive repugnance to building his life round a permanent appointment as an organist was surely well founded, and the sacrifice of the dubious blessings of service in security was not without compensation. It ensured him freedom of movement in which he could build up a reputation as an executant, and combine this with a cosmopolitan experience of organs to a degree quite unapproached by any great musician in his own era, and scarcely equalled before or since.

16

The Clavier in Mozart's Life

THERE were, so far as is known, only four instruments on which Mozart distinguished himself as a performer. In boyhood and adolescence his competence as a violinist won eulogies from a perhaps rather uncritical father and from other contemporaries. But after finally leaving Salzburg in 1781 he gave up the violin almost entirely in favour of the viola which he played, however, only in chamber music. On the organ, it is no exaggeration to say that his reputation was European, for, as the previous chapter shows, he never lost an opportunity of playing on famous or unfamiliar instruments wherever he travelled. But in continuous and decisive influence, organ, violin, and viola were far exceeded by the clavier, which really dominated his whole career. Some interesting questions suggest themselves. What kind of an instrument was it that Mozart played? How far was it related to his theory of performance, and how far did his own playing exemplify this? What was his attitude to teaching, and how remunerative was it? What part did playing have in his social life? Although most of the facts from which some answer can be given to these different but closely connected questions are by no means unknown, they are widely scattered and do not appear to have been correlated anywhere in detail.

At the outset, let us try to define clavier, which has won general acceptance as a convenient term to cover the three keyboard instruments used by Mozart at different stages of his career—the clavichord, harpsichord, and 'fortepiano'. For which of these it was that he wrote his many works with keyboard-solo, in chamber music or in concertos, is a complicated problem to which, as a whole, there is no absolutely definite answer. It need not be discussed here, as there is an excellent article by Nathan Broder, 'Mozart and the Clavier',[1] in which all the evidence is presented and weighed. Broder's conclusions are that Mozart did not compose specifically for the clavichord, and that his keyboard works written before 1782 were, with a few possible exceptions, for the harpsichord, those after that date for the 'fortepiano', as we may call it for the purpose of this chapter. All three instruments were available in the Mozart household and he went on playing the clavichord in private right up to 1789. But there is nothing to suggest that he continued to play the harpsichord once the 'fortepiano' had become generally available, for the latter suited perfectly the needs of his rapidly evolving style of playing and composing.

In Salzburg, which was musically unprogressive, the 'fortepiano' was slow to be introduced, but on his travels Mozart had met it in Mannheim as early as 1777. His enthusiastic account, written in a letter of 17 October of that year, must be quoted in full:

This time I shall begin at once with Stein's pianofortes. Before I had seen any of his make, Späth's claviers had always been my favourites. But now I much prefer Stein's for they damp ever so much better than the Regensburg instruments. When I strike hard, I can keep my finger on the note or raise it, but the sound ceases the moment I have produced it. In whatever way I touch the keys, the tone is always even. It never jars, it is never stronger or weaker or entirely absent; in a word, it is always even. It is true that he does not sell a pianoforte of this kind for less than three hundred gulden, but the trouble and the labour which Stein puts into the making of it cannot be paid for. His instruments have this special advantage over others that they are made with escape action. Only one maker in a hundred bothers about this. But without an escapement it is impossible to avoid jangling and vibration after the note is struck. When you touch the keys, the hammers fall back again the moment after they have struck the strings, whether you hold down the keys or release them. He himself told me that when he has finished making one of these claviers, he sits down to it and tries all

kinds of passages, runs and jumps, and he polishes and works away
at it until it can do anything. For he labours solely in the interest
of music and not for his own profit: otherwise he would soon finish
his work. He often says: 'If I were not myself such a passionate lover
of music, and had not myself some slight skill on the clavier, I
should certainly long ago have lost patience with my work. But I do
like an instrument which never lets the player down and which is
durable.' And his claviers certainly do last. He guarantees that the
sounding-board will neither break nor split. When he has finished
making one for a clavier, he places it in the open air, exposing it to
rain, snow, the heat of the sun and all the devils in order that it may
crack. Then he inserts wedges and glues them in to make the instrument very strong and firm. He is delighted when it cracks, for he can
then be sure that nothing more can happen to it. Indeed he often
cuts into it himself and then glues it together again and strengthens
it in this way.

What, then, was the appearance and nature of this instrument,
and how was it specially suitable for Mozart's music?[1] The
Flügelklavier, as it is generally known on the Continent, from
its graceful winglike shape, had a compass of five or five-and-
a-half octaves, and was about seven feet in length. So light was
the action that the force needed to depress the keys was only
about one-quarter of that on the modern pianoforte. The strings
were mostly of thin steel wire, those of the bass often of brass,
being barely half as thick as those in the top octave of the
modern 'grand'. The hammers were covered in thin wash-
leather, and their swift contact and rebound from the strings
produced a clear, singing tone, sonorous and vibrant in the bass
and silvery in the middle and upper octaves. The natural quality

[1] Technical and historical data are given in Hans Brunner's *Das Klavierklangideal Mozarts und die Klaviere seiner Zeit* (Augsburg, 1933), and in Eva Hertz's *Johann Andreas Stein* (Wolfenbüttel, 1937). Some of Brunner's conclusions were disputed in an article by Rudolf Steglich, 'Studien an Mozarts Hammerflügel', in the *Neues Mozart Jahrbuch* for 1941, in which volume also Gottfried von Franz wrote on 'Mozarts Klavierbauer Anton Walter'. Cf. also R. M. Haas, 'Ein neuer Walterflügel' in his *Bach und Mozart in Wien* (Wien, 1951), pp. 35-44, and the list of makers on p. 49; Victor Luithlen, 'Klaviere von A. Walter', in *Festschrift für Müller von Asow* (Berlin, 1942). An early nineteenth-century account of the instrument is given in an anonymous pamphlet *Kurze Bemerkungen über das Spielen, Stimmen und Erhalten der Fortepianos* (Regensburg, 1837), copy in BM (Hirsch 1516).

of the sound was enhanced by the whole instrument being constructed of wood. Apart from Stein, the maker most favoured by Mozart was Anton Walter of Vienna, one of whose instruments he acquired at some time, according to Broder, between 1782 and 1784. (It is now preserved and used in the Mozarteum in Salzburg.) The principal contemporary makers in England were Stodart, Clementi, and Broadwood. While there were considerable differences in constructional principles between these and the Continental makers, and hence in quality, their general effect was much the same. All were as perfect of their kind, musically and technically, as harpsichords by Ruckers, Tschudi, or Kirkman.

From 1785 onwards Mozart regularly used a pedal-board to reinforce the volume of his instrument, both for concert and teaching purposes. The evidence for this, though scanty, is quite conclusive, and so important that it is extraordinary that it should apparently have escaped the notice of English writers on the history of the 'fortepiano', and on Mozart as an executant. On 12 March 1785 Leopold wrote to his daughter: 'He has had a large fortepiano pedal made, which is under the instrument and is about two feet longer and extremely heavy. It is taken to the Mehlgrube every Friday and has also been taken to Count Zichy's and to Prince Kaunitz's.' In 1790 the presence of the pedal board was noticed by Joseph Frank, when taking lessons from Mozart (cf. p. 256). We can form a clear picture of the nature of the attachment from an article published in 1806.[1] The salient passages run as follows:

The pedal is built like the fortepiano, with similar hammers, dampers, etc., but the keys are much enlarged and so disposed that they can be played with the feet. The pedal can be placed under any instrument so that the player can easily use both together. Generally

---

[1] *AMZ*, vol. ix, 1806–7, cols. 565–70. Quoted by G. Kinsky in 'Mozart-Instrumente', *Acta musicologica*, vol. xii, 1940, pp. 12, 13. A misleading and inaccurate account of the matter is given by Marcia Davenport, *Mozart* (New York, 1932), p. 388 (London, 1933), p. 315. Bory, *La Vie et l'œuvre de W.-A. Mozart par l'image* (Geneva, 1948), p. 128, reproduces a poster of 10 Mar. 1785, announcing a concert at which Mozart would use a 'forte-piano' with a pedal 'beym Phantasieren'.

it comprises about only 2 octaves, from lowest C up to middle C, but in the so-called 16-foot tone, i.e. an octave deeper than our keyboard instruments . . . obviously a skilful player can, with the help of the pedal, accomplish much that is otherwise impossible. Many compositions, otherwise only playable with the accompaniment of another instrument, can easily be arranged so that by means of the pedal the accompanying instrument can be dispensed with.

A specimen of the instrument, dating from a little after Mozart's time, is preserved in Salzburg.[1]

Plainly this pedal attachment had many uses. It could be used for increasing volume, by simple doubling of the lower or middle notes of any passage and it could serve to add harmonic richness, tonal variety, antiphonal or contrapuntal effects. With its aid the 'fortepiano' could be used for practising organ works with a pedal part, just as the pedal clavichord had been for generations. (How long into the nineteenth century the pedal remained generally in favour does not appear to be known, but that it never died out is proved by the fact that Schumann, Gounod, and Massenet composed for it.) We may be certain that Mozart used his skill as an organist to obtain the best possible effects from his massive pedal. Its power is a factor which should be taken into account by modern attempts to recapture the elusive tonal values of this period, possibly by the use of electrical amplification.

Thus, the distinctive qualities of the 'fortepiano' emphasize its right to be restored to its proper status as a concert instrument, ideal for the performance of the keyboard music of Mozart, of Haydn, and of Beethoven up to about his Fourth Concerto, op. 58, of 1805. The 'fortepianos' of Stein and Walter are in regular concert use in Salzburg, Vienna, Munich, and other south German towns, and those by Chickering and the early American firms are in demand in the United States. (The Mozart concerto in G major, K. 453, has been recorded on a Nixa record by

[1] *Alte Musik-Instrumente in Museum Carolino-Augusteum, Salzburg.* Führer . . . von Karl Geiringer, 1932, p. 17, no. 70. Mozart's own instrument, 'Fortepiano mit Pedal', as it is described in the inventory of his effects, was valued after his death at 80 florins. See Schurig, *Konstanze Mozart* (Dresden, 1922), p. 153.

Ralph Kirkpatrick, using a Viennese-type 'fortepiano', made by John Challis, an American maker.) Admittedly original German specimens are rare in England,[1] but why should not their English counterparts be given a fair trial? It is quite illogical to revive the harpsichord for Bach and Handel, yet to deny Mozart and his near contemporaries their rightful instrument. The modern iron-framed grand pianoforte can no more approach the tonal qualities of the 'fortepiano' than those of the harpsichord. Only when the 'fortepiano' is revived for concert use as an alternative shall we be able to appreciate the main principles of keyboard technique as Mozart understood them and embodied them in his own playing. It is especially worth noting that the veiled *una corda* effect, discreetly used, gave a range and variety of expression unattainable with the soft pedal of the modern instrument. In concertos particularly, a revival of the 'fortepiano' would allow a substantial reduction in the number of strings needed, thus giving the wind and brass a more brilliant prominence, and restoring something of Mozart's ideals of blend and contrast which have too long been forgotten by performers.

His letters contain a number of passages giving valuable information about the keyboard playing of others, and, largely by inference, about his own style and teaching.[2] A description of the playing of Nanette Stein, a child prodigy of Augsburg, deserves quotation from a letter of 23 October 1777:

> Anyone who sees and hears her play and can keep from laughing, must, like her father, be made of stone. For instead of sitting in the middle of the clavier, she sits right up opposite the treble, as it gives

---

[1] No definitely identifiable 'fortepiano' by Walter and only one by Stein have been recorded on this side of the Channel. The latter belongs to C. F. Colt, and was heard at a paper read to the Royal Musical Association on 'The Classical Grand Pianoforte, 1780–1820', by Hugh Gough, in 1951: cf. also his article 'The Classical Forte-Piano', *Music*, April 1953. Gough is of the opinion that the Viennese 'fortepiano' illustrated in Philip James's *Early Keyboard Instruments* (London, 1930), pl. lxi, from the Rushworth and Dreaper Collection, Liverpool, is not a Stein, but may possibly be a Walter. Gough has constructed, on classical principles, a 'fortepiano' which has been used in concert performance.

[2] See also an informative article by John F. Russell, 'Mozart and the Pianoforte', *MR*, vol. i, no. 3, Aug. 1940.

her more chance of flopping about and making grimaces. She rolls her eyes and smirks. When a passage is repeated, she plays it more slowly the second time. If it has to be played a third time, then she plays it even more slowly. When a passage is being played, the arm must be raised as high as possible, and according as the notes in the passage are stressed, the arm, not the fingers, must do this, and that too with great emphasis in a heavy and clumsy manner. But the best joke of all is that when she comes to a passage which ought to flow like oil and which necessitates a change of finger, she does not bother her head about it, but when the moment arrives, she just leaves out the notes, raises her hand and starts off again quite comfortably—a method by which she is much more likely to strike a wrong note, which often produces a curious effect. I am simply writing this in order to give Papa some idea of clavier-playing and clavier-teaching, so that he may derive some profit from it later on. Herr Stein is quite crazy about his daughter, who is eight and a half and who now learns everything by heart. She may succeed, for she has great talent for music. But she will not make progress by this method—for she will never acquire great rapidity, since she definitely does all she can to make her hands heavy. Further, she will never acquire the most essential, the most difficult and the chief requisite in music, which is, time, because from her earliest years she has done her utmost not to play in time. Herr Stein and I discussed this point for two hours at least and I have almost converted him, for he now asks my advice on everything. He used to be quite crazy about Beecke; but now he sees and hears that I am the better player, that I do not make grimaces, and yet play with such expression, that, as he himself confesses, no one up to the present has been able to get such good results out of his pianofortes. Everyone is amazed that I can always keep strict time. What these people cannot grasp is that in tempo rubato in an Adagio, the left hand should go on playing in strict time.

Mozart's account of his teaching Rosa Cannabich at Mannheim contains the following interesting passages (letters of 14–16 November):

The Andante [of the sonata K. 309] will give us most trouble, for it is full of expression and must be played accurately and with the exact shades of forte and piano, precisely as they are marked. She is very smart and learns very easily. Her right hand is very good, but her left, unfortunately, is completely ruined. I can honestly say that I often feel quite sorry for her when I see her struggling, as she so often does, until she really gets quite out of breath, not from lack of skill but simply because she cannot help it, for she has got into the habit of doing what she does, as no one has ever shown her any other way. I have told her mother and I have told her too that if I were her regular teacher, I would lock up all her music, cover the keys with a handkerchief and make her practise, first with the right hand and then with the left, nothing but passages, trills, mordants and so forth, very slowly at first, until each hand should be thoroughly trained. I would then undertake to turn her into a first-rate clavierist.

Next year, 1778, Mozart had some severe strictures to pass on Vogler's playing in a letter of 17 January:

He took the first movement prestissimo—the Andante allegro and the Rondo even more prestissimo. He generally played the bass differently from the way it was written, inventing now and then quite another harmony and melody. Nothing else is possible at that pace, for the eyes cannot see the music nor the hands perform it. Well, what good is it?—that kind of sight-reading—and shitting—are all one to me. The listeners (I mean those who deserve the name) can only say that they have seen music and piano-playing. They hear, think and—feel as little during the performance as the player himself. Well, you may easily imagine that it was unendurable. At the same time, I could not bring myself to say to him, *Far too quick!* Besides, it is much easier to play a thing quickly than slowly: in difficult passages you can leave out a few notes without anyone noticing it. But is that beautiful music? In rapid playing the right and left hands can be changed without anyone seeing or hearing it; but is that beautiful? And wherein consists the art of playing prima vista? In this; in playing the piece in the time in which it ought to be played and in playing all the notes, appoggiaturas and so forth, exactly as they are written and with the appropriate expression and taste, so that you might suppose that the performer had composed it himself. Vogler's fingering too is wretched; his left thumb is just like that of the late Adlgasser and he does all the treble runs downwards with the thumb and first finger of his right hand.

Another contemporary of whom Mozart notoriously disapproved on technical grounds was Clementi. On 12 January 1782 he wrote:

Clementi plays well, so far as execution with the right hand goes. His greatest strength lies in his passages in thirds. Apart from this, he has not a kreutzer's worth of taste or feeling—in short he is simply a *mechanicus*.

Again, on 16 January, in almost the same words:

He is an excellent cembalo-player, but that is all. He has great facility with his right hand. His star passages are thirds. Apart from this, he has not a farthing's worth of taste or feeling: he is a mere *mechanicus*.

On 7 June 1783 he warned his sister against Clementi's sonatas:

Everyone who either hears them or plays them must feel that as compositions they are worthless. They contain no remarkable or striking passages except those in sixths and octaves. And I implore my sister not to practise these passages too much, so that she may not spoil her quiet, even touch and that her hand may not lose its natural lightness, flexibility, and smooth rapidity. For after all what is to be gained by it? Supposing that you do play sixths and octaves with the utmost velocity (which no one can accomplish, not even Clementi) you only produce an atrocious chopping effect and nothing else whatever. Clementi is a *ciarlatano*, like all Italians. He writes *Presto* over a sonata or even *Prestissimo* and *Alla breve*, and plays it himself *Allegro* in 4/4 time. I know this is the case, for I have heard him do so. What he really does well are his passages in thirds; but he sweated over them day and night in London. Apart from this, he can do nothing, absolutely nothing, for he has not the slightest expression or taste, still less, feeling.

About G. F. Richter, a successful contemporary, Mozart expressed himself thus on 28 April 1784:

He plays well so far as execution goes, but, as you will discover when you hear him, he is too rough and laboured and entirely devoid of taste and feeling. Otherwise he is the best fellow in the world and is not the slightest bit conceited. When I played to him he stared all the time at my fingers and kept on saying: 'Good God! How hard I work and sweat—and yet win no applause—and to you, my friend, it is all child's play.' 'Yes', I replied, 'I too had to work hard, so as not to have to work hard any longer.'

Although the evidence from all these criticisms is partly negative, it does enable us to form some idea of at least the theoretical basis of Mozart's own approach to the keyboard. We can also see, incidentally, something of his mental limitations, especially in regard to Clementi, whose advances in technique he failed to appreciate. Nor did Mozart realize how different was the touch of the shallow-bedded keys of the 'Viennese' action compared with the deeper, less responsive touch of the English 'fortepiano' to which Clementi was accustomed. When all is said, our exact knowledge of Mozart's playing is scanty. Accounts given by contemporaries are rather vague, and perhaps err on the side of adulation. But it seems fairly certain that though he may have been surpassed in technique by some of his contemporaries, such as Kozeluch and Sterkel, in depth, feeling, and imaginative power, he stood alone. There was, moreover, one aspect of Mozart's playing that earned him especial renown, his prodigious power of extemporization. When his imagination was roused, he was identified with his instrument to an extraordinary degree. Perhaps the most eloquent of many testimonies is to be found in Schichtegroll's *Nekrolog* of 1793:

> His whole countenance would change, his eye became calm and collected; emotion spoke from every movement of his muscles, and was communicated by a sort of intuitive sympathy to his audience.

To this may be added the following more factual but highly illuminating description preserved by Vincent Novello. It occurs in a passage of his diary which mentions his meetings with Viennese composers in 1829:

> He [Abbé Stadler] communicated to me the following curious anecdote, on my enquiring what were the most favourite pieces with Mozart when he was in private among his intimate friends. The Abbé said that he usually played *extemporaneously*, but that his imagination was so inexhaustible and at the same time his ideas were

so symmetrical and regularly treated that Albrechtsberger could not be persuaded but that they were regular pieces that he had studied beforehand. One evening when Mozart, the Abbé Stadler and Albrechtsberger were together, the latter asked Mozart to sit down to the instrument and play something. Mozart directly complied, but instead of taking a subject of his own he told Albrechtsberger to give him a theme. Albrechtsberger accordingly invented a subject on the spot and which he was quite certain that Mozart could not possibly have ever heard before; he also selected the most trivial features he could think of in order to put Mozart's ingenuity, invention, and creative power to the severest test.

This extraordinary genius immediately took the theme that had been given him thus unexpectedly and played for upwards of an hour upon it, treating it in all possible variety of forms of fugue, canon, from the most simple to the most elaborate counterpoint, until Albrechtsberger could hold out no longer, but exclaimed in transport: 'I am now perfectly convinced that your extemporaneous playing is really the thought of the moment, and that you fully deserve all the fame you have acquired for this wonderful talent.'[1]

It is most interesting to compare these passages with the following sentences taken from a description of him as a child of ten:

He was sometimes involuntarily attracted to his harpsichord as by a secret force, and drew from it sounds, which were the lively expression of the idea with which he had just been occupied. One might say that at these moments he is himself the instrument in the hands of music and one may imagine him as composed of strings harmoniously put together with such skill that it is impossible to touch one without all the others being also set in motion.[2]

Truly, the child was father to the man, whose chosen instrument offered such effortless intimacy of expression.

Mozart must have found it depressing that comparatively few pupils approached his own standards either in virtuosity or powers of expression. 'You happy man', he once remarked to Gyrowetz,[3] who was about to start on a journey to Italy; 'as for

---

[1] *A Mozart Pilgrimage*, pp. 167–8.
[2] Quoted in their full context, in Chapter 8, pp. 135–6.
[3] Gyrowetz, *Selbstbiographie*, 1848, p. 14.

me, I am off now to give a lesson to earn my bread.' While his attitude fluctuated in regard to the whole matter of keyboard performance and to the principle at stake in devoting so much time and energy to teaching, he seems ultimately to have accepted it as a necessary part of his life, and as one which was not without its compensations. 'Unless you wear yourself out', he wrote to his father from Paris on 31 July 1778, 'by taking a large number of pupils, you cannot make much money.' That some of them were extremely stupid may be inferred from several remarks in his letters, and we can only guess at the drudgery involved, of which there is a hint on a single sheet in Mozart's autograph (in the Fitzwilliam Museum, Cambridge, cf. p. 92) containing five-finger exercises. Nevertheless, he could take pains with a backward pupil and a good one caused him pride. On 9 June 1784 he wrote to his father: 'I am fetching Paisiello in my carriage, as I want him to hear both my pupil and my compositions.' This pupil was Barbara Ployer, for whom he had composed his Concertos in E flat (K. 449) and G (K. 453). Another girl in whose playing he delighted was Franziska von Jacquin, of whom he wrote on 14 January 1787: 'I have never yet had a pupil who was so diligent and who shewed so much zeal—and indeed I am looking forward to giving her lessons again according to my small ability.' We have a hint of the bond between himself and some of those he taught when we read in his father's letter of 19 November 1784, that, to celebrate his name-day, he 'gave a small musical party, at which his pupils performed'.

We may conjecture that Mozart was not an ideal teacher, owing to certain flaws in his character. He never suffered fools gladly, and in his earlier years, about the time of his stay in Paris, proved too lazy to apply himself to the business of instruction. Later, despite his spasmodic and harassed way of life, he made an effort to keep to a routine, although his irregular concert engagements and travels must have been a source of continual difficulty. In February 1782 it was his custom to teach from nine to one: exactly two years later he wrote to his father on 10 February: 'I spend the whole morning giving lessons, so I have only the evening to spare for my beloved task—composition.'

The fees which his teaching brought him are a matter of considerable interest. Occasionally, when in difficult circumstances, he taught for nothing except a return in kind. This happened at Mannheim in the winter of 1777 when he gave lessons to Thérèse Serrarius, a girl of fifteen, in order to secure free lodging, firewood, and light for himself and his mother. Earlier, during the same sojourn, Mozart wrote that he expected to be paid one *louis d'or* (= approximately £1) for each of two pupils, but he did not say how many lessons he was giving. At Vienna, on 16 June 1781, he wrote to Leopold that his terms were six ducats for twelve lessons. As a ducat was equivalent to about 9s., one lesson cost 4s. 6d. Apparently this was a high charge, for he also said that if he lowered his terms he could have more pupils. Soon, however, though the terms remained the same, his attitude hardened, for on 22 October 1781 he wrote: 'I compose until ten, when I give a lesson to Frau von Trattner, and at eleven to the Countess Rumbeck, each of whom pays me six ducats for twelve lessons and to whom I go every day, unless they put me off. I mean that, if I do not find her at home, I am at least to get my fee; but Frau Trattner is too economical for that.' This was confirmed in January 1782, for he then decided to alter the basis of his terms. He wrote on the 23rd: 'I have three pupils now, which brings me in eighteen ducats. I no longer charge for twelve lessons, but monthly. I learnt to my cost that my pupils often dropped out for weeks at a time; so now, whether they learn or not, each of them must pay me six ducats. I shall get several more on these terms, but I really need only one more, as four pupils are quite enough.'

Mozart's straits were so desperate by May 1790 that he wrote to his generous friend Puchberg on the 17th: 'I now have two pupils and should very much like to raise the number to eight. Do your best to spread the news that I am willing to give lessons.' We do not know what Mozart's fees were in the last months of his life, nor whether he charged his aristocratic pupils at a different rate from those drawn from his own circle. Nor have we any definite evidence as to the length of time for which he taught any one pupil. Our lack of precise information on these and other relevant points is due to the fact that almost the only source lies in casual remarks made in the course of irregular correspondence. But it is almost certain that he had altogether many more pupils than those whose names, barely a dozen in all, have been preserved.

Among the nobility, we hear several times of Countess Rumbeck between March 1781 and September 1782, and once of the Countesses Zichy and Countess Palfy. In October 1782 it seemed possible (cf. letters of the 5th and 12th) that Mozart might have become music-master to Princess Elizabeth of Württemberg, but in the end a nonentity named Georg Summer received the coveted post which carried a salary of 400 gulden (about £40) a year. Competition for such prizes as this was undoubtedly keen, so it was perhaps not without a touch of 'sour grapes' that Mozart wrote: 'You can easily understand that you cannot act as independently towards a pupil who is a princess as towards other ladies. If a princess does not feel inclined to take a lesson, why, you have the honour of waiting till she does', and added that although at that time he could have had as many pupils as he liked, he preferred to have only two, from whom he earned about the same as Summer's salary, while preserving some independence.

Within Mozart's own circle and on his own social level, his relation with his pupils were certainly easier. Besides Gottfried von Jacquin, his sister Franziska (mentioned above), and Barbara Ployer, he taught from 1781 onwards a girl named Josephine Aurnhammer, who was so gifted that he composed for her, and several times played with her, the Sonata K. 448 for two claviers.[1] Rosa Cannabich, Thérèse Serrarius, a Mlle Pierron

---

[1] According to the *Magazin der Musik*, 1787, vol. ii, p. 1274, she superintended Artaria's engraving of many of Mozart's sonatas and variations.

(mentioned only in a letter of 22 February 1778), all of Mannheim, and Nanette Stein of Augsburg were among his earlier pupils. For Thérèse von Trattner, wife of a well-known Viennese music publisher, Mozart had considerable regard. Her exceptional ability can be inferred from his dedication to her of the Sonata and Fantasia in C minor (K. 457, 475). He is said to have written to her two letters, now unfortunately lost, giving his views on music, and, we may surmise, on the performance of these pieces. F. J. Freystädter (1768–1841), a minor composer, and J. N. Hummel are the only two male pupils mentioned in the letters. The latter was an especial favourite. There is nothing to show that musicians such as Attwood, Eberl, and Süssmayr, who were Mozart's pupils in theory and composition, also took lessons in playing the 'fortepiano': while probable, it remains unproven though Anton Liste (1774–1832) may have done both from 1789 onwards.[1] Among non-musicians, there was Joseph Frank, a Viennese doctor who received twelve lessons in 1790. His account runs:

I found Mozart a little man with a large head and plump hands, and was somewhat coldly received by him. 'Now', said he, 'play me something.' I played a Fantasia of his own composition. 'Not bad', said he, to my great astonishment: 'but now listen to me play it.' It was a miracle! The clavier became another instrument under his hands. It was strengthened by a second clavier which served him as a pedal. Mozart then made some remarks as to the way in which I should perform the Fantasia. I was fortunate enough to understand him. 'Do you play any other pieces of my composition?' 'Yes', I answered: 'your Variations on the theme "Unser dummer Pöbel meint" [K. 455], and a Sonata with accompaniments for violin and violoncello.' 'Good, I will play you that piece; you will profit more by hearing me than playing them yourself.'[2]

Anyone as sociable as Mozart was bound to be in continual demand at informal and semi-private gatherings to provide entertainment at the keyboard. Of the many accounts of his

---

[1] Refardt, *Musik-Lexikon der Schweiz* (Zürich, 1928), p. 191.
[2] *Deutsches Museum* (Leipzig, 1854), vol. ii, p. 27.

feats, one of the less familiar deserves quotation. It is taken from Kelly:[1]

> He favoured the company by performing fantasias and capriccios on the piano-forte. His feeling, the rapidity of his fingers, the great execution and strength of his left hand particularly, and the apparent inspiration of his modulations, astounded me. . . . He was kind-hearted, and always ready to oblige; but so very particular, when he played, that if the slightest noise were made, he instantly left off.

Another sociable form of music to which Mozart was partial was the playing of four-hand duets. Here Kelly may be quoted again[2] about the sister of his venerable friend Padre Martini:

> When I was admitted to her conversaziones and musical parties, she was in the vale of years, yet still possessed the gaiety and vivacity of a girl, and was polite and affable to all. Mozart was an almost constant attendant at her parties, and I have heard him play duets on the piano-forte with her, of his own composition. She was a great favourite of his.

It is indeed probable that all Mozart's duets were composed with his own performance primarily in view, although we know, from a letter of 29 May 1787, that he recommended one of them, K. 521, to Franziska von Jacquin.

He also regularly performed with his sister, his partner from the time of their early travels together until much later. A correspondent of Burney's heard them play in Salzburg (prior to 1773), and recently a document has come to light in Augsburg showing that their partnership lasted until they were both adult. This is a letter of 10 March 1781[3] from a local dignitary named Ströbl, mentioning a visit (hitherto unknown) paid to Augsburg by Leopold Mozart with his son and daughter, who played on two 'fortepianos'. Later, the youthful Hummel provided Mozart with another partner. When visiting Mainz in 1790 Mozart took the opportunity of playing his F major Duet with

---

[1] Vol. i, pp. 222, 223.

[2] Vol. i, p. 249.

[3] Quoted by Richard Schaal, 'Neues zur Mozart Biographie', in *Acta Mozartiana* (Augsburg, 1954), Hft. i.

a gifted young local musician named P. C. Hoffmann[1] and also with Ignaz Beecke, an old acquaintance, who shared a performance of one of Mozart's own concertos, arranged for four hands.[2] Probably he had many other partners whose names are now lost. Duet-playing undoubtedly gave him much pleasure, which, from references in the letters, we may conjecture to have been fully equalled by participation in his many other chamber works which had a 'fortepiano' part.

In a letter already referred to, that of 7 February 1778, Mozart told his father that he regarded the keyboard as a sideline, 'though, thank God, a good one'. On 2 June 1781, he wrote: 'Vienna is certainly the land of the clavier.' Three years later, in March 1784, he sent his father a list of twenty-two concerts which he was giving between 26 February and 3 April inclusive. On 12 March 1785 Leopold Mozart wrote to his daughter: 'If only the concerts were over! It is impossible to describe the rush and bustle. Since my arrival your brother's fortepiano has been taken at least a dozen times to the theatre or to some other house.' This pace, while it lasted, was a killing one, and although the rate of concert-giving slackened somewhat in 1790 and 1791, there is no doubt that the intense strain of performing combined with teaching was one of the factors which weakened Mozart's constitution and made him more susceptible to illness when it came.

Yet it was impossible for him to have done otherwise. For the clavier was the lodestar to which he was drawn by the need to keep his self-respect, by legitimate ambition, and by dire need. He must have realized, however, well before the crisis of 1789 that the fluctuating amount he could earn by teaching and playing could never secure his livelihood. Furthermore, the amount he received from his various publishers was a mere drop in the ever-widening pool of debts, and of course he gained nothing from the pirated editions that had appeared all over

[1] G. von Schilling, *Encyclopädie der gesammten musikalischen Wissenschaften*, 1835–40, s.v. 'Hoffmann'. Cf. also, p. 15.
[2] Lipowsky, *Baierisches Musiklexikon* (Munich, 1811), p. 16.

Europe, and had spread his fame more widely than had his actual playing. Modern research has revealed the surprising fact that of all the editions of Mozart's works printed before his death as high a proportion as nearly one-third was of his clavier music.[1] Even among the larger disappointments and tragic ironies of his life, this adds emphasis to the sad fact that all the renown earned by prolonged exertions as teacher and virtuoso availed him so little in his struggle against poverty.

[1] Cf. the summary given on p. 9.

Appendix 1

A SUBSCRIPTION LIST TO *COSÌ FAN TUTTE*

ABOUT the year 1830 the Brunswick firm of Meyer published an edition of Mozart's opera *Così fan tutte* in vocal score. Its title reads: 'Così fan tutte. Weibertreue. Komische Oper in zwei Aufzügen von W. A. Mozart. Clavier-Auszug mit ital. u. deutsch. Texte.' No editor or arranger is mentioned. The music is printed in a rather undistinguished style from engraved plates. The two copies examined belong to the Hirsch Library[1] in the British Museum, and each contains a subscription list that is unusually long for this kind of edition. It runs to four pages and presents several features of interest.

It raises at the outset the question why an ordinary working edition of an opera originally composed in 1789 and published in twenty editions or more should have been circulated so widely in the German-speaking world. For this list contains the names of 274 subscribers who took, between them, 1,329 copies. Little is known of the number of copies which at this period comprised an edition of an engraved piece of music, so that it is hard to say with certainty whether many more copies of this Mozart opera were printed for the non-subscribing public. Since about 2,000 copies could be printed from well engraved plates without much loss of clarity, it seems likely that general sale was allowed for by a larger printing. But the actual reason for subscription remains obscure. It does not seem to be connected with any contemporary revival of the opera.

Of the 274 subscribers 122 are booksellers or publishers, thirty-six are music-sellers or publishers, and the remainder private persons. Besides covering most of the large towns in Germany the firm of Meyer obtained subscribers from places as far from Brunswick as Amsterdam, Bern, Lemberg, Warsaw, Copenhagen, Rotterdam, Riga, Vienna, and Prague. Of the booksellers, the heaviest subscriber was the Hamburg firm of Schuberth & Niemayer who took 105 copies. Cranz, of the same town, headed the German music-sellers with seventy-four, which was actually exceeded by the Copenhagen

[1] Pressmarks: M. 325, and IV. 1212.

firm Lose, who took eighty-four. Two other foreign music publishers, Berra of Prague (one of the first publishers of Lanner), and
Theune of Amsterdam, stand high with sixty-two and sixty-four
copies respectively.

Besides the large subscribers, some of the small are equally interesting for different reasons. The Warsaw firm of Brzezina (twenty
copies) was at this time associated with Chopin. Peters in Leipzig
only took six, presumably because they had enough Mozart on their
hands already. Probably for the same reason André of Offenbach
took only two. Haslinger of Vienna, where Mozart was by now
almost a drug on a market that was by 1830 more profitably
receptive to Beethoven and Schubert, took seven copies. The Dresden
firm of Meser, soon to be closely associated with Wagner, also
found seven copies enough: the same sufficed for Trautwein of
Berlin, who were shortly to be interested much more in Haydn than
in Mozart.

Among the names of private persons are found very few of the
aristocracy who were the chief source of support for musical subscription lists of the pre-Napoleonic era. This modest Mozart edition
found support from one baron, one count, and one countess, all
in Grätz, but from no other people of quality. On the other hand,
the new middle and professional classes are well represented, especially the musical world, singers, teachers, and choirmasters. In
Brunswick the subscribers include two ordinands, one commis-
sioner of police, and one clergyman: in Hildesheim, two leather-
manufacturers; in Driberg, the solitary subscriber is an inspector
of wells! There is no doubt that the study of more lists of this period
would throw valuable light not only on the distribution of music
through trade-channels, but on the changes in taste and patronage
which went on everywhere during the first half of the nineteenth
century.

Appendix 2

THE FIGURE

AS USED BY MOZART AND BY EARLIER AND LATER COMPOSERS

MOZART's uses of the sequence of four notes that open the Finale of the 'Jupiter' symphony are as follows:

1764/5. Symphony in E flat (K. 16), Andante, bars 7–10.
1768.   Symphony in B flat (K. 45b), Allegro, bars 25–32, &c.[1]
1772?   Tantum ergo (K. 197, doubtful), first repeat of 'veneremur'.
1774.   Mass in F (K. 192), *passim*.
1776.   Mass in C (K. 257), Sanctus.
1776.   Wind Sextet (K. 240), first movement, after double bar.
1778.   Sinfonia concertante (K. 297b), Adagio, bars 5–8.
1779.   Symphony in B flat (K. 319), first movement, development.

1782.   String Quartet in G (K. 387), Finale ⎫ Derivative, expanded to five
1783.   String Duo in B flat (K. 424), Adagio ⎬ notes.

1783.   Five Divertimenti (K. 439b, No. 4), first movement, bars 5, 6, 10, 11.
1785.   Violin Sonata (K. 481), first movement.
1791.   *Die Zauberflöte*, Act 2, finale (p. 175 of full score), 'Schwingt er sich aus Erde'.

The intervals of the first three notes appear to have some relation to folk-music, particularly Celtic;[2] they are also identical with the opening of the third Gregorian psalm-tone. Some uses of

---

[1] Information from Dr. Mosco Carner.
[2] Cf. Cecil Sharp, *English Folk Song* (London, 1954), p. 86.

the sequence of four notes by other composers, with varying note-values, are as follows:

1584. Palestrina. 'Delectus meus mihi', 5-part motet, 'super montes Bether'.

c. 1625. Antonio Ferrabosco the younger. 'Four-note Pavane.' BM Add. 17792–6, no. 25, and BM Egerton 3665, f. 505b, 508a.

1703. A. Scarlatti. 'Missa Clementina I.' Kyrie.[1]

1744. J. S. Bach. 'Das wohltemperierte Klavier.' Book 2, E major fugue.[2]

1746. Handel. *Judas Maccabaeus.* (Act 3, 'Father of Heaven'.)

1767. F. J. Haydn. Symphony No. 13. Allegro.

1787. J. M. Haydn. Gradual. No. 3 in *DTÖ*, xxii, 1 ('Alleluia').

1801. Beethoven. Sonata. Op. 27, no. 2. Trio, bars 2–5.

1807. Hummel. Pianoforte Sonata in F minor. Op. 20. 'Presto'. *Passim*, modelled closely on 'Jupiter' finale.

1814/15. Schubert. Mass in F. *GA*, p. 58.

1836. Mendelssohn. St. Paul. (No. 30. 'For so hath the Lord Himself commanded.')

1853. Brahms. Pianoforte Sonata. Op. 5. Andante.

1860.	,,	Four Duets. Op. 28, no. 1. *Passim.*
1865.	,,	Trio for Pianoforte, Horn, and Violin. Op. 40. Scherzo. *Passim.*
1869.	,,	Harzreise. Op. 53. Opening.
1871.	,,	Schicksalslied. Op. 54. *Passim.*
1871.	,,	Capriccio, F sharp minor. Op. 76, no. 1.
1877.	,,	Nine Songs. Op. 69, no. 2. End of each stanza.

It is an interesting coincidence that the keys of Brahms's four symphonies form, successively, the same sequence of these notes as used in the 'Jupiter'.[3]

1897. Indy. String Quartet in E major. Op. 45. The motto theme dominating the whole work.

---

[1] Quoted by Reissmann, *Allgemeine Geschichte der Musik* (Leipzig, 1864), vol. iii, p. 39. A nineteenth-century copy of the Mass is in BM Add. 32071.

[2] Mozart's devotion to Bach's '48' is discussed on p. 171.

[3] Cf. Robert Kahn, 'Memories of Brahms', in *ML*, Apr. 1947.

Appendix 3

THE ORIGIN OF THE TITLE 'THE "JUPITER" SYMPHONY'

THE origin of the title 'Jupiter' has been generally regarded as completely obscure; Jahn and Abert could only conjecture that it was coined some time after Mozart's death. It appears likely, however, to be older than has been generally supposed, and possibly to have originated in England. The London correspondent of the *Allgemeine musikalische Zeitung*, writing in June 1822 (col. 410), said: 'Das dritte [Konzert] am 25ten März, unter Spagnoletti's und Potter's Anordnung, begann mit der hier so sehr beliebten, und unter dem Namen Jupiter bekannten Sinfonie in C dur von Mozart.' This implies that the name had been current some time; and it had previously been used to describe the Symphony on 26 March 1821, in a programme of the Philharmonic Society.[1] The title was known in Scotland as early as 1819, when it appears in a programme (BM, Smart Collection) of the Edinburgh Music Festival of 20 October. Mozart's son Wolfgang Amadeus told Vincent Novello[2] that the sobriquet was coined by the London violinist and impresario J. P. Salomon. Scholes[3] mentions J. B. Cramer as the possible originator of the description. The earliest known illustrated edition of the work bearing the title 'Jupiter' is shown on Pl. 1 (frontispiece). Its watermark date is 1822.

[1] See M. B. Foster, *History of the Philharmonic Society* (London, 1913), p. 50.
[2] *A Mozart Pilgrimage*, p. 99. Salomon died in 1815, after a long illness.
[3] *Oxford Companion to Music* (ninth ed., London, 1955), p. 689.

GENERAL INDEX

Abert, Hermann, 36, 64, 68, 69.
Aiblinger, J. C., 121.
Albert, Father, 126 n. 3.
Albert, Prince Consort, 97.
Albrechtsberger, J. G., 121, 235, 252.
Ambros, A. W., 67.
André, C. A., 96, 111, 113, 114, 119.
André, J. A., 10, 82, 90, 95, 97, 111, 114, 115, 128, 218.
André's heirs, 91, 93, 98.
Anton, King of Saxony, 17.
Antwerp, Cathedral, 229.
Aristophanes, 194.
Asioli, B., 5 n. 3.
Attwood, Thomas, 5, 83, 92, 95, 171, 256.
Auber, D. F. E., 26, 214 n. 2.
Augener, Messrs., 61 n. 1.
Augsburg, 231, 240, 257.
Augsburg, Cathedral, 233, 234.
Augsburg, Monastery of the Holy Cross, 232.
Augsburger Tafelkonfekt, 149.
Aurnhammer, J., 255.

'Baar', —, 85.
Bach, Carl Philipp Emanuel, 15, 146, 200.
Bach, John Christian, 106, 220.
Bach, Johann Sebastian, 1, 32, 34, 44, 49, 50, 57, 64, 66, 149, 165, 170–3, 178, 179, 211, 234, 247, 263 n. 2.
Bach, Otto, 34.
Bach, Wilhelm Friedmann, 64.
Bach Society, 2.
Bachmann, S., 230.
Baini, G., 66.
Balfour, Arthur J., 61 n. 1.
Baring, Edward, 61 n. 1.
Barrett, W. A., 62 n.
Barrow, W., 94.
Bayer, N., 232.
Beazley, Sir John D., 217.
Beck, F., 48.
Beecham, Sir Thomas, 45, 50, 52.
Beecke, I., 248, 257.
Beethoven, Ludwig van, 2, 18, 19 n. 3,
26, 27, 30, 36, 41, 44, 50, 58, 59, 66, 68, 80, 81, 82, 88, 113, 149, 185, 195, 200, 205, 246, 261, 263.
Benda, G., 146.
Biber, H., 156.
Bibernach, 230.
Bibliothèque cantonale, Lausanne, 139.
Bibliothèque nationale, Paris, 102.
Biedenfeld, Baron F. L. K. von, 8.
Bishop, Sir Henry R., 13.
Bizet, Georges, 29.
Blech, Harry, 52.
Blom, Eric, 19 n. 1, 21.
Blume, Friedrich, 65.
Boïeldieu, F. A., 113 n. 1.
Botticelli, S., 2.
Brahms, Johannes, 26, 29, 50, 60, 62, 67, 159, 185, 263.
Breslauer, Martin, 89.
Breughel, Peter, 180, 181.
Bridge, Sir John F., 95.
British Museum, 78–91, 98, 117, 128, 129, 132, 161 n. 2, 260.
Brixi, F. X., 237.
Broadwood, John, 245.
Brown, A. Curtis, 94.
Browning, Oscar, 40, 61 n. 1.
Brunsvik, Countess J. von, 202.
Bupleurum Koechelii, 56.
Burckhardt, J., 67.
Busoni, Ferruccio, 47.

Caecilia, 114.
Cagliostro, A., 199.
Caldara, A., 94.
Cambridge, King's College Chapel, 190.
Cannabich, Karl, 220, 232.
Cannabich, Rosa, 248, 255.
Carey, Clive, 45, 51.
Carl Eugen, Prince of Württemberg, 138.
Carpani, G., 23.
'Casino' concerts, 176.
Catel, C. S., 113 n. 1.
Cecilian Society, 26.
Challis, John, 247.
Chappell, Messrs., 62 n.

Chapuis, A., 199 n. 2.
Cherubini, Luigi, 200.
Chickering & Sons, 246.
Chladni, E., 1.
Chopin, Frédéric François, 26, 180, 182, 261.
Chrismann, F. X., 235.
Christie, John, 46, 51.
Chrysander, Friedrich, 66, 68.
Cimarosa, Domenico, 23 n. 3, 144.
Città Castellana, Cathedral of Santa Maria, 230.
Clark, J. E. T., 199 n. 1.
Clarke, Mary Cowden, 80.
Clementi, Muzio, 18, 113, 143, 144, 215 n. 1, 245, 250, 251.
Cobbett, W. W., 69 n. 1.
'Collo, J. H.', 144.
Cologne, Elector of. *See* Maximilian Francis, Elector and Archbishop of Cologne.
Colt, C. F., 247 n. 1.
Concert Spirituel, 220.
Conservatoire, Paris, 98.
Corelli, Arcangelo, 153.
Cornet, A., 223 n. 1.
Cornetti, —, 223.
Cramer, Carl Friedrich, 3, 16 n. 3.
Cramer, Johann Baptist, 18, 113–19, 264.
Croft-Murray, Edward, 200 n. 1.
Curzon, Clifford, 94.
Cusins, Sir William G., 62 n.
Czerny, Carl, 112–14, 116.

Dante Alighieri, 159.
Da Ponte, Lorenzo, 224.
David, J. N., 64.
Delaval, Madame, 104.
Demmler, J. M., 233.
Denmark, King of. *See* Frederick VI.
Dent, Edward J., 51.
Deutsch, Otto Erich, viii, 96, 144.
Deym von Střitež, Count J., 198, 201–2, 204, 211, 215.
Dittersdorf, Carl Ditters von, 7, 177.
Doles, J. F., 178 n. 2, 225, 235.
Domenichino, Il, 23.
Donaldson, Sir George, 90.
Donne, John, 52.
Dragonetti, Domenico, 81.
Droz, E., 199 n. 2.
Dulau, Messrs., 62 n.

Duleep Singh, Maharajah, 61 n. 1.
Dürnitz, Baron T. von, 220.
Dvořák, Antonín, 29.

Eberl, A., 256.
Eberlin, E., 89, 172.
Edinburgh Music Festival (1819), 264.
Edmund, Father, 123, 125, 126, 127, 129.
Einstein, Alfred, 62, 63, 64, 88, 131.
Elizabeth, Princess of Württemberg, 255.
Ella, John, 87.
Ellis, William Ashton, 28 n. 3.
Emerson, Ralph Waldo, 158.
Emery, Walter, viii.
Epictetus, 191.
Erfurter Enchiridien, 156.
Espagne, F., 59, 62.
Esterhazy, Prince Nicolas, 200.
Exner, C., 97.
Eybler, J. E. von, 121.

Ferguson, Howard, 106 n. 2.
Ferrabosco, Antonio, the younger, 263.
Fishmongers' Hall Exhibition, 92.
Fitzwilliam Museum, 91, 253.
Forkel, J. N., 66.
Fouché, Mrs., 79.
Frank, Joseph, 245.
Frankfurt, Church of St. Katherine, 235.
Frederick the Great, King of Prussia, 201.
Frederick VI, King of Denmark, 17.
Frederick William II, King of Prussia, 17.
French, —, 91.
Freystädter, F. J., 256.
Friedrich, Archduke, 55.
Fry, Roger, 188, 197.
Fuchs, Aloys, 37, 56, 95.
Fürstenberg, Prince Joseph Wenzeslaus zu, 218.
Fux, J. J., 165.

Gabrieli, Andrea, 175.
Gabrieli, Giovanni, 66, 175.
Gál, Hans, 117.
Gardiner, William, 16, 17.
Gasser, H., 24.
Gassmann, F., 146.
Gelinek, J., 6.
Gemmingen, Baron O. von, 221.
Gerber, E. L., 223 n. 1.
German Handel Society, 61.

General Index

General Index 267

Ghent, Church of the Bernardines, 229.
Girod de Vienney, Louis Philippe Joseph, Baron de Trémont, 129, 130.
Glasenapp, C. F., 67.
Gluck, Christoph Willibald von, 36, 66, 117, 118, 119, 145, 147, 152, 154, 201.
Goethe, Johann Wolfgang von, 30, 182, 188 n. 1.
Goldschmidt, Otto, 60, 90.
Görner, —, 235.
Goss, Sir John, 95.
Gossec, F. J., 48.
Gough, Hugh, 247 n. 1.
Gounod, Charles François, 246.
Gozzi, Carlo, 221.
Grassalkovics, Prince, 5.
Greco, El, 2.
Grétry, A. E. M., 146, 154, 201.
Grieg, Edvard Hagerup, 47.
Griffin, Ralph, 91, 92.
Grimm, Baron F. M. von, 74, 138, 233.
Gropius, W., 52.

Haarlem, 230.
Haas, Otto, 93, 132.
Haas, Robert Maria, 205 n. 1.
Hagenauer, L., 100.
Haibel, J., 122.
Hall, Royal Convent, 230.
Hallé, Sir Charles, 62 n.
Halle, J., 160 n. 1.
Hamilton, C. J., 86.
Hamilton, Miss Nisbet, 62 n.
Handel, George Frideric, 2, 23 n. 3, 32, 34, 36, 49, 57, 66, 170, 171, 200, 247, 263.
Hartenstein, G., 68.
Hässler, J. W., 14, 234.
Haydn, Franz Joseph, 2, 6, 7, 23 n. 3, 27, 62, 66, 113, 144, 146, 153, 155, 166, 167, 180, 181, 200, 202 n. 2, 211, 214, 226, 246, 261, 263.
Haydn, Johann Michael, 89, 121, 126, 169 n. 2, 177, 200, 263.
Hellbrun, Palace of, 125, 199.
Henderson, Mrs. Inge, 94.
Henkel, H., 97.
Henschel, Sir George, 62 n.
Hertz, E., 244 n. 1.
Heyer, Wilhelm, 37, 92, 96.
Heyer Collection, 214.
Hill, Arthur F., 94.

Hiller, Ferdinand, 25 n. 1.
Hinterberger, Heinrich, 91, 205 n. 1.
Hirsch, Mrs. Olga, 92.
Hirsch, Paul, viii, 92, 132, 144.
Hirsch, Robert P., 92.
Hoboken, Anthony van, 37.
Hoffmann, E. T. A., 42.
Hoffmann, P. C., 15, 258.
Hollander, Benno, 46.
Holmes, Edward, 87, 128.
Holzbauer, Ignaz, 143, 232.
Homer, 159.
Hook, Theodore, 4 n.
Horatius Flaccus, Q., 70.
Hughes-Hughes, Augustus, 81 n. 1.
Humboldt, A. von, 67.
Hummel, J. N., 15, 82, 113 n. 1, 256, 257, 263.
Humphries, Charles, 104 n. 2.
Hunt, Leigh, 32.
Hunt, Lydia B., 79.

Ictinus, 191.
Indy, Vincent d', 263.
International Foundation Mozarteum, 54 n. 1.
Ipps, 228.

Jacquin, Baron Gottfried von, 221, 255.
Jacquin, Franziska von, 253, 255, 257.
Jahn, Otto, 27, 56, 66–77.
James, Philip, 247 n. 1.
Janiewicz, A., 223.
Joachim, Joseph, 60, 87.
Jonson, Ben, 185.
Joseph II, Emperor of Austria, 143, 170, 202, 224.
Justen, F., 62 n.

Kafka, J., 95.
Kalbeck, Max, 67.
Kant, Immanuel, 199.
Kaunitz, Prince, 245.
Keats, John, 32.
Kees, F. B. von, 221.
Kirkpatrick, Ralph, 247.
Kirnberger, J. P., 92, 156, 202.
Kite, J. E., 93.
Kittel, J. C., 234.
Köchel, Ludwig Ritter von, 27, 37, 55–65, 223 n. 1.

Kozeluch, L., 6, 8, 80, 178.
Kurze Bemerkungen über das Spielen . . .
  der Fortepianos, 244 n. 1.

Lachner, F. L., 25 n. 1.
Lachnith, L. W., 13.
Lambach, 234.
Latilla, G., 6.
Laudon, Field-Marshal E. G., 202.
'Laudon-Mausoleum', 202, 204.
Le Gros, J., 220.
Leichtentritt, H., 199 n. 1.
Leipzig, Karl Marx Universität, 214.
Leipzig, Thomaskirche, 234, 235.
Leipzig University, 214.
Leitzmann, A., 131.
Lenz, Wilhelm, 32.
Lesure, François, 111 n. 1.
Lichtenthal, Pietro, 16.
Liepmannssohn, 97.
Ligniville, Marquis E. de, 166.
Lind, Jenny, 90.
Lindpaintner, P. J. von, 25 n. 1.
Liste, A., 256.
Liszt, Franz, 42, 62.
Lodron, Countess A., 230, 234.
Loft, Abram, 21.
Lohelius, Father, 237.
Löhr, G. S., 62 n.
London Theatre Concerts, 52.
Lortzing, G. A., 51.
Lowes, John Livingston, 161 n. 1.
Ludwig, Prince of Württemberg, 138–40,
  218.

Mahler, Gustav, 45.
Mainwaring, John, 66.
Mainz, Church of the Holy Ghost, 229.
Mainzer, Joseph, 120–30.
Mälzel, J. N., 200.
Mannheim, 232, 243, 254.
Manning, W. E. Westley, 94.
Maratti, C., 136.
Marchand, Henri, 223.
Marchand, Marguerite, 221.
Marie Antoinette, Queen of France, 201.
Marschner, H. A., 25 n. 1.
Marshall, Julian, 80.
Martini, — (sister of G. B. Martini), 257.
Martini, Giovanni Battista, 74, 153,
  165 n. 1, 166, 201.
Marx, A. B., 66.

Marxfelder, A., 232.
Massenet, Jules, 246.
Maximilian Francis, Elector and Arch-
  bishop of Cologne, 81, 224.
Mayseder, J., 113 n. 1.
Meck, Najeda von, 29.
Melk, Abbey of, 230.
Mendelssohn-Bartholdy, Felix, 26, 68,
  81, 263.
Menken, S., 58 n. 1.
Mesmer, F. A., 199.
Messier, C., 55.
Metastasio, P., 29.
Meyerbeer, Giacomo, 25 n. 1, 26.
Meyerstein, E. W. H., 89.
Micha, F. V., 177.
Millar, Eric, 89.
Milton, John, 52, 159, 185.
Monn, Georg, 177.
Moscheles, Ignaz, 27, 113 n. 1.
Moser, A., 58 n. 1.
Mosoriak, Roy, 199 n. 1.
'Moyart, A.', 108, 109.
Mozart, Constanze, afterwards Nissen,
  Constanze von, 10, 14, 17, 24, 56, 75,
  79, 82, 89, 97, 116, 122, 123, 126, 129,
  170, 218.
Mozart, Karl, 91.
Mozart, Leopold, 90, 131, 219, 254, 257.
Mozart, Maria Anna (Marianne, or
  Nannerl), afterwards Sonnenburg,
  Baroness M. A. Berchtold zu, 72, 74,
  79–80, 106, 123–5, 127–30, 218–57.
Mozart, Maria Anna Thekla, 75.
MOZART, Wolfgang Amadeus the
  Elder.

The first number is that of the work
in the third edition of Köchel, edited
by Einstein. The page references,
when printed in italic figures, refer
to an autograph.

Masses and sacred pieces

20. Motet. 'God is our Refuge', *90*, 164.
49. Mass in G, 165.
93. Psalm. 'De profundis clamavi', *80*.
93 a. Psalm. 'Memento, Domine,
  David', *80*.
166 h. Psalm. 'In te Domine, speravi', *91*.
192. Mass in F, 166, 262.
197. 'Tantum ergo' in D (doubtful),
  262.

257. Mass in C, 262.

297 a. Eight pieces supplementary to a 'Miserere' by Ignaz Holzbauer, 220.

317. Mass in C, 166.

341. Kyrie in D minor, 14, 169.

427. Mass in C minor, 166.

626. Requiem. 14, 20, 26, 32, 75, 162, 166, 216.

App. 232. 'Twelfth Mass', 26.

— Mass in C. (Supposititious: arranged mainly from *Così fan tutte*), 16, 74.

Church sonatas

241. G major, 64.

263. C major, 64.

329. C major, 238.

336. C major, 238.

Cantatas, &c.

471. *Die Maurerfreude*, 156.

477 a. *Per la ricuperata salute di Ophelia*, 224.

566. Handel's *Acis and Galatea*. Re-orchestration, 208.

572. Handel's *Messiah*. Reorchestration, 208.

591. Handel's *Alexander's Feast*. Re-orchestration, 208.

592. Handel's *Ode on St. Cecilia's Day*, 208.

Operas and other works for the stage

35. *Die Schuldigkeit des ersten Gebotes*, 97.

51. *La Finta Semplice*, 150.

135 a. *Le Gelosie del seraglio* (Ballet for *Lucio Silla*), 64.

208. *Il Rè pastore*, 26.

299 b. Ballet music for *Les Petits riens*, 156.

315 e. *Semiramis*. Duodrama, 220, 221.

344. *Zaide*, 33, 146.

345. Incidental music to *Thamos, König in Ägypten*, 75, 143, 150.

366. *Idomeneo, Rè di Creta*, 11, 13, 26, 29, 45, 46, 75, 115, 118, 143, 145, 146, 151, 152, 154, 155, 157.

384. *Die Entführung aus dem Serail*, 11, 13, 25, 74, 115, 118, 146, 150.

422. *L'Oca del Cairo*, 33.

430. *Lo Sposo deluso*, 33.

492. *Le Nozze di Figaro*, 11, 13, 20 n. 2, 25, 45, 64, 79, 94, 96, 124, 145, 154, 156, 175, 183, 193, 196.

527. *Don Giovanni*, 8, 10, 11, 12, 13, 19, 21, 25, 29, 30, 31, 45, 64, 74, 98, 115, 124, 160 n. 1, 193.

588. *Così fan tutte*, 11, 13, 16, 46, 74, 157, 260, 261.

620. *Die Zauberflöte*. 8, 10–13, 20, 25, 45, 65, 115, 141–63, 178, 186, 200, 262.

621. *La Clemenza di Tito*, 11, 13, 29, 74, 97, 147.

Arias, &c., with orchestra

72 b. Aria 'Misero non tu sei', 219.

315 b. Scena for G. F. Tenducci, 200.

365 a. Recitative and aria for Gozzi's *Le Due nozze affanose*, 221.

569. Aria 'Ohne zwang, aus eignem Triebe', 223.

577. Rondo 'Al desio, di chi t'adora', 79.

615. Final chorus 'Viviamo felici in dolce contento' for Sarti's *Le Gelosie villane*, 223.

Songs with clavier

523. *Abendempfindung*, 184.

524. *An Chloe*, 124, 125, 184.

596. *Sehnsucht nach dem Frühling*, 192.

597. *Im Frühlingsanfang*, 192.

598. *Das Kinderspiel*, 192.

Canons

507. 'Heiterkeit und leichtes Blut', 92.

508. 'Auf das Wohl aller Freunde', 92.

508 a. Eight two- and three-part canons, 90.

555. 'Lacrimoso son' io', 94.

557. 'Nascoso è il mio sol', 94.

559. 'Difficile lectu mihi Mars', 97.

560 b. 'O du eselhafter Martin', 97.

562. 'Caro, bell' idol, mio', 94.

562 a. Four-part canon, without text, 94.

572 a. Double canon, 'Lebet wohl, wir sehn uns wieder' and 'Heult noch gar, wie alte Weiber', 224, 225.

App. 109[x]. Four-part canon by Kirnberger, resolved by Mozart, 92.

Clavier solo

Sonatas and fantasias

33 d–g. 218.

MOZART, Wolfgang Amadeus the
Elder (*cont.*)
281. B flat, 154.
282. E flat, 157.
283. G major, 47, 158.
284. D major, 169.
309. C major, 248.
310. A minor, 149, 182.
331. A major, 48 n. 2.
457. C minor, 47, *84, 86*, 173, 256.
475. C minor, 47, *84, 86*, 256.
498 a. B flat (partly supposititious), 157.
545. C major, 47.
570. B flat, *89*, 157.
576. D major, 178.

Variations

21 a. A major, 217.
353. On 'La belle françoise', *94*.
455. On 'Unser dummer Pöbel meint',
256.
613. On 'Ein Weib ist das herrlichste
Ding', 206.

Miscellaneous pieces

15 a–15 ss. The 'London sketch-book',
64, 164 n. 1, 218.
32 a. 'Capricci', 217.
41 e, f. Fugues, 219.
236. Andantino in E flat, 112–19.
284 a. Four preludes, 220.
284 f. Rondo, 220.
395. Capriccio in C major, 238.
485 a. Minuet, *95*.
494. Rondo in F major, 47, 158, 174,
206.
511. Rondo in A minor, 47, 174, 181.
533. Allegro in F major, Andante in
B flat, 47, 177.
540. Adagio in B minor, 24, *84, 86*.
574. Gigue in G major, 47, 178.
App. 284 i. Rondo in B flat, now attributed to Beethoven, *80*.

Clavier duets (4 hands, and 2 claviers)

19 d. Sonata in C major, 64, 100–11,
130.
358. Sonata in B flat, *79, 80*, 104 n. 1,
130.
381. Sonata in D major, *98*, 101, 125–7.
426. Fugue in C minor, 18, *88*, 173, 178.
497. Sonata in F major, *91*, 106 n. 1,
130, 150, 175, 184, 257.

521. Sonata in C major, *91*, 106 n. 1,
110, 111, 130, 257.
App. 284 g. Gavotte, allegro, and march
in C minor, now attributed to Beethoven, *80*.

Clavier and violin

7. Sonata in D major, 124 n. 1.
8. Sonata in B flat, 124 n. 4.
9. Sonata in G major, 124 n. 1.
296. Sonata in C major, 3.
304. Sonata in E minor, 169, 182, 194.
359. Variations on 'La Bergère Célimène', *84, 86*.
360. Variations on 'Hélas, j'ai perdu
mon amant', *84, 86*.
376. Sonata in F major, 3.
377. Sonata in F major, 3, 145.
378. Sonata in B flat, 3.
379. Sonata in G major, 3.
380. Sonata in E flat, 3.
454. Sonata in B flat, *84, 86*, 181.
481. Sonata in E flat, 151, 176 n. 1, 183,
262.

Duets for violin and viola

424. B flat, 262.

Trios

404 a. Six three-part fugues for strings.
Arranged from J. S. Bach and W. F.
Bach, with introductory adagios,
four by Mozart.
496. Clavier trio in G major, 105.
542. Clavier trio in E major, 29, 225.
562 e. String trio in G major, *91, 92*.
563. String trio in E flat, *98*, 154, 157,
178, 192.
564. Clavier trio in G major, 48, 105.
App. 149. Clavier trio in B flat (arr.
from K. 589), 105.
App. 284 h. Clavier trio in D major,
now attributed to Beethoven, *80*.

String quartets

155. D major, 167.
156. G major, 167.
157. C major, 167.
158. F major, 167.
159. B flat, 167.
160. E flat, 167.
168. F major, 167, 206.
169. A major, 167.

170. C major, 167.
171. E flat, 145, 167.
172. B flat, *81*, *91*, 167.
173. D minor, *96*, 167.
387. G major, *83*, *87*, 153, 172, 226, 262.
421. D minor, 5, 29, *83*, *87*, 115, 118, 226.
428. E flat, *83*, *87*, 226.
458. B flat, 4, *83*, *87*, 115, 146, 182, 226.
464. A major, 4, 41, *83*, *87*, 115, 157, 174, 183, 226.
465. C major, 4, 5, 32, *83*, *86*, *87*, 183, 226.
499. D major, *84*, *86*, 87.
575. D major, *83*, *86*, *87*, *161*, 178.
589. B flat, *83*, *86*, *87*, 157, *161*, 178, 186.
590. F major, *83*, *86*, *87*, 178.
546. Adagio and Fugue in C minor, *84*, *86*, *88*, *98*, 177.
Anh. 210–13 (doubtful. The 'Milanese' quartets), 64.

Other quartets

285 a. Flute and Strings. G major, 64.
478. Clavier and Strings. G minor, 6.
493. Clavier and Strings. E flat, 6, *91*, *93*.

String quintets

406. C minor, *80*, *84–86*.
515. C major, 184, 190.
516. G minor, 26, *92*, 184, 195, 279.
593. D major, *84*, *86*, *94*, 178, 186, 206.
613 a. E flat, 34.
614. E flat, *84*, *86*, *97*, 106 n. 1, 115, 147, 178, 186, 213.

Other quintets

452. Clavier and wind. E flat, 192.
581. Clarinet and strings. A major, 154.
617. Armonica, flute, oboe, viola, violoncello. C minor-major, *97*, 157, 204.

Symphonies

16. E flat, 262.
16 a. A minor, 217.
16 b. C major, 217.
19 a. F major, 217.
19 b. C major, 217.
45 b. B flat, 262.
183. G minor, 168.
199. G major, 168.
297. D major, 169.

319. B flat, 169, 262.
338. C major, 169.
425. C major, 148.
504. D major, 175, 186.
543. E flat, 19, 176, 184, 189.
550. G minor, 145, 184, 189.
551. C major, 19, *88*, 173–8, 184, 189, 262–4.

Divertimenti, serenades, and cassations

41 a. Six divertimenti, 218.
41 b. Wind pieces, variously scored, 218.
41 g. Serenade, 219.
62. Cassation. D major, 219.
187. Divertimento. C major, 118.
188. Divertimento. C major, 156.
240. Divertimento. B flat, 262.
246 b. Divertimento. D major, *93*.
247. Divertimento. F major, 152, 230.
250. Serenade. D major, 150.
252. Divertimento. E flat, 145.
253. Divertimento. F major, 152, 158.
287. Divertimento. B flat, 230.
289. Divertimento. E flat, *98*.
334. Divertimento. D major, 194.
361. Serenade. B flat, 16 n. 1, 169.
375. Serenade. E flat, 151, 182.
388. Serenade. C minor, 173.
439 b. Divertimenti. 262.
522. 'Musikalischer Spass', 194.
— Cassation (1771), 219.

Miscellaneous orchestral pieces

41 c. Marches, 218.
291. Fugue (by J. M. Haydn), 169 n. 3.
311 a. Overture. B flat, 64.
408. Three marches, *96*.
477. Maurerische Trauermusik, 175, 178.

Orchestral dances

41 d. Minuets, variously scored, 218.
104. Minuets, *96*.
176. Minuets, *79*.
267. Kontretänze, *91*.
585. Minuets, 157.
602. Deutsche Tänze, 147.
609. Kontretänze, *97*.
App. 293 a. Minuet and trio. C major, now attributed to Beethoven, *81*.

MOZART, Wolfgang Amadeus the Elder (*cont.*)

Clavier concertos
175. D major, 168, 174.
242. F major (three claviers), 155, 230.
271. E flat, 65, 107, 153.
365. E flat (two claviers), 151.
382. D major (rondo), 168.
386. A major (rondo), 64, *94*, *95*.
413. F major, 46, 147, 173.
414. A major, 173.
415. C major, 172.
449. E flat, 46, 253.
450. B flat, 155.
453. G major, 41, 46, 157, 174, 246, 253.
456. B flat, 41, 46, 182.
459. F major, 155, 157, 168, 172, 174, 175, 178.
466. D minor, 26, 46, 47, 115, 173, 175, 183, 196.
467. C major, 46, 183.
482. E flat, 46, 183.
488. A major, 46, 107, 183.
491. C minor, 18, 41, 46, *89*, 195, 196.
503. C major, 46, 175, 184, 186.
537. D major, 46.
595. B flat, 46, 186, 212.
626 a. Cadenzas to: K. 40. D major, *89*; K. 246. C major, *95*.

Other concertos
Strings: strings and clavier
206 a. Violoncello. F major, 220.
219. Violin. A major, 154.
315 f. Violin and clavier. D major, 225.
320 e. Violin, viola, violoncello. A major, 34, 225.
365. Violin and viola. E flat, *95*, *96*.

Wind
47 a. Trumpet, 219.
191. Bassoon. B flat, 220.
196 d. Bassoon. F major, 219.
293. Oboe. F major, *91*.
297 b. Oboe, clarinet, horn, bassoon. E flat, 152, 262.
314. Flute. D major, 147.
315. Flute. G major, 149.
447. Horn. E flat, *96*.
622. Clarinet. A major, 161.

App. 230 a. Bassoon. (Doubtful.) B flat, 64.

Mechanical organ
593 a. Fragment in D minor, 209, 210·
594. Adagio and allegro. F minor-major, 88 n. 1, 178, 186, 202, 204–6, 208–11, 238.
608. 'Fantasie.' F minor-major, 18, 178, 186, 202, 204–6, 208–11, 238.
616. Andante. F major, 204, 208, 210–15, 238.
616. (Sketch for), 214.

Miscellaneous
33 a. Solos for flute, 218.
33 b. Solos for violoncello, 218.
33 h. Piece for horn, 218.

Mozarts Unterricht in der Komposition, 152.
Verzeichnüss aller meiner Werke, 56, *96*, 182, 205, 216, 223.

Mozart, Wolfgang Amadeus, the Younger, 23, 113, 116.
Mozart Festivals:
Darmstadt, 25.
Elberfeld, 25.
Glyndebourne, 46.
Koschirsch, 25.
Salzburg, 24.
Vienna, 25, 58 n. 1.
Mozart-Gemeinde, 36.
Mozarteum, Salzburg, 24, 217.
Mozartstiftung, Frankfurt, 24.
Müller, August Eberhard, 15.
Müller, Josef. *See* Deym von Střitetž.
Müller, Wenzel, 178.
Müller von Asow, E. H., 216 n. 1.
'Müller'sche Gebäude', 202, 211.
'Müller'sche Kunstgalerie', 201.
Myslivecek, J., 153.
Mystères d'Isis, 13.

'Nagenzaun', 126 n. 3.
Nancy, 231.
Napoleon I, Emperor of France, 201.
National Gallery Concerts, 52.
New York Public Library, 88 n. 1.
Newman, Ernest, 32, 67.
Niederrheinische Musikfeste, 14.
Niemecz, Father P., 200.

Nissen, Constanze von. *See* Mozart, C., afterwards Nissen, C. von.
Nissen, Georg Nikolaus von, 17, 90, 101, 114, 115.
Nottebohm, Gustav, 59, 62.
Novello & Co., 64 n., 94, 95.
Novello, Mary Sabilla, 80.
Novello, Vincent, 14, 32, 79, 80, 81, 94, 127, 128, 166, 264.

Oakley, Herbert, 61 n. 1.
O'Brien, Justin, 50.
Odling, T., 95.
Oldman, Cecil Bernard, viii, 14, 37, 64, 95, 103, 116 n. 1.
O'Reilly, R. B., 98.
Österreichische Nationalbibliothek, Vienna, 224 n. 3.
Otter, J., 165 n. 1.
Ottobeuren, Monastery at, 190.

'P., Baron von', 74, 140, 239 n. 1.
Padua, Church of San Giustino, 230.
Paisiello, Giovanni, 6, 66, 146, 253.
Palestrina, Giovanni Pierluigi da, 32, 175, 263.
Palfy, Countess J. G., 255.
Panizzi, Sir Antony, 98.
Pantheon, 98.
Parhammer, Father I., 219.
Parthenon, 190, 191.
Paul Petrovich, Grand Duke of Russia, 221.
Payne, Humfry, 217.
Pelegrini, J., 121.
Pendlebury, R., 61 n. 1.
Pergolesi, G. B., 23 n. 3.
Petri, Egon, 47.
Philharmonic Society, 14, 116, 117, 264.
Philidor, F. A., 147.
Piccini, N., 23 n. 3, 143.
Pierron, Mlle, 255.
Plato, 30, 191, 193.
Pleyel, Ignaz, 48.
Plowden, C. H. Chichele, 86.
Plowden, Miss Harriet, 86.
Ployer, Barbara, 253.
Pohl, C. F., 85, 97.
Poissl, —, 121.
Pope, Alexander, 52.
Posch, Leonhard, 204.
Potter, Cipriani, 34, 94, 264.

Prado, The, 2.
Prague, Church of the Premonstratensians, 236.
Prod'homme, J. G., 129, n. 2.
Promenade Concerts, 51.
Proske, K., 26.
Prout, Ebenezer, 32, 62 n.
Prussia, King of. *See* Frederick William II.
Puccini, Giacomo, 51.
Puchberg, Michael, 160, 254.
Purcell, Henry, 21.
Pushkin, A. S., 31.
Puttick & Simpson, 85, 91.
Pye, K. J., 94.

Quantz, J. J., 200.

Racine, Jean, 133.
Radiciotti, G., 67.
Ranelagh, 229.
Raphael, 21, 22, 23.
Ravell, John, 87 n. 2.
Ravenna, Church of San Vitale, 190.
Reeves, William, 95, 96.
Reid Concerts, 51.
Reinecke, Carl, 60.
Reissmann, August, 263 n. 1.
Reissiger, K. G., 25 n. 1.
Rembrandt, 180, 181.
Reutter, G., 80.
Richelieu, Cardinal A. J. du P. de, 201.
Richter, G. F., 250.
Riemann, Hugo, 69.
Rietz, J., 59, 62.
Rio de Janeiro, 14.
Rolle, J. H., 144.
Romano, G., 23.
Romberg, B., 113 n. 1.
Romsey Abbey, 190.
Rose, William, 188 n. 2.
Rosetti, F. A., 48.
Rossi, —, 221.
Rossini, Gioacchino Antonio, 14, 26, 67, 121.
Roubier, H., 33.
Rousseau, Jean Jacques, 138.
Roveredo, Church of St. Mark, 230.
Rowley, Alec, 103.
Ruckers, family of, 245.
Rudorff, Ernst, 60.
Rumbeck, Countess, 254, 255.

Rushworth and Draper Collection, 247 n. 1.

St. James's Palace, London, 229.
St. Marx, Cemetery of, Vienna, 24.
Saint-Saëns, C. C., 46.
Salieri, A., 223.
Salomon, Johann Peter, 14, 98, 264.
Salzburg, Archbishop of. *See* Schwarzenburg.
Salzburg, Cathedral, 239, 240.
Salzburg, St. Peter's Church, 239.
Salzburg, University Church, 190.
Sandberger, A., 64.
Sarti, G., 5, 223.
Sattler, —, 89.
Savioli, Countess, 220.
Saxony, King of. *See* Anton.
Scarlatti, Alessandro, 263.
Scharschmied, F. von, 55.
Schechner, N., 121.
Scheibe, J. A., 1.
Schelling, F. W. J. von, 188 n. 1.
Scheurleer, D. F., 37.
Schikaneder, E., 143, 160, 221.
Schindler, A., 66.
Schinn, J. G., 165 n. 1.
Schlesinger, Thea, 115 n. 1.
Schlösser, C. W. A., 87.
Schlosser, J. A., 94, 114.
Schmid, Ernst Fritz, 65, 88 n. 1, 201.
Schobert, J., 48.
Schoelcher, Victor, 81.
Scholes, Percy, 120.
Schottenfeld, 235.
Schubert, Franz Peter, 28, 50, 62, 261, 263.
Schumann, Georg, 146 n. 1.
Schumann, Robert Alexander, 246.
Schünemann, Georg, 165 n. 3, 218.
Schwarzenburg, F. J. C. von, Archbishop of Salzburg, 23 n. 4.
Sechter, Simon, 169 n. 2.
Seiffert, Max, 64.
Serov, A. N., 32.
Serrarius, Thérèse, 254, 255.
Seyfried, I. X. Ritter von, 126.
Shakespeare, William, 2, 30, 194.
Sharp, Cecil, 262.
Sharp, Geoffrey, 108 n. 1.
Shaw, George Bernard, 41.
Shelley, Percy Bysshe, 32.
Shield, William, 223.

Sigl, Madame, 121.
Silbermann, J. A., 233, 240.
Simonides, 191, 192.
Smart, Sir George, 81.
Smart Collection, 264.
Société d'études mozartiennes, 45.
Soldan, Kurt, 64, 65.
Sonnenburg, Baron J. B. Berchtold zu, 123 n. 3, 160 n. 1.
Sonnenburg, Baroness M. A. Berchtold zu. *See* Mozart, M. A., afterwards Sonnenburg.
Sophocles, 191.
Sotades, 191.
Sotheby & Co., 91, 94, 96.
Spagnoletti, P., 264.
Späth, F. X., 243.
Speyer, Edward, 37, 95, 96.
Spiegl, Fritz, 209 n. 1, 214 n. 2.
Spitta, Philipp, 60, 66.
Spohr, Louis, 25 n. 1, 113 n. 1.
Spontini, G., 26.
Squire, William Barclay, 86, 115, 200 n. 1.
Stadler, Maximilian, 94, 126, 251.
Stamitz, family, 48.
Steggall, Reginald, 92.
Stein, J. A., 231, 240, 243–5, 248.
Stein, Nanette, 247, 256.
Stendhal, i.e. H. M. Beyle, 50.
Sterkel, J. F. X., 6.
Stodart, R. S. and W., 245.
Stone, E., 134.
Storace, Ann (Nancy), 224.
Storace, Stephen, 104 n. 1, 224.
Strasbourg, Neukirche, 233.
Strasbourg, Thomaskirche, 233.
Strauss, Richard, 45, 51 n. 1.
Street, Joseph E., 91.
Streicher, J. B., 82, 90.
Ströbl, 257.
Stumpff, Johann Andreas, 81–85, 87, 88, 97, 98, 116.
Summer, G., 255.
Süssmayr, F. X., 256.
Swieten, Baron Gottfried von, 170.

Tappert, W., 153 n. 1.
Tarchi, Angelo, 13.
Taylor, Sedley, 161 n. 3.
Tenducci, G. F., 220.
Three Choirs Festival, 14.
Tiersot, J., 201.

Tintoretto, 23 n. 3.
Titian, 23 n. 3, 185.
Tomkison, May. *See* Fouché, Mrs.
Tournefort, J. P. de, 134.
Tovey, Sir Donald F., 46, 51.
Townsend, Pauline, 68.
Trattner, Thérèse von, 254, 256.
Trémont, Baron de. *See* Girod de Vienney.
Tschudi, B., 245.

Uppsala University Library, 214.

Valentin, Erich, 36.
Verdi, Giuseppe, 26, 29, 50.
Vergilius Maro, P., 159.
Veronese, P., 23 n. 3.
Versailles, 233.
Viardot-Garcia, P., 98.
Victoria, Queen of England, 97.
'Vierzehnheiligen', Church of the, Franconia, 190.
Vogler, G. J., 75, 232, 249.
Voltaire, F. M. Arouet de, 199.

Wagner, Richard, 26, 34, 36, 50, 67, 261.
Walker, Frank, 5 n. 4.
Wallace, Lady Grace, 33.
Walmsley, T. A., 92.
Walter, Anton, 245, 246, 247 n. 1.
Wandering Minstrels, 90.

Wanhal, J. B., 6, 178.
Ward, Mrs. Humphrey, 29.
Warren, E. P., 89.
Wasserburg, 229.
Weber, Carl Maria F. E. von, 14, 18, 66, 81, 113.
Weber, Max Maria von, 18 n. 4, 66.
Weigl, J., 113 n. 1.
Werthes, F. A. C., 221.
Weyhe, E., 129.
Whinfield, E. W., 62 n.
Winter, Peter von, 6, 8.
Winterfeld, K., 66.
Wirtenberg, Duke Louis of. *See* Ludwig, Prince of Württemberg.
Wölfl, G., 105 n. 4.
Wollheim, H., 64.
Wood, J. L., viii.
Wordsworth, William, 162, 163.
Wranitzky, Paul, 20, 146, 152.
Würzburg, Palace at, 190.

Young, Charles, 79.
Young, Winslow, 79, 80, 128.

Zichy, Count S. or Count K., 245.
Zichy, Countess A. M. A., 255.
Zichy, Countess M. T., 255.
Z–n, Mr., 222.
Zulehner, Carl, 16.
Zweig, Stefan, heirs of, 96.

INDEX OF SOURCES AND AUTHORITIES
CITED

Abert, Hermann, 20, 40, 68–74, 77, 103
n. 1, 118, 127 n. 1, 131, 144, 146, 155
n. 2, 156, 234 n. 1, 235 n. 1, 264.
Albert, C. E. R., 22.
Allgemeine Musikalische Zeitung, 264.
Amiel, H. F., 29, 191.
Amsterdamsche Courant, 229.
Analytical Review, 108.
Anderson, Emily, viii, 10, 38, 72, 101,
111, 160 n. 1.
Aristide, ou le Citoyen, 131–40.
Arnold, I. F., 16.
Augsburger Intelligenz-blätter, 137.

Bach, A. B., 22.
Barna, I., 155.
Barrington, Hon. Daines, 138, 140, 164.
Belmonte, Carola, 41 n. 1.
Bennett, Joseph, 25 n. 2.
Berger, L., 143.
Berlinische Musikalische Zeitung, 234.
Blaschitz, Mena, 217.
Blume, Friedrich, 51.
Blümml, E. K., 41 n. 1, 73.
Bory, R., 38, 96, 245 n. 1.
Botstiber, Hugo, 66.
Brahms, Johannes, 193.
Broder, Nathan, 243.
Brunner, Hans, 76 n. 1, 244 n. 1.
Bülow, H. G. von, 53 n. 2.
Busoni, Ferruccio, 42–44, 190.
Butler, Samuel, 35.

Caecilia, 143, 146.
Calendrier musical universel, 109, 110.
Carner, Mosco, 262 n. 1.
Chantavoine, Jean, 40, 76, 142, 144–6,
150, 155, 159.
Chopin, Frédéric François, 29.
Clough, F. C., 50.
Cœuroy, André, 45 n. 2.
Corte, A. della, 143.
Cuming, Geoffrey, 50.
Curzon, Henri de, 37.

Da Ponte, Lorenzo, 223 n. 1.
Davenport, Marcia, 245 n. 1.
Deininger, H. F., 73, 239 n. 1.
Deiters, Hermann, 68–70, 74, 77, 144.
Delacroix, Eugène, 29.
Dennerlein, H., 73, 214 n. 2, 238 n. 1.
Dent, Edward J., 16 n. 1, 21, 40, 42, 47,
141, 146 n. 4, 161 n. 3.
Deutsch, Otto Erich, 8, 19 n. 1, 41 n. 1,
72, 76, 80 n. 3, 81 n. 1, 83 n. 1, 105,
126, 201, 202 n. 3, 203, 224 n. 1.
Dickinson, G. Lowes, 40.
Dittersdorf, Carl Ditters von, 4, 47.
Dörffel, A., 25 n. 4.
Dwight's Journal of Music, 32.

Ebert, A., 236 n. 1, 237.
Eckermann, J. P., 20.
Einstein, Alfred, 13, 40, 73, 110, 145,
146 n. 2, 170 n. 1, 225, 238 n. 2. *See also*:
Köchel, L. Ritter von, *Mozart-
Verzeichnis*, 1937 edn.
Ella, John, 25 n. 2, 83 n. 1, 98.
Engel, Hans, 31 n. 3.
Engländer, Richard, 214 n. 1.

Farmer, Henry George, 73.
Fehr, Max, 139 n. 3.
Ferrari, G. G., 5, 18 n. 3.
Fleischer, O., 56 n. 3.
Foster, Myles Birket, 25 n. 2, 264 n. 1.
Frank, Joseph, 256.
Franz, G. von, 244 n. 1.
Freeman, Andrew, 238 n. 3.
Freischütz, Der, 138.
Friedländer, Max, 149 n. 1.
Frimml, Theodor, 81 n. 1.
Fritz, O., 51 n. 1.

Ganzer, R. C., 102, 103.
Gathy, August, 117.
Geiringer, Karl, 246 n. 1.
Gide, André, 50.
Girdlestone, C. M., 40, 47.

Glock, William, 49.
Goethe, Johann Wolfgang von, 20, 21.
Goschler, I., 32.
Gounod, Charles François, 28, 197.
Gray, Cecil, 47.
Gruber, C. A. von, 23 n. 1.
Gyrowetz, A., 221, 222, 252.

Haas, Robert Maria, 73, 103 n. 2, 145, 244 n. 1.
Hadow, Sir William Henry, 41.
Hallé, Sir Charles, 25 n. 3, 29.
Harthan, John P., 22.
Haushalter, C., 25 n. 1.
Hauswald, G., 73.
Heuss, A., 42.
Hill, Richard S., 131, 132, 139 n. 3.
Hiller, Ferdinand, 56 n. 3.
Hiller, Johann Adam, 138.
Hirsch, Paul, 37.
Hochfürstlich bambergische wöchentliche Frag- und- Anzeige-Nachrichten, 138.
Hoffmann, E. T. A., 21, 22.
Holmes, Edward, 32, 66, 171, 216 n. 1.
Hummel, Walter, 24, 58 n. 1.
Hussey, Dyneley, 21.

Jahn, Otto, 8, 16 n. 1, 32, 38, 40, 66–77, 85, 131, 144, 155, 181, 239 n. 1, 264.
Joachim, Joseph, 58 n. 1.
Joseph II, Emperor of Austria, 3, 4.
Journal des Luxus und der Moden, 6.
Junk, V., 21.

Kahn, R., 263 n. 3.
Keats, John, 22.
Keller, Otto, 37, 71, 72.
Kelly, Michael, 3, 222, 224, 257.
Kinsky, Georg, 214 n. 2, 245 n. 1.
Kirkegaard, S. A., 30.
Köchel, Ludwig Ritter von, *Mozart-Verzeichnis*, 1862 edn., 34, 57, 60, 65, 68. 1905 edn. (revised by Waldersee), 37, 58 n. 1, 62, 112. 1937 edn. (revised by Einstein), 37, 62, 63, 72, 73, 81 n. 1, 82, 113, 117, 161, 216–19.
Komorzynski, Egon, 73.
Köstlin, K., 30.
Kreitmaier, J., 38.
Küsche, L., 102, 103.

Lach, R., 40, 152 n. 1.

Latham, Peter, 53.
Lehmann, N., 236, 238.
Lert, Ernst, 40.
Lipowsky, F. J., 258.
Loewenberg, Alfred, 13, 45.
Lorenz, Franz, 33, 56, 65.
Lysons, Daniel, 14.

Macdowell, Edward, 42.
Magazin der Musik, 3, 4, 6, 9, 255.
Mansfield, Orlando A., 238.
Maty, Mathew, 90.
Meadmore, W. S., 52 n. 1.
Meilichofer, L., 23 n. 4.
Michaelis, A., 67 n. 1.
Morhardt, M., 131, 138.
Mörike, Eduard, 30.
Moser, H. J., 58 n. 1.
Mozart, Leopold, 4, 9, 38, 72, 98, 102, 138, 218, 229, 231, 245, 258.
Mozart, Maria Anna (Marianne, or Nannerl), afterwards Sonnenburg, Baroness M. A. Berchtold zu, 101, 102.
Mozart, Wolfgang Amadeus, the Younger, 264.
Müller, K. F., 64 n.
Müller von Asow, E. H., 64 n. 3, 75.
Musikalische Monatsschrift, 7.
Musikalische Zeitung, 7.
Musikalisches Wochenblatt, 101.

Nägeli, H. G., 19.
Naumann, Emil, 27, 28.
Nerval, Gérard de, 45 n. 2.
Nettl, Paul, 20, 41 n. 1.
Neuestes Sittengemählde von Wien, 203.
Newman, William S., 109, 110.
Niemetschek, F. P., 3, 16, 236.
Nissen, Georg Nikolaus von, 6, 32, 72, 100, 121, 123, 137 n. 1, 146, 216 n. 1, 230 n. 2.
Nohl, Ludwig, 33.
Nottebohm, Gustav, 37, 38, 101, 128 n. 1.
Novello, Vincent, 251.

Oldman, Cecil Bernard, 8, 10, 75, 105, 111 n. 1.

Parke, W. T., 20, 222.
Parry, Sir Charles Hubert H., 41.
Paumgartner, Bernhard, 72, 73, 126.

Perger, R. von, 25 n. 5.
Pfannhauser, K., 80.
Pohl, C. F., 14, 33, 58 n. 1, 66, 72, 176 n. 2, 235.
Pole, William, 33.
Prieger, K., 18 n. 5.
Public Advertiser, 100, 229.

Reeser, E., 109, 110.
Refardt, E., 256 n. 1.
Reinecke, Carl, 46.
Richter, Hans, 53 n. 2.
Rochlitz, J. F., 6 n. 2, 16, 171 n. 1, 225.
Rockstro, William S., 42.
Rossini, Gioacchino Antonio, 27.
Russell, John F., 247 n. 2.

Saint-Foix, Count Georges de, 38, 39, 63, 64, 73, 77, 101, 102, 103, 104, 106 n. 2, 118, 141.
Schaal, Richard, 257 n. 3.
Schachtner, Andreas, 140.
Scheurleer, D. F., 229 n. 1, 230 n. 1.
Schiedermair, L., 38, 72, 101.
Schilling, G. von, 258 n. 1.
Schlichtegroll, A. H. F. von, 16, 251.
Schmid, Ernst Fritz, 73.
Scholes, Percy, 264.
Schopenhauer, Arthur, 21 n. 5.
Schubert, Franz Peter, 18, 19.
Schumann, Robert Alexander, 191.
Schünemann, Georg, 64.
Schurig, A., 39, 73, 75, 126, 246 n. 1.
Smith, Henry, 73.
Sonnenburg, Baroness M. A. Berchtold zu. *See* Mozart, M. A., afterwards Sonnenburg.

Speyer, Edward, 87.
Spohr, Louis, 18 n. 5.
Steglich, R., 244 n. 1.
Stendhal, i.e. H. M. Beyle, 22, 23.
Storch, L., 82.
Stumpff, Johann Andreas, 24.

Tchaikovsky, Peter I., 29.
Tenschert, R., 90.
Thackeray, William, 31.
Thayer, Alexander Wheelock, 18 n. 1, 66, 68, 81 n. 1.
Tissot, S. A. D., 131, 139.
Torrefranca, F., 39.
Tovey, Sir Donald F., 41, 117.

Ulibichev, A. D., 31, 32, 72.
Ullrich, H. J., 77 n. 1.

Valentin, Erich, 51 n. 1, 72, 127.
Vigny, Alfred de, 31.

Wagner, Richard, 28, 29.
Waldersee, Count Paul von. *See* Köchel, L. Ritter von, *Mozart-Verzeichnis*, 1905 edn.
Warde Fowler, William, 29, 87, 162, 191, 193.
Weber, G., 20.
Whistling, K. F., 12, 129 n. 3.
Wiener Zeitung, 202.
Wörsching, J., 239.
Wurzbach, Constantin von, 33, 34, 37, 117.
Wyzewa, Theodor de, 38, 39, 63, 73, 77, 118, 141, 142, 148, 149, 158, 161.

Zschorlich, P., 45 n. 1.

INDEX OF PUBLISHERS

André, J. A., 15, 33, 56, 75, 90, 105, 261.
Andrews, Hugh, 104, 108, 109, 111.
Artaria, 5, 8, 105, 215 n. 1, 224, 255 n. 1.

Berra, M., 261.
Birchall, Robert, 12, 103, 104, 105, 106.
Birchall & Andrews, 104, 105 n. 1.
Breitkopf & Härtel, 10, 11, 12, 34, 47, 57–61, 68, 101, 119, 128, 144, 148 n. 1, 205, 217, 218.
Brzezina, 261.

Calkin & Budd, 85.
Chappell & Co., 83.
Chappell, S., 113.
Cocks, Robert, & Co., 113, 114.
Cianchettini & Sperati, 11.
Cimador, G. D., 18.
Cramer & Co., 113, 117.
Cranz, August, 260.

Diabelli, Anton, 205.
Dunnebeil, H., 103.

Edwards Bros., 63, 65.

Frey, J. J., 12, 129 n. 3.

Goulding & Co., 110.

Härtel, G. C. See Breitkopf & Härtel.
Haslinger, Tobias, 94, 261.
Heckel, F., 12.

Henning, 105.
Hoffmeister, F. A., 6.
Hummel, J. J., 5.
Hurst, Chance & Co., 113.

Lavenu & Mitchell, 105.
Longman & Broderip, 224 n.
Lose, 261.

Magasin de l'imprimerie chymique, 11.
Mechetti, 17.
Meser, C. F., 261.
Meyer, G. M., 11, 260.

Novello & Co., 65.

Peters, C. F., 261.
Pleyel, Ignaz, 11.

Richault, S., 12, 33.
Roullede, de, 102, 105, 106, 109, 110, 111.

Schlesinger, Martin, 12.
Schott, 103, 110.
Schuberth & Niemayer, 260.
Semen, A.
Simrock, 11.
Spehr, J. P., 10.
Steiner, S. A., 11.

Theune, 261.
Trattner, J. T. von, 256.
Trautwein, T., 261.

PRINTED IN
GREAT BRITAIN
AT THE
UNIVERSITY PRESS
OXFORD
BY
CHARLES BATEY
PRINTER
TO THE
UNIVERSITY